Critical Moments

in Religious History

Critical Moments

in Religious History

edited and with an introduction by

Kenneth Keulman

Mercer University Press

ISBN 0-86554-411-5   MUP/H334

The paper used in the publication meets the minimum
requirements of American National Standard
for Information Sciences—Permanence of Paper
for Printed Library Materials, ANSI Z39.48-1984.

Library of Congress Cataloging-in-Publication Data

Critical moments in religious history / edited
and with and introduction by Kenneth Keulman.
viii+230pp. 6x9" (15x23cm.).
"The essays in this book originated as papers delivered
at a conference on critical moments in religious history
at Rice University in 1984." —CIP data sheet.
Includes bibliographic references and index.
ISBN 086554-411-5 : $24.95.
1. Religions—Congresses.
2. Religion and culture—Congresses.
3. Religion and state—Congresses.
4. Religious pluralism—Congresses.
I. Keulman, Kenneth, 1942–
BL87.C77   1993
200'.9—dc20   93-14386   CIP

Contents

Preface

Most of the essays in this book originated as papers delivered at a conference on "Critical Moments in Religious History" at Rice University in 1984 under the auspices of the Rice Alumni Institute. Several other studies on related subjects have been added to round out the spectrum of viewpoints needed to further develop the theme. All the authors focus on "critical moments in religious history" from a range of perspectives.

The themes under consideration come into sharp focus against the background of a pluralistic world. There exist multiple options in various cultural spheres, and these various political options exist beside versions of Native American religions, Buddhism, Judaism, Christianity, and Islam. This volume investigates the ramifications of pluralism. A number of the essays ask how religion affects political modernization, exploring mutual acceptance in a world that is frequently more of a global battlefield than a global village. The book asks whether religious toleration is derived from political differentiation or if political exigencies contribute to a spectrum of theological expressions. It reflects on this as a question fundamental to the fate of the world's religions in the twentieth century, and wonders if it applies differently in the individual traditions.

The essays are concerned with the relationships existing among culture, religion, law, nationalism, and society. They examine the way in which the notion of pluralism defines culture within the construct of social systems. A number of the essays reveal some of the systemic difficulties inherent in legal systems as these systems are used to accommodate divergent cultures. Overall, the essays examine the dilemmas of culture and religion by assessing the impact they have on various communities. The methodology employed implicitly reflects the technique of narrative which has become a critical strategy in historical scholarship.

The volume is cross-cultural in its orientation: Buddhism is considered in light of the Great Persecution in China; Judaism in the context of the destruction of the Temple; Islam is viewed against the background of the Iranian revolution; American Indian religion through the pacification and transformation of the Plains Indians. Christianity is seen in its relation to Gnosticism and also in terms of the question "Conquest or Inculturation?" within the missionary impulse of Christianity. Christian Fundamentalism comes under scrutiny in essays on the beginning of the Southern Bible Belt and the transformation of Fundamentalism between the World Wars. The biblical justification of apartheid in Afrikaner civil religion is also considered. The question of war and peace in the Christian tradition is considered vis-à-vis the United States Roman Catholic Bishops' pastoral letter on nuclear weapons.

I want to acknowledge the contributors to this volume. Their competence and cooperation set a high standard for the type of collaborative effort represented here. I am particularly grateful to Werner Kelber for his continued encouragement in bringing this project from the oral tradition into its present status as text. We also owe a debt of gratitude to Edd Rowell, senior editor of Mercer University Press, for the care he took in editing the manuscript.

Allen Matusow, dean of Humanities at Rice University, graciously provided financial assistance in the final stages of this project, as did the Association of Rice Alumni. The Office of Grants and Research at Loyola University also awarded a research grant. Carol Cortazzo typed the manuscript with exceptional diligence. I express my gratitude to all the individuals behind the institutional nomenclature, who have facilitated the production of this work.

—Kenneth Keulman

Introduction

Between the Indian summer of the *ancien régime* and the evanescent "restoration" of postrevolutionary continental Europe, perceptions of the upwardly mobile intellectual classes took a decisive turn from nostalgia to anticipation, from criticism to intimations of dynamism. When Boulanger wrote in the *Encyclopedia* that "the mind of men living in civilized states has been more or less the same throughout the ages: the difference lies only in the way it ['civilization'] is used,"[1] he was reflecting the Enlightenment's confidence in human nature, man's place in the world, and the causal reliability of the universe. But not half a century later, beyond the Revolution, that natural posture of harmony is shattered; a romantic like Novalis can write of recent events as the "stirrings of a puberty crisis."[2]

An understanding of other times is dependent upon the contours of evidence. Historical writing can be initiated only when a present is sundered from a past. An act of separation divides present time from past time. The historian's perception of duration is delineated by what is recorded as past. Once this disparate form of time is constituted, interpretation is validated, theory unfolds, and writing is initiated.

The project of historical writing can be situated in the forms of narrative or configurations of recounted occurrences, thus underscoring the way in which one can conceive of the action of language enhancing the sense of history. Thus the archival project remains incomplete. Local blocks of information are created from research that is particular, fragmentary, and limited. Historians work upon the limits decreed by their field. From the complexities of research methods, the historian constructs "local" representations of the past. The incomplete character of the project, however, indicates the possibility of garnering generalities from analysis of minutiae. One may perceive structures through patterns underlying the randomness of historical circumstance. At any time, only a restricted number of

---

[1] "Prodige," *Encyclopédie ou Dictionnaire raisonné des arts, des sciences et des métiers*, 17 vols. (Paris, 1751–1765) 13:423.

[2] Novalis, *Blütenstaübe*, no. 105 *Gesammelte Werke*, 5 vols., ed. C. Seelig (Herrliberg-Zurich, 1943) 2:36. The entire quotation is from George Armstrong Kelly, *Idealism, Politics, and History* (Cambridge: Cambridge University Press, 1969) 1.

representations can be fashioned. These discursive formations generate the ideological spectrum of representation. Thus historiographers are able to hint at an intimation of the whole by means of the figures that play between interpretation and knowledge. Inquiry into specific questions can provide insight into unconscious totalities as adequately as the mythic omniscience the historiographer had sought during other periods.

Former blocks of history are studied in terms of the process that formed the contour of their development. Self-enclosing designs that generate an "author," a "period," an "epoch," or even a "critical moment" are valid subjects of analysis. Their forms of appropriation are significant. The latter indicate forces of self-legitimation that mirror the investments the present places in the past for its own ends. A symmetry—the intention that a project or a discipline proclaims for itself—participates in the rapport that allegory has with the production of information. In previous forms of historical writing, the historian fashioned schemes that would apply to and comprehend a complete block of information. The task of the historian today involves deciphering obscure connections that existed in discourses of other times. The desire to produce self-contained blocks of knowledge is enervated by the actual methods used to bring form and symmetry to knowledge.

Historiography today emphasizes the way events are described, how they are thought to be significant, how they become worthy of record. The historian who discerns them is influenced by the presuppositions, ideologies, and dispositions of the writers and observers of former times, of the chroniclers who have fashioned the archives of the modern historian. This background influences the ways events are selected and interpreted. In this way, events may be compared with coded tropes that "read" or allegorize the past.[3] By approaching history through theories of religion, we view language and mimesis as forces informing most collective relations. Since modern historiography cannot fail to analyze the erosion of the symbolic shapes of religion, it must always return to question the narratives and legends that give birth to a communally significant past.

The traditional tendency in historical writing is to emphasize the dimension of continuity in past ages. For most historians contemporary history does not make up a distinct period with unique hallmarks of its own; they regard it rather as the most recent phase of a continuous process and, wary of admitting that it is different in quality or kind from earlier history, treat it simply as that part of "modern" history that is nearest in time.

This orientation is problematic. Continuity is not the most obvious feature of the historical landscape. At every turning point of the past one is confronted

---

[3]These remarks on the nature of historical writing are based on Tom Conley's translator's introduction to Michel de Certeau's, *The Writing of History* (New York: Columbia University Press, 1988).

by the fortuitous and the unforeseen, the dynamic and the revolutionary. At such times, the ordinary arguments of causality are insufficient in themselves to explain the next stage of the narrative, the next turn of events.[4] There is little problem in identifying moments when the human race swings out of its old paths onto a new plane, when it leaves the well-trodden route and turns off in a different direction. One such time was the explosion 40,000 years ago of new types of bone and stone tools, artwork, elaborate burials and many other prototypical patterns of human behavior. The first half of the twentieth century likewise has all the marks of a period of revolutionary change and crisis. Here we encounter one of the central issues in the writing of history—the issue of periodization. What we should look out for as important are the differences rather than the similarities, the elements of discontinuity rather than those of continuity. In brief, contemporary history should be considered as a unique period of time, with qualities of its own which mark it off from the preceding period, in much the same way as what we call "medieval history" is marked off from modern history.

Thus one of the primary responsibilities of historians is to articulate the distinguishing features of an era and its boundaries. In doing so there is need to be wary of false categories. We have to remember that all sorts of life-forms last over from one period to another, just as all types of realities regarded as "typically medieval" persisted into Elizabethan England; and we should not expect to assign fixed dates to changes which, in the last analysis, are simply changes in balance and perspective. Unless we keep our eyes open for what is different, we shall all too easily miss the essential—that is, the sense of living in a new period. Only when we have the gulf between the two periods fixed in our minds can we begin building bridges across it.

Historians are thus interested in discerning irregularities in rates of change—that is, reasons why continuity and stability exist in some places and times, and accelerated rates of change exist in others. They want to understand the reasons that change does not materialize in tranquil periods, why it takes place so quickly when it does arrive. An understanding of the reasons for relative change or continuity over time of a particular phenomenon, is thus a significant element of historical research. Some historical studies try only to describe a particular culture at a specific period. Yet they are actually part of the same project, for they specify chronological landmarks with greater accuracy and ordinarily describe a "plateau" period, consequently providing significant ballast to the analysis of more turbulent times.

The use of the words *reasons* and *why* in the preceding description demands comment. The notion of causality is not in good repute among cultural historians.

---

[4]This is a theme of Herbert Butterfield in *The Present State of Historical Scholarship* (Cambridge: Cambridge University Press, 1965).

They usually substitute the word "significance" to report analogues; however, when they do so the notion of "cause" still does not disappear. Even though there are problems implicit in the idea of causality, we still must consider important the attempt to answer "why" questions regarding the past—why a given result and not another one, took place. A straight narrative history, or a merely evocative history, can escape these problems. But then it approaches its subject with an assumption of inevitability. An attempt to analyze alternative outcomes provides us with an historical universe far more vital than narrow accounts of specific struggles from the inside, although the sense of what it was like to be alive inside such a struggle may well communicate what was at issue.

In the history of any subject, a description of significant turning points in that history needs to be articulated. Whether or not ideas can be treated independently is a central issue between some intellectual and social historians. Do ideas form discarnate abstractions apart from any origin in or implication for the fabric of human life? A good portion of contemporary writing in intellectual history appears to share this assumption.

Yet, human history is first of all social history. Any specific city or nation-state may be perceived as a composite of social groups. These aggregates are the constituents of social history. Usually, even in intellectual history, we deal with social aggregates, and attempt to describe stasis or innovation within such collectivities. Intellectual history would look upon itself as advancing a specific type of explanation of motivation vis-à-vis historical outcomes in communities. Today it is possible to look at the spectrum of human motivation, at the types of categories ordinarily fashioned to explain it, in a more complex manner than in the former, two-sided juxtaposition of "material forces" and "ideas." A word needs to be said about the classification of motives that historians of the present time seem to follow in their research, about the types of explanations historians most frequently put forward.

Social historians prefer to stay near to what they consider to be "social reality"—behavior patterns or institutional structures that demand only a utilitarian notion of mental processes. They may go so far as to prefer to leave out or only quickly acknowledge entrenched cultural standards which may affect historical outcomes. Demographers, for instance, may give the impression that human existence is simply a matter of birth and death, overlooking the in-between cultural content as insignificant.

These are excesses which have taken place during the ascendancy of social historians. Ordinarily in theory, and frequently in practice, such historians do in fact allow scope for the study of patterns of thought functioning beyond the extent of social mobility in the culture. Even the *Annales* historians assign a significant role to the analysis of *mentalité* or collective states of mind. In fact, some of the most important studies by social historians focus on divergences between group self-perception and structural reality.

Any study of the relations between social realities and formal systems of thought, faces another range of questions. On the one hand, collective mentalities are present. On the other, formal systems of thought exist. Social historians ordinarily do not trespass on this area, but for some intellectual historians, the historical evidence to be relegated to this segment is crucial. These intellectual historians form a counterpart, at another end of the spectrum, to economic or social historians who limit themselves to social realities. They, along with some representatives of *mentalité*, may even attempt to depreciate the autonomous existence of social realities in the classical sense of philosophical idealism. This might also lend itself to distortion. The types of information aggregated under "social realities," are diverse, including everything from the breeding of Paul Revere's horse to epidemiological studies.[5]

One of the dilemmas of historical discourse is that, like all language, it unfolds in strictly linear fashion, whereas, to escape oversimplification, one ought to be able to recall at every point the entire network of relationships discerned there. "Effective history deprives the self of the reassuring stability of life and nature, and it will not permit itself to be transported by a voiceless obstinacy toward a millennial ending. It will uproot its traditional foundations and relentlessly disrupt its pretended continuity."[6]

In this spirit, it seems useful to offer these essays dealing with critical historical moments, which may provide a means of grasping the correspondence between the structure of historical narrative and the structure of the symbolic properties attached to social groups. This is not meant to encourage readings which will reduce the similarities between systems of differences to direct, mechanical relationships between groups and properties; or that will encourage ensconcing the historian in the role of omniscient seer.

Such readings would be correlative with the modern crisis of representation, in which an essentially realistic epistemology, conceiving of representation as the reproduction, for subjectivity, of an objectivity that lies outside it—projects a mirror theory of knowledge, whose fundamental evaluative categories are those of adequacy and accuracy. Yet it may well be that it is the very rhetoric of crisis itself which offends any plausible sense of continuity, and prevents us from dealing with what turns out to be genuinely unprecedented circumstances. This

---

[5]The direction of this argument on the importance of historical discontinuity is indebted to Lawrence Veysey's essay "Intellectual History and the New Social History," in *New Directions in American Intellectual History*, ed. John Higham and Paul Conkin (Baltimore: Johns Hopkins University Press, 1979).

[6]Michel Foucault, *Language, Counter-Memory, Practice*, ed. Donald Bouchard (Ithaca NY: Cornell University Press, 1977) 154.

is to move along the borders of the issue of power as a representational model. From this perspective, to analyze the ideological aspects of symbolic orders is to examine the way structures of signification are mobilized to legitimate the sectional interests of hegemonic groups.

A word on some of the methodological issues underlying the essays in this volume. By way of example: a collapse of religious practice occurs in France during and after the Revolution. This dramatic change demands an explanation: something must have happened earlier so that this break could occur. "The fact that this change occurred very quickly under the effect of the shock of the Revolution, gives us reason to believe that minds were ready to accept it."[7] What does an historian do, if not call chance into question, put forth reasons—that is, understand? But understanding does not imply retreat into ideology, nor supplying an identity for that which remains obscure. It means having to discern through the actual historical data what permits it to be conceived.

This investigation has a number of effects. It allows a series of indications to be put forward that had not been analyzed until then and which, from that point, become acknowledged because one generally understands the functions to which they correlate. But the investigation can also interrogate the ideas, the historical levels of analysis, that had been adopted up to that time. Consequently, the notion of "Christianization" in the seventeenth century needs to be rethought;[8] so may the disjunction of an *ancien régime* as a reality unassociated with the events that follow it.[9]

The attention given to comprehending the process of religious change has increased substantially as the pace of global religious development has accelerat-

---

[7]Etienne Gautier and Louis Henry, *La Population de Crulai, paroisse normande* (Paris: Presses Universitaires de France, 1958) 119.

[8]In *Le catholicisme entre Luther et Voltaire* (Paris: Presses Universitaires de France, 1971) Jean Delumeau maintains that: "In order to be de-Christianized, it is certainly necessary that they [populations] at one time had been Christianized! It is the measure of this *Christianization* which will reveal the measure of *de-Christianization*" (326). At the opposite pole, if one comes back from the breakdown of religious practice to its antecedents (the shallow nature of Christian practices), it is possible to measure more accurately the degree of Christianization, and possibly even do away with this idea. Quoted and annotated by de Certeau, *The Writing of History*, 123n.2.)

[9]The break between "modern" and "contemporary" history has become relativized through the study of demographic, economic, cultural, and other continuities, or by the fashioning of discontinuities which are not correlative with the break at the end of the eighteenth century. (Cf. de Certeau, *The Writing of History*, 123n.3.)

ed. The more informed advocates of various religious communities have begun to understand that a greater awareness of the dynamics of the generation and assimilation of innovation is essential for their own particular orientations. Simultaneously, scholars of religion have begun to analyze significant historical "critical moments," in studying the emergence of new movements, and in coming to terms with the issues of secularization and modernization. Up to now, though, the analysis of religious change has been the province principally of the historians of specific religious traditions and of anthropologists and sociologists involved in understanding the role of religion in society.

Historians of specific religious traditions have contributed a great deal by specifying elements of innovation, and by tracing the development of new constellations of doctrine and praxis in specific traditions. Sociologists have written comparative monographs on the subject; but the end of such inquiry has been the interpretation of *cultural* change or *social* change rather than the significance of religious transformation itself. These cross-cultural analyses have also been conducted within the context of the sociopolitical concern with the issues of modernity; consequently the ideas and methods articulated in these monographs have a restricted utility in understanding religious development in premodern cultures.

It is thus crucial for historians of religions to go forward with the project of developing an orientation that will combine the analysis of adaptations and new configurations in various traditions with the analysis of cross-cultural patterns and interpretations. The acknowledgement of the desire to investigate this type of subject is founded on the realization that a comprehension of religious change is vital for any understanding of what religion *is* and how it intersects with other aspects of culture.[10]

This volume concentrates on specific transitions and transformations that have taken place in five religious traditions: Buddhism, Judaism, Christianity, Islam, and American Indian, during various periods from the first century CE to the present. From a cross-cultural perspective, these essays highlight patterns of religious change.

A number of the essays in this volume are in one way or another concerned with law. The first one, "The Destruction of the Temple and the Rise of Judaism," by Baruch Brody, emphasizes that concern in a decisive way.

The history of Judaism is marked by the development of legal precepts and theological concepts. Both precepts and concepts involve a Jew's relationship with his or her own people, the world, and God. In every period of its history,

---

[10]See the introduction to Frank E. Reynolds and Theodore M. Ludwig, *Transitions and Transformations in the History of Religions: Essays in Honor of Joseph M. Kitagawa* (Leiden: E. J. Brill, 1980).

Judaism has been gifted with expositors who were highly skilled in the interpretation of both precepts and concepts. Consequently Judaism and not only the Judaism of the rabbinic period, is made up of *halacha,* law and *agada*, theology. In the Judaic tradition, both *halacha* and *agada* are of equal importance.

The rabbinic deliberation and instruction encoded in the laws for conduct—*halacha* —applied to all human activity. Faithfulness to the covenant was a way of living out the Jewish calling. Jews who observed Torah as interpreted by rabbinic *halacha* were considered by the rabbis to complete their human destiny in this life and to gain their place in the future world. Although the Roman Empire was politically dominant, Jewish belief maintained that Yahweh was the actual sovereign of the world. The messianic kingdom would be brought to fruition through Israel's faithfulness to *halacha*, and though it was useless to oppose Rome by armed rebellion, fidelity to the covenant could still eventually influence the course of history.[11]

The conflict between the Pharisees and the Sadducees was over the comprehensiveness of the Torah and the authority to interpret it. The Pharisees maintained that their more inclusive method of interpretation was in closer harmony with an oral law that originated with the Sinai covenant. They claimed that only an Israelite who excelled at and accepted as divine both the oral and the written law was qualified to teach Torah. This notion of authority made the Pharisees the precursors of the rabbis. Some scholars maintain that the Pharisees were a "Populist" party that called into question the rights of the privileged minority. The controversies between the Sadducees and Pharisees were most likely debated and occasionally adjudicated in the Sanhedrin, a legislative and judicial council created in the Hellenistic era which was made up of both the Pharisees and the Sadducees. The Sadducees maintained that the Torah did not include the numerous oral traditions that had developed after the written scroll appeared. They also argued that the Torah be interpreted by the proper priestly authorities.[12]

Brody criticizes the thesis that Judaism can be strictly identified with the religion portrayed in the Hebrew Bible. He sketches an account of the origins of Judaism that does not identify it with biblical religion. He argues that the institutions of modern Judaism (such as the synagogue) barely appear in the Hebrew Bible. Judaism is not the religion of the Hebrew Bible, nor is the type of religious sensibility portrayed there Judaism, because the central institutions of one are not the central institutions of the other.

Brody's essay also focuses on Pharisaic Judaism, the community most closely identified with the concerns of the majority of the Jews of their time.

---

[11]Niels. C. Nielsen, ed., *Religions of the World* (New York: St. Martin's Press, 1983) 444.

[12]Ibid., 436-37.

While the Pharisees believed that salvation came by following the law, they also maintained a certain flexibility and spirit of innovation. For the modern Western reader, especially in the United States, these notions are problematic in the sphere of law most familiar to citizens: civil law. Lawyers, no matter how elevated their private commitments may be, ordinarily are professionally concerned with the interests of their clients, not the interests of justice. And considered as a whole, the activities of lawyers cannot rise higher in the pursuit of justice than the projects of their clients. Justice is left to the beneficence of the Invisible Hand.[13]

The ancient near east, as this essay points out, did not view law as a series of technical rules which lawyers could manipulate for the benefit of a client. It perceived law, instead, as a way of ordering relationships among the citizenry so that justice could be accomplished. The Pharisees, in fact, developed a doctrine of transcending the requirements of law: the law establishes the standards which all must follow, but there are higher standards to which all must aspire.

The essay, then, argues that modern Judaism is the product of a party that arose in the last two centuries BCE, the Pharisaic party. The party was vigorous in part because of its teaching, but also in part because its opposition was destroyed by the Romans in 70 CE with the destruction of the temple.

With the temple burnt to the ground Israel was destroyed. Jews throughout the Greek-speaking world began to ask painful questions about the providence of Yahweh. The overall religious situation of the Roman Empire was in flux, as well. This is the cultural milieu that forms the backdrop for Werner Kelber's essay on "Gnosis and the Origins of Christianity."

The populace, particularly the wealthy, was invited to take part in this situation by the very character of the educational system, which was differentiated from any cult. Greek was the prevalent language of the empire and it was particularly the language of education, commerce, and philosophy. Greek, both as a language and a culture, was altering the Roman perspective on religious experience. The religion of the Greeks, like that of the Romans, originated as a succession of city-cults, public demonstrations of gratitude, respect and fear toward the local gods of the city-state. Alexander's vision of a Hellenic empire had revamped the city-states into a far-flung territorial complex, in which the free citizen usually did not participate directly in civic affairs. The individual thus had leisure and incentive to cultivate a private life. Consequently, under the aegis of Greek inspiration, an era of personal religion dawned. What had previously been a matter of racial, tribal, state or social convention now became an issue of indi-

---

[13]See the introduction to David Luban, *Lawyers and Justice* (Princeton: Princeton University Press, 1988).

vidual consideration. Fundamental questions about the meaning of life were being posed with increasing frequency, and not just by Greeks. The Romans were experiencing a comparable period of liberation from all-encompassing civic obligation. It may well be that the world-empire itself liberated many from the obligations of public responsibility and provided them with time for thought. In the schools, the emphasis was on the teaching of ethics, mainly Stoic in character. Lists of virtues and vices, and the reciprocal responsibilities of husbands to wives, fathers to children, masters to slaves were drawn up.

Yet this was a form of morality not fundamentally at variance with municipal codes of behavior. The schools were not equipped to come to terms with the types of inquiries which had to do with the nature of the person, and its relationship to the world and eternity. When such questions were posed, they remained. There is a certain sense in which the world was intellectually prepared for Christianity. Yet it is an open question whether the Hellenic world could have fashioned such a religion solely from its own—though formidable—devices.

The religious situation, though highly varied, was thus beginning to take shape. New types of voluntary religious association were beginning to come into being. There was a pronounced orientation toward monotheism. In the syncretic Hellenic culture, the emerging gnostic cults, which offered new perspectives on the world, were based on monotheistic beliefs, even as they posited a dualistic cosmos presided over by contending powers of good and evil. The ancient city and national creeds were rendered useless except as aids to public order and the oriental mystery cults, though syncretized and made complex by Hellenistic philosophy, still were not able to give an adequate explanation of the human condition.[14]

In his essay, Kelber reminds us that the spirit of late antiquity was marked by a pervasive anxiety about the nature of human existence. He connects this *zeitgeist* with decisive changes encompassing the ancient world. Hellenization, with its internationalizing tendency, shattered national governments and overturned ethnic identities. The monarchy, with its ancient roots, had to give way to more democratic forms of city government. Greek literacy, the technology of alphabet writing, spread expeditiously and threatened entrenched patterns of classical rhetoric and oral communication.

It was in this kind of situation that both orthodox Christianity and Gnosticism developed. Overcome by change, and haunted by the experience of physical destruction and the death of the gods, gnostic Christianity strove to make sense of the predicament by tracing its roots to the creator God. The problem of evil thus found a clever explanation.

---

[14]A popular account of this situation may be found in the first chapter of Paul Johnston's, *A History of Christianity* (New York: Atheneum, 1976).

The Nag Hammadi Christians affirmed Jesus as the figure of salvation, yet their understanding is at variance with that of the orthodox tradition. On the question of Christology, the gnostics believed that if the redeemer figure is to be efficacious in an evil world, he must have no real contact with the world. He is able authentically to redeem the world only if he mirrors divine wholeness without entering into the flesh of the human condition.

On the basis of the information provided by the Nag Hammadi library, Kelber makes a plea for the reconstruction of early Christianity in its historical fullness, not merely from its orthodox perspective. Understanding a world in upheaval casts a ray of light on the development of both orthodox Christianity as well as Gnosticism.

The discoveries of Nag Hammadi raise foundational questions. They intimate that Christianity may have matured in disparate ways or that Christianity as we are familiar with it might never have endured. Had Christianity remained variegated, its very diversity may have weakened it so that it would not have possessed the cohesiveness necessary for survival in a hostile world. It may well be that the survival of Christian tradition is owed to the theological and organizational framework that the nascent church developed. The religious beliefs of the Christian creed dovetail with sociopolitical issues in the development of orthodox Christianity.[15]

From the persecution of gnostics by "orthodox" Christians, we now examine a turning point in the religious history of China: the massive purge of Buddhism in the years 841–845 CE. The year 845 was a pivotal date, marking the end of the high point and the beginning of the decline of Buddhism. The dynamics of the persecution provide a revealing look at the relationship between T'ang factional politics and religious issues. The persecution—the most extensive of its kind in Chinese history—dealt Buddhism a blow from which it has never recovered. Besides permanently damaging Buddhism, the persecution virtually destroyed the other foreign religions then existing in China. Richard Smith's essay on Buddhism and the "Great Persecution" in China is an exercise in understanding the complex process by which religion as a cultural system interacts with its sociopolitical environment.

Both archaeological and literary evidence demonstrate that Buddhism arrived in China during the first century of the common era. Once Buddhism had reached China, it encountered many difficulties: a sprawling empire and a civilization ruled by political and social concepts and standards that had developed over many centuries. Particularly among the cultural elite, these paradigmatic

---

[15]See Elaine Pagels, *The Gnostic Gospels* (New York: Random House, 1979) 142-43.

themes went against the grain of some of the most basic tenets of Buddhist teaching. As examples of traditional Confucianism, the Chinese intelligentsia maintained a secular and pragmatic outlook. Even at its apex, Buddhism was subaltern to the secular order.

As a teaching, Buddhism was destined to encounter censure from the Confucian elite, who held that the fundamental aims of human existence are to be achieved in this life, and that beliefs should be evaluated according to their sociopolitical productivity rather than according to their transcendent attributes. Confucianism considered the search for personal salvation to be egocentric: the person can become individuated only within society. Taoism, the principal non-Confucian indigenous tradition of philosophical and religious thought in China, also shares these views. In this tradition as well, the aims are palpable ones—integration with nature and the prolongation of life. In light of this type of orientation, Buddhism, once it arrived in China, had to endure many tensions. Its evaluation of existence as chimerical and its credence in notions such as rebirth, the principle of moral causality: actions and the law that regulates their effects (*karman*), and the quest of transcendent goals, such as *nirvāna* , that had been customary in India, were seen as peculiarities that were opposed to the teachings of the most respected teachers in China. The foreign origin of Buddhism was enough to brand it as inappropriate to be taught throughout the country.[16]

Conflicts were even more apparent at the institutional level. Buddhist clergy had traditionally claimed to be free of responsibility for any secular commitments and dispensed from government aegis. In China, the notion of such a foreign element within the sovereignty was viewed as both improper and dangerous. It became an area of conflict that lasted for centuries, until, in late imperial times, Buddhist clergy were forced to give up their prerogatives. They thus forfeited even the appearance of autonomy.

Nonetheless, Buddhism did become solidly established in China and developed into a significant element in Chinese culture. This was in part because its constitutive stage corresponded at points with a time of political breakdown, combined with a transient deterioration of Confucianism. When the Han empire fell in 220 CE, Buddhism had survived in obscurity in China for more than 150 years and afterwards expanded into an important religious bloc in the time of conflict (311–589 CE) when the empire had crumbled, and "barbarian" dynasties dominated vast sections of China. During that period, the influence of Confucianism was attenuated. This worked to the advantage of Buddhism. Once the empire was again consolidated, Buddhism was in a stable position, in spite of antago-

---

[16]Erik Zürcher, "Buddhism in China," *The Encyclopedia of Religion*, ed. Mircea Eliade (New York, Macmillan, 1987) 2:414-16.

nism from the Confucian element.[17] Smith's essay spells out the culturally inspired antecedents of the actual persecution of 841–845 CE, among them the attack on the alien origins of Buddhist doctrine, its undermining the foundations of imperial rule, and its influence in corrupting popular customs. He argues that the significance of the Hui-ch'ang suppression itself did not change the status of Buddhism in China so much as it reflected and, in a way, preceded a number of other events and trends which together produced long-term effects on both the theory and practice of Chinese Buddhism.

Buddhism, in various of its stages, has been a sectarian religion, a civilizational religion, and an imperial religion. During the ninth and tenth centuries, Buddhism in China was attacked both internally and externally. Repeated invasion by Uighurs and Turkik peoples, as well as official persecutions and the revival of the Confucian tradition, led to a decisive weakening of institutional Buddhism in the country.

The nationalistic impulse in China can be traced back to the denial of self in favor of the collectivity.[18] And the prohibition of contention in deference to the value of orderly status relations had an impact in the majority of Asian cultures which, from a Western perspective, suggests the notion of authoritarianism. But since these cultures shared a very different notion of power, it is only partially accurate to view the relationship of superior and inferior as authoritarian. The intolerance of adversaries and the insistence on conformity do validate the charge of authoritarianism, and occasionally even of despotism. But since the Asian understanding of power was not one of command and decision making, the hierarchical status relations were in reality not endowed with the sense of domination inherent in real authoritarianism. The impact of this difference was to advance the evolution of types of paternalistic authority, and the stifling of criticism in paternalistic authoritarianism is of a different nature from the denial of criticism in which power is connected with the furtherance of policies.[19]

Smith's essay presents a view of the cultural dimensions of authority—an instance of the methods of exercising authority and power in Asia.

C. J. McNaspy's essay on "Conquest or Inculturation" deals with events surrounding Mateo Ricci's introduction of Christianity to China, Jesuit presence in India during the 16th century, and the Paraguayan Reductions.

---

[17]Ibid.

[18]Lucian Pye, *Asian Power and Politics* (Cambridge MA: Harvard University Press, 1985) 194.

[19]Ibid., 50.

When on May 20, 1499, Vasco de Gama cast anchor at Calcutta, the world had all of a sudden literally expanded. The Age of Discovery—and colonization—was in full swing.

The exotic geographical ventures and colonial exploitations, in particular, had special significance for Christianity—the millennial kingdom of Christ was close at hand. The Christian order in its institutional form, though, was not ready to face the various cultures and strange inhabitants of these lands. Eventually Christianity became the exclusive preserve of Europeans: non-Christian cultures were considered simply as pagan. Armed with a sense of destiny and confident in their own superiority, missionaries departed from Europe in order to convert the world, and in the process, to westernize it.

Any adaptation of the European way, let alone any compromise of Christian doctrines, was considered godless.[20] Yet Christianity did possess a tradition of accommodation: the disciples carried Jewish cultural forms with them into the Greco-Roman world. In diverse ways, the early Christian community appropriated Latin and Greek expressions, accepted pagan rites, and actually encouraged the preservation of diverse aspects of native cultures. It was a policy of accommodation calculated to bring any alien culture into the Christian fold.

The Society of Jesus (Jesuits), organized 1534 by Ignatius of Loyola (with papal confirmation in 1540), facilitated a revival of the tolerant spirit; in fact, the Jesuit policy of accommodation was developed through a long series of trials and errors in the mission fields. In the beginning there was an absence of any concrete plan to implement a policy as such, as well as a lack of official sanction from the papacy. But when the Society found success with its adaptive style in Ethiopia and Ireland (both had earlier known Christianity), its leadership decided to experiment further with the rediscovered strategy. The testing ground was Asia, and it was Francis Xavier (1506–1552), who gave meaning to the approach of accommodation and decided upon its basic contents. Briefly, these mandated that missionaries must learn to speak and write in the language of the culture; they should understand and prepare themselves for the central role of intellectuals in Asian society (Xavier himself requested that learned missionaries be sent to Japan and its universities to debate the Buddhist bonzes). He also came to realize the overwhelming importance of China as a mission field.

Xavier died on Sancion Island in 1552, never realizing his goals for the Middle Kingdom. But there was no doubt in the mind of the man who followed in his footsteps that "Xavier was the first to realize the aptitude of the innumerable people of the vast empire [of China] for absorbing the truth of the Gospel."

---

[20]This point is made in a number of places in John Phelan, *The Millennial Kingdom of the Franciscans in the New World*, 2nd ed. rev. (Berkeley: University of California Press, 1970).

Born in the year of Xavier's death, this successor, an Italian named Matteo Ricci, would discover later that it would be necessary to transcend Xavier's mandate. Ricci (1552–1610), known to his Chinese contemporaries as Li-ma-tou, was the West's first "sinologist." From the very beginning, he was convinced that the conversion of all the Chinese was possible "if someone would be favorably received by the King [of China]."[21] Thus, the principal concern of the Jesuit missionaries in China was to involve a search for ways to compromise with the local culture without modifying basic Christian doctrines.

Confrontation and misunderstanding seem to be the accepted approach in an East-West environment. The Sinologist Jacques Gernet depicts the impact of Christianity on China as a function of disparities between distinct languages with different "logics," "modes of thought," and "visions of the world and man." Ricci strove both for cultural toleration and transcendence. Yet, he went beyond the stage of understanding another culture. He attempted to synthesize the central values of two vastly different thought systems. Ricci's East-West synthesis demands the need to understand how it was first conceived, and what it meant in the intellectual exchanges between China and the West.

A similar attempt at adaptation and acculturation also occurred in India. In 1580, three of Ricci's confreres were involved in intercultural philosophical and theological dialogue with the emperor Jalal-ud-din Muhammad Akbar. It was one of these confreres, Roberto de Nobili, who initiated one of the most significant breakthroughs in Western mission history, that of adaptation to the intellectual and cultural life of the land. But when de Nobili tried to make Sanskrit the official liturgical language for Indian Christians, he met resistance from local church theologians and officials. While he later received support from Pope Gregory XV, de Nobili's methods of acculturation were short-lived, though they have been vindicated today in their acceptance by many Christian Indians.

Throughout Latin America the Indian villages organized in the sixteenth century often took on the more ordered form called reductions in the seventeenth and eighteenth centuries. Particularly, the Franciscans, Jesuits, and Dominicans established reductions in the areas of Mexico and California, Venezuela and Colombia, Peru and Ecuador, Paraguay, Brazil, and northern Argentina. The more than thirty reductions of Paraguay, with 3,500 or more Indians in each, occupied an area of 53,904 square kilometers. The total population reached 150,000 in 1743.

The Indians who entered the reductions were bound for life to the mission. Some were born in the village; others entered by personal choice or as a penalty for crimes; as prisoners of war; and some as purchased property.

---

[21]Matteo Ricci, *China in the Sixteenth Century: The Journals of Matthew Ricci, 1583–1610*, trans. Louis Gallagher (New York: Random House, 1953) 296.

After the expulsion of the Jesuits in 1767 by the Portuguese and Spanish kings, the missions fell into decadence. Natives had not been schooled to provide leadership to ward off the attacks of the encroaching Portuguese or Spanish seeking lands and slave labor, or to adapt to the new political and social context. Within thirty years half the Indians in Brazil and Paraguay had scattered, many to the nearly inaccessible interior. By the early nineteenth century, no missions were left.

The success of the missions in colonial times is a controverted issue. The positions held by various scholars disagree with respect to the relative degree of change or adaptation brought about by evangelization. Some maintain that the result was only an external imposition of liturgy and ecclesiastical forms upon pagan religion. Others believe that a kind of syncretism was accomplished, whether by an amalgamation or a juxtaposition of paganism and Christianity. Still others hold that an incomplete evangelization resulted, producing a genuine change through progressive catechesis. A final position is that the Indians basically became Christians; the purity of their faith depended much on the methods of evangelism employed.

In *Violence and the Sacred* (1972), René Girard presents an important new theory of religion founded on the phenomenon of sacrifice. For Girard, religion develops in connection with some human activity basic to social life and in all its aspects is fundamentally a human construction. Girard asks why the relationship between violence and religious sacrifice is so rarely investigated. From the way in which historians of religion treat the subject of sacrifice, it would be difficult to know whether scholarly objectivity or some form of secret discretion influences their orientation. Girard's work provides a point of entry into Jesse Nash's essay on the pacification and transformation of Plains Indian religion.

Ancient literature seems to suggest that substitution is the foundation for the practice of sacrifice: that is, the ritual victim is an "innocent" who expiates for a "guilty" party. Modern anthropological fieldwork and later theoretical reflection reenforce this hypothesis (though a number of anthropologists pay little attention to this notion or reject it outright). Girard takes a more nuanced position, maintaining that, in sacrifice, a society attempts to reflect upon a relatively indifferent victim, the violence that would otherwise be unleashed on its own members, the people it most wants to protect.[22]

For Girard, violence is endemic to human culture, and no solution exists to this problem except the one provided by religion. Since that solution is provided in rituals of killing and their rationalization as "sacrifice," the answer religion

---

[22]René Girard, *Violence and the Sacred* (Baltimore: Johns Hopkins University Press, 1977) 4.

gives is also an act of violence. Girard ultimately sees the phenomenon of sacrifice at the very core of human life. Sacrifice is the most crucial and fundamental of rites, it is also the most commonplace.[23] All social systems that give structure to society have sprung up from it: language, kinship systems, codes of etiquette, taboos, patterns of exchange, rites, and civil institutions. A theory of sacrifice generates an all-encompassing account of human social formation, religion, and culture.

According to Girard, the commonly accepted notions of "sacrifice," meant as clarifications of the significance of sacrificial rituals, belong to the level of mythic rationalization. In order to penetrate beyond this, it is necessary to be aware of what occurs in rituals of sacrifice, and to ask why mythic rationalizations have developed over time. What takes place, of course, is a killing. There is a growing body of anthropological evidence relating to the incidence and importance of ritual slaying in the most varied forms of human culture. Since the core of ritual is a reenactment of a "prior event," it needs to be analyzed under two aspects: the way in which ritual represents or substitutes for the "prior event"; and the way in which both the ritual and prior event interpret the act of killing. From Girard's perspective, the "prior event" that all ritual slayings rationalize and represent in various "substitutions" is a collective murder, an act of mob violence. "Sacrifice" then becomes a word that can be employed to refer to the complex phenomenon of the collective killing of a human victim, its mythic rationalization, and its ritualization.[24]

Jesse Nash's, "'No More War Parties': The Pacification and Transformation of Plains Indian Religion," argues that Plains Indian religion has been misunderstood in the past. In particular, the Plains Indians did practice human sacrifice, if we remember that the scalp once belonged to a human being. When the white settlers came and pacified the Plains Indians, their religion was naturally affected but mainly because killing was a religious act, an act which was now illegal. Killing was such an integral part of the Plains Indian religion, a part of a tribal sacrificial complex, that the pacification of that religion ended its vitality. To wage war no more meant that the Indians could no longer truly be religious.

The persistence of a strong religious sensibility in an increasingly modernized culture is a striking feature of the southern United States. The imperviousness of the South to the erosion of traditional orthodox religion is a salient characteristic of the region. This runs counter to stereotypical notions about the type of cultural impact that the modernization process ordinarily exerts on a society.

---

[23]Ibid., 300.
[24]Robert Hamerton-Kelly, ed., *Violent Origins*. (Palo Alto: Stanford University Press, 1987); cf. the introduction by Burton Mack, at 7-8.

The South, so such notions would maintain, might be expected to jettison evangelical religion. Secularization should be developing into the dominant cultural mode. Yet, while it is true that secularization has burgeoned in the South, it does not seem to have had an overwhelming effect on southern religiosity.[25] An element in the tradition of that religiosity is detailed in John Boles's essay on "The Beginning of the Southern Bible Belt."

The new social history has mainly concentrated on the late colonial and antebellum periods. The fundamental issue confronted by social historians in relation to the antebellum South is, What was the social importance of evangelical Christianity? Their studies have indicated several answers: It resulted in "marks of civility" and provided form, structure, and coherence to the lives of its adherents. It was a contributing factor in the social organization of the Old South. Evangelical Christianity was also a significant component of the "moral economy" of that culture. Other analyses have maintained that evangelical religion was a contributing factor in the decentralization of the society.[26]

Evangelicals applied their religious principles to political life. They did so because they perceived civil government not simply as a human invention, but as an institution ordained by God to secure peace and order among a fallen human race. Consequently both magistrates and citizens were obliged to carry out their political duties in accordance with those eternal laws given to regulate individual and social behavior.[27] Thomas Smyth maintained that "Christianity prescribes for citizenship, as well as for domestic or industrial life, and its ethics should be taught in the former department as freely as in either of the latter." One of the functions of the pulpit was to be "the means of instructing Christians in the Christianity of their political relations."[28]

While arguing for the application of religious principles to political life, evangelicals also supported the separation of church and state. They had no difficulties with disestablishment or the voluntary system. The evangelical outlook on church-state relations was capsulized by Smyth in a tract on "The Relations of Christianity to Civil Polity." Smyth claimed that "the political principles of the Bible held that there were two governments, civil and ecclesiastical, both instituted by God, each "independent and distinct" in its obligations and sphere of in-

---

[25]Cf. the introduction to Samuel Hill, *Varieties of Southern Religious Experience* (Baton Rouge: Louisiana State University Press) 1988.

[26]Ibid., 5.

[27]See the chapter on "The Church in the World," in Anne Loveland, *Southern Evangelicals and the Social Order: 1800–1860* (Baton Rouge: Louisiana State University Press, 1980).

[28]Thomas Smyth, "National Righteousness," *Southern Presbyterian Review* 12 (April 1859): 25-26; quoted in Loveland, *Southern Evangelicals*, 108.

fluence. The role of the state was to promote justice and maintain order; the role of the church was to facilitate personal sanctity. The state employed coercion to bring about compliance with its measures, while the church used spiritual methods. Though "independent and distinct," state and church had a reciprocal relationship. The state protected the church in the free exercise of its authority, rights, and powers. The church, reciprocally, upheld the authority, rights, and powers, of the state, counseling the Christian obligation of obedience to civil authority. Smyth held that state and church were "coordinate and conducive to the common good . . . ; so that while they can never commingle, they can never be safely disjoined." This was the foundation for his belief that Christianity was "the grand requisite in civil government." He and other evangelicals maintained that religion was essential to the preservation of the American republic. They held that the United States had been established as a Christian nation, and that the virtue, peace, prosperity and liberty of the country depended on the spread of Christianity. In fact, evangelicals seem to have placed more confidence in religion than in government as the guarantor of order and peace.[29]

While evangelicals believed that ministers should respect civil authority and preach compliance with the state, they also believed that ministers should make themselves heard on political issues that involved religious and ethical principles. Because of their belief that Christianity was essential for the vitality of the nation, evangelicals maintained that ministers should demonstrate the relevance of religious principles to the society, admonishing citizens and public officials when required. The editor of the *Christian Index* stated: "We claim the right, and shall exercise it, of expressing our opinion on any subject that involves the religious interests of our country, whenever we think proper to do so, let who will take offence thereat. We believe the political and moral interests of our country are inseparably connected; and we feel just as free to censure what we believe to be injurious in its tendency, in the judge upon the bench or the representative in the council halls of the nation, as in the humblest mendicant."[30]

The South as the United States' Bible Belt of evangelical Protestantism is an early nineteenth-century development. It was the Great Revival of 1800 that set the region on the road to evangelical ascendancy and consequently altered the historical contours of the area. The camp-meeting revivals on the southern frontier at the beginning of the early nineteenth century were a cultural turning point for the South; their origins, development, and consequences are the subject of Boles's essay.

---

[29]Loveland, *Southern Evangelicals*, 109-10.
[30]*Christian Index*, 9 March 1848, 77; quoted in Loveland, *Southern Evangelicals*, 111-12.

For complex demographic, social, and theological reasons, societal tensions and perceived crises, the Southern United States at the end of the 1790s was prepared for religious revival. American historians use various interpretive frameworks to provide reasons for the events leading up to this outbreak of revivalism. They advert to social tensions resulting from rapid migration and the transformation of the southern economy; they employ social science terms such as hysteria, mass psychology, and revitalization movements to instantiate their narrative of events. While Boles employs these notions correlative with the discourse of cultural anthropology and functionalism—to provide an explanation of what apparently took place, he also attempts to view events from the perspective of the actors themselves.

By 1803 the South was caught up in a wave of revivalism, and after 1805, the area was on the road to becoming the evangelical Protestant Bible Belt of the United States. Boles spells out the cultural consequences of the Great Revival. Southern evangelicalism, for instance, was highly privatized and individualistic. There were, accordingly, a number of ways southern white evangelicals rationalized their compromise with slavery. One way was to consider slavery a matter of civil society and consequently place the institution of slavery beyond their religious responsibility. The need to divide life into legal or civil spheres and moral spheres thus became more pronounced. A consequent emphasis on individual morality, not on social reform, developed. In its southern expression mainline evangelical religion in the antebellum period acknowledged and legitimated a stratified society even as individuals in the church thought of themselves as belonging to a religious community. Boles implicitly raises intriguing issues about the nature of civil society and the consequences which develop when the legal and moral spheres are sundered.

Within the context of that segment of the historical development of evangelicalism just sketched, many reasons have been put forward to explain the reemergence of a hard-edged, conservative evangelical movement in the United States. The electorate, it is maintained, is disillusioned with the federal government and state-sponsored social programs which benefit the poor and minorities. Liberals, we are told, no longer have the ideas or fortitude of the past. Americans are rebelling against the assault on traditional values which played so disruptive a part in the cultural politics of the 1960s and early 1970s. William Martin's essay, "The Transformation of Fundamentalism between the World Wars," specifically articulates the dynamics involved in the transformation of fundamentalism between the world wars.

There is probably truth in some, and conceivably all, of these explanations. Jimmy Carter's success in the 1976 election is testimony in part to the popular revulsion at official corruption, discontent with government programs that fail to meet expectations, and reaction against the adversary culture's contempt for cherished principles. Ronald Reagan, in his two campaigns, played variations on the same themes. Reagan won his stunning victory in November 1980, not because the country as a whole went "conservative," but because the conservatives—especially the white Moral Majority—gave him such massive support, according to an ABC News-Harris Survey. Thus, the power of the "Moral Majority" proved to be real.

In this age of space exploration and computer technology, the ideas of evangelicals appear as an aberrant intrusion on the modern age—a relic from a bygone era that is tolerated in our midst, like a piece of ancient architecture that has withstood the assault of centuries past. Yet before such ideas are dismissed simply as curious sociological diversions, it should be noted that at least one survey taken in 1979 indicated that there were more than 45 million evangelical Christians in the United States.

This indicates that there have existed, for quite a while, two different Americas. Since the press pounded out their last line of copy at the Dayton, Tennessee Scopes Trial in 1925, however, evangelical America has been a virtual nonstory—with the exception of an occasional report on anticommunist sects or possibly a Billy Graham rally. Evangelical America is the silent majority that Nixon and Agnew spoke to and for during the turbulent years of the late sixties and early seventies. Now this silent majority is finding its own voice, and that voice is starting to attract a larger and more attentive constituency.

Evangelicals are today determinedly building their own Christian community. The evangelical Christian communications system is more highly developed and effective than at any time in this country's history. The same is true for the infrastructure of evangelical life throughout the nation. The evangelical community is amassing a base of potential power that dwarfs many other competing interests. A careful look at the evangelical communications infrastructure and network would convince even the skeptic that it is now a significant "alternative" cultural force.

Martin's essay maintains that the First World War and the Russian Revolution of 1917 provided Fundamentalism with what was to become one of its most significant themes: religious nationalism. The combination of prewar nativism, war-heightened patriotism, the rise of communism and the outbreak of strikes, bombings, and espousal of radical causes at the war's end helped create the "Red Scare," and Fundamentalists were among the groups that responded most strongly to all these events. The conservative Protestant denominations advocated religion as a bulwark against radicalism and tended to identify Christianity and patriotism.

Martin deals explicitly with the Fundamentalist Controversy, which was marked by two distinct elements. One was the fight against Darwinian evolutionary theory, in which antievolutionists throughout the South and Southwest made concerted efforts to prohibit the teaching of evolution in public schools. The other element was the struggle against biblical criticism. This was occasioned by the steady increase in acceptance of German biblical criticism into Protestant churches and seminaries. Biblical criticism undercut the idea of the special inspiration of scripture. Its authors were seen to be quite human, fashioning a sacred literature by the same processes used to create secular literature. This made it difficult to maintain claims of inerrancy and of the absolute authority of the Bible. Thus, Fundamentalists found it imperative to oppose the movement of biblical criticism.

Biblical interpretation also figures importantly as a theme in Robert Hamerton-Kelly's essay, "Biblical Justification of Apartheid in Afrikaner Civil Religion." Apartheid is an ideology with its roots in race, nationalism, Calvinist doctrine, and South African history. No coherent legal theory has ever been expounded by the adherents of apartheid. Yet, a number of jurisprudential strains have greatly influenced the legislative and judicial strategies of apartheid and may consequently be considered the jurisprudential foundations of the South African state. A form of anti-humanism is one of the strains that has been invoked on various occasions in order to justify legislative or judicial action, but usually it has functioned unobtrusively to aid in the fashioning of a state based on legislative supremacy and judicial subordination, in which the concept of legally protected individual rights plays no role.

It is no easy task to describe the influence of Calvinism on South African jurisprudence. Calvinism has had a major impact on the life and legal institutions of the country through the Dutch Reformed Churches, which govern the religious life of the Afrikaner people. But whether Calvinism, as usually understood, can be blamed for the authoritarian nature of the Afrikaner rule and the denial of human rights is not so certain. Interpreters of Calvinist legal theory hold that Calvinism envisages the legal protection of human rights, though it rejects humanism as a foundation for such rights.[31] Calvinism may consequently have been inappropriately invoked to support the approach to law of the national Party Government. On the other hand, it is certain that it has been so invoked. In particular it has been invoked in order to discredit institutions such as the Rule of Law and a Bill of Rights on the grounds that their humanistic foundation contradicts the teachings of Calvinism.

A prominent Afrikaans legal scholar, Professor Venter, rejected in 1973 the Rule of Law, as expounded by A. V. Dicey and South African liberal lawyers, for the reason that it "presupposes the notion of 'fundamental rights' accruing to the individual against (State, Government) authority" and consequently reflects

---

[31]J. D. Van der Vyver, *Seven Lectures on Human Rights* (1976) 120; J. D. Van der Vyver, "The Bill of Rights Issue," *Lawyers for Human Rights*, bulletin no. 1 (February 1983): 68, 70.

a humanist philosophy which is not acceptable in the country. The author bases his conclusion on the preamble and section two of the South African Constitution of 1961, in which the sovereignty of God is acknowledged, and maintains that "the Christian premise of the sovereignty of God stands in radical opposition to the humanistic point of departure which makes *man* the sovereign consideration."[32] Venter goes on to suggest that South African lawyers should not approve the Rule of Law but rather embrace "Christian government, necessarily including juridical ordering and administration of justice with a distinct Christian accent."

Venter's ideas received total support from the constitutional committee of the President's Council charged with the task of considering the desirability of including a Bill of Rights in the 1983 Constitution. It put forth as one of the main reasons for a negative attitude "toward the adoption of a Bill of Rights the humanist emphasis it placed on individual right, vis-à-vis the authority of the state, whereas particularly the Afrikaner with his Calvinist background is more inclined to place the emphasis on the State and the maintenance of the State."[33] In view of this resistance, it was not surprising that the Constitution Bill presented to Parliament contained no guarantees for personal freedom and that the government rejected a proposal of the Progressive Federal Party that a Bill of Rights be included in the new Constitution.[34]

Since the accession of President F. W. de Klerk, the release of Nelson Mandela, and the legalization of the African National Party, attitudes toward a Bill of Rights are changing among the ruling Afrikaner elite. Although a number of racist laws have been repealed, full equality before the law and the statutory recognition of human rights are far from being realized. Blacks still do not have the vote.

Mr. de Klerk has done away with the obstacles to constitutional negotiation: black leaders are out of prison, their organizations unbanned. The president now confronts the even more difficult task of persuading blacks not to repeat his own party's past failings. He is critical of big government, though apartheid regulated every part of the lives of the people. He wants a bill of rights, upheld by an independent judiciary. Yet during the rule of his National party South Africa has had no such charter, while both legislature and judiciary have been bypassed more and more by executive decree.

President de Klerk's constitutional planners have come up with various proposals, all of which limit state power. They include: a bill of rights, separation

---

[32]"The Withering of the Rule of Law," (1973) 8 *Speculum Juris* at 86-88.

[33]"Second Report of the Constitutional Committee of the President's Council," PC/41982 9.10.

[34]House of Assembly Debates, cols. 13-14 (31 January 1986).

of powers, checks and balances, a mixed executive, devolution of power to federal and even smaller regions, and a two-chamber parliament.

Hamerton-Kelly's consideration of the manner in which the Afrikaner churches have attempted to find a biblical basis for apartheid, spells out the way that history is turned into myth in order to promote the political interests of the mythmakers. His essay seeks to understand the role that the Bible played in the Afrikaner civil religion which issued eventually in the policy of apartheid.

The civil religion that sustained the Afrikaners until recently was given form in the late nineteenth and early twentieth centuries, under the impulse of British imperialism and Dopper Calvinism. Racism, though, was a more influential factor than Calvinism in the politics of the Afrikaners, who today practice a much more pragmatic rather than ideological politics based in this racism.

The notion that human "races" are unassimilable, is at the core of Afrikaner nationalist mythology and of the political economy that it legitimates. The Dutch Reformed Church has traditionally based its argument in support of racial separation on five biblical texts. Hamerton-Kelly maintains that this argument is founded on defective hermeneutical principles which permit the misuse of the Bible to justify the actions of national self-interest. He draws the wider conclusion that the use of the Bible to justify a cultural or political program is riddled with ambiguity, and raises questions for current theologies of liberation.

The separation between politics and religion has been an important issue in Judaism since the destruction of the second Temple and the destruction of the Jewish state in the ancient period. It is also treated in Islamic medieval political theory (for instance, in the writings of ibn Khaldun). The dialectical relationship between politics and religion is instantiated in the fundamental arrangement of Hindu state ideology and is also articulated in considerations of Buddhist states at least since Akbar. In both the Hindu and Buddhist cases the king is given legitimation by religious figures (the Brahmins in the Hindu instance, and the sangha in the Buddhist example). The responsibility of the king in the Buddhist case is to maintain the sangha uncorrupt.

The formulation of problems posed by relations between politics and religion, and the possible solutions to those problems, thus arises in varied cultural traditions. There exist other religious traditions in which politics and religion are construed differently, and in which consequently, the problems and solutions vary greatly from Western ones. The Islamic tradition in its worldwide membership and universalist aspirations, can be compared with Christianity. Michael Fischer's essay, "The Iranian Revolution: Five Frames for Understanding," concentrates on a critical moment in modern Islamic history: the Iranian revolution.

The struggle and mutual interaction between these rival civilizations has now perdured fourteen centuries. It commenced in the seventh century with the birth of Islam, and continues to the present. The relationship has been marred at times by crusades and jihads, but the interaction with Islam also provided Europe with access to the worlds of classical learning that generated the Renaissance and modernity. The decolonization processes of the post-World War II period have seen the rise of nationalist and fundamentalist nativisms in many areas of the Islamic world, which with the demographic shifts from rural to urban populations and peripheralization of the economies of many of the states of the Middle East have led to revolutionary processes not unlike those which Europe experienced in the eighteenth and nineteenth centuries, and which most dramatically exploded in the Iranian revolution of 1977–1979. For some time a reaction has been intensifying against Western primacy and a need to reaffirm Islamic principles and restore Muslim glory. Today much of the Muslim world is once again seized by an intense—and violent—resentment of the West.

The foundation of secularism in the West may be discerned in two circumstances—in early Christian doctrines and, even more, experience, which fashioned two institutions, church and state; and in later Christian controversies, which separated the two. Muslims also experienced equivalent religious conflicts resulting in such situations as the Safavid Empire becoming Shi'a in the sixteenth century, while the Ottoman Empire became Sunni. These were analogous to the kind of antipathy that characterized Christian struggles between Protestants and Catholics, which eventually motivated Christians to develop a position of separation of church and state. By taking away coercive power from religious institutions, Christian civilization was able to prevent the intolerance and persecution that Christians had inflicted on members of other religions and, especially, on those who avowed other forms of their own. Muslim societies also developed functional equivalents: for instance, the millet system of the Ottoman empire. Although paying lip service to religious authority, institutions and reforms analogous to the secular state in Europe emerged, and were embodied in the very operation of multireligious, multilinguistic, multiethnic/national empires such as the Ottoman, Mughal, and Safavi-Qajar ones.

Comparative history demonstrates that when there exists a disjunction between political and hierocratic domination, granted the supremacy of the deity over worldly powers, theocratic monism may well be the next step taken down the road. Political-hierocratic dualism frequently contains seeds of hierocratic monism which may or may not take root depending on historical circumstances.

The catalyst for the evolution of assertions of hierocratic monism out of Qajar political-hierocratic dualism originated with the politicization of Islamic identity in conflict with Western (that is, Ottoman, Russian, as well as West European) cultural and political hegemony. The pessimistic appraisal of the political domain can sometimes develop into a pessimistic evaluation of the political domain with the objective of its subjection to religious authority—that is, espousal of hierocratic monism.[35]

Periodically there was a threat from within Shi'ism to the solidity of the binary structure of domination in the reorganized Shi'ite political order of premodern Iran. This is how the Safavid state itself was created, and there were many religiopolitical movements that took a similar shape, of which the most significant was probably the movement which eventually turned into a schism and the establishment of a new religion (Baha'ism) and in political terms was a suppressed civil war. There was also an external danger in the form of imperialist advance, and of the influence of the West on the modernization of the state.

Probably the most significant area of divergence between Christianity in the West and Islam, is often considered to be the lack of a structurally independent hierocracy. In the Ottoman Empire, the Islamic clergy (*ulama*) were educated and employed in state institutions; but in Iranian Shi'ism there were religious taxes paid directly to the clergy that gave them at times great independence. During the first half of the nineteenth century, Shi'ism started to become more like Christianity in the West in the sense that, as was the case with the medieval papacy, it was the institutional translation of the separation of the political and the religious domains that eventually awarded the Shi'ite hierocracy immense political influence as the autonomous guardians of sacred law and religious tradition. Simultaneously, the entrenched predeliction toward disengagement from the daily grind of politics at the highest echelon of the hierocracy heightened the effectiveness of their occasional intrusions in political crises.

The disjunction of hierocratic domination from political domination in the nineteenth century had implications that are still in evidence. In the context of the idea of the two powers, the hierocracy asserted the leadership of the nation with the support of the merchants when, in conflicts between the Shi'ite majority and foreign states, the ruler was perceived as inadequately fulfilling his duty to guard the best interests of the nation.

In the crucial time of nationalist unrest and anti-imperialist conflict, the period of the nationalization of oil (1950–1953), the Shi'ites in Iran were able to find a secular leader in Musaddiq. Yet while Musaddiq was secular, his National Front depended on the support of Ayatullah Kashani, and when Kashani withdrew his support, the coalition started to come apart. In the case of the rebellion against the shah as the presumed front for American imperialism and propagator of a foreign culture, the hierocracy once more took on national leadership in the political crisis of 1978. But now the contending monarchical

---

[35]Cf. Said Amir Arjomand, *The Shadow of God and the Hidden Imam: Religion, Political Order, and Societal Change in Shi'ite Iran from the Beginning to 1890* (Chicago: University of Chicago Press, 1984) 264-65.

state shattered. The hierocracy took over the state from its last secular leader on February 11, 1979.[36]

Fischer's essay focuses specifically on the Islamic form of the Iranian revolution as part of the anthropology and sociology of the Islamic world, as well as on the possibilities for revolution today, and on the role of ideologies in relation to transformations in class structure. He poses some provocative questions about the role of religion in sociopolitical context. Fischer specifies some class-linked differences in the interpretations of Islam and maintains that variations in religious interpretation can provide a significant tool for understanding critical social cleavages within a society.

Shifting back to the West, the debate over the morality of nuclear weapons has become a pivotal event in church-state relations. "The Challenge of Peace," the United States Roman Catholic Bishops' pastoral letter of 1983, aroused a storm of national controversy. My essay, "Nuclear Ethics—'The Challenge of Peace'," analyzes certain themes of the controversial Pastoral Letter on War and Peace.

Yet to understand the statement only as the result of ecclesiastical doctrine or even of the bishops' personal convictions would be inappropriate. Behind the bishops' stance on nuclear weapons policy lies a series of institutional changes that over the last two decades have thrust politics more and more to the center of the life of the church. The period since Pope Paul VI's pronouncement on birth control—*Humanae vitae* (1968)—which prohibited artificial contraception for Catholics, has been marked by self-doubt and much dissension within the Church. Yet at the same time, there has been a concerted growth in that part of the Church's institutional resources dedicated to social justice. Much of it can be traced to 1967, when Pope Paul issued an encyclical on third world development. In its own way the 1967 document, *Populorum progressio*, was almost as controversial as *Humanae vitae*. It criticized the wealthier nations for indifference to the poorer, and fixed the blame for third world poverty on Western exploitation. *Populorum progressio* culminated a series of council documents and encyclicals—Pope John XXIII's *Mater et magistra* (1961) and *Pacem et terris* (1963), and Vatican Council II's *Gaudium et spes* (1965)—in which the Vatican set forth a new political teaching the themes of which reflected the temper of the times: a more conciliatory attitude toward Communism, a new accent on disarmament and peace, empathy for the third world. To put forward these interests, Pope Paul established a Pontifical Commission on Justice and Peace to oversee the development of the Church's social teaching. In brief, after over two

---

[36]Ibid., 265.

decades of inner turmoil, it is the Church's politically oriented institutions that have emerged the most unscathed and vital.

"The Challenge of Peace" is marked theologically by an effort to make a case for the "complementarity" of both the just-war tradition and pacifism as viable ethical perspectives. The statement's difficulties in this regard were intensified by what may best be summarized by the question: Must we mean what we say? The real dilemma is actually not between the just-war tradition and nonviolence, as set out in the letter, but between the just-war tradition and pacifism (the principled refusal to take a human life, even in a "just" cause).

Given the nature and rapidity of international political developments since 1983, we can say now that, had the bishops more carefully analyzed the connection between the drive for national autonomy (even then on the horizon) and peace—had they placed the debate about nuclear weapons in the context of the need for constructive political change in adversary nations as an important element of the peace process—the pastoral letter might not appear quite so much the product of a particular moment in the political culture of the United States. Events of the past several years prove that progress on follows changed political attitudes and behaviors. The threat of global war appears less imminent today than in 1983, not because there are fewer nuclear weapons, but because of changed behavior on the part of the former Soviet Union.

Current changes obviously go far beyond the bilateral U.S./Soviet relationship. The linchpin in the collapse of communist regimes in Eastern Europe is related to the reality that change in the former Soviet Union has been paralleled by a process of de-Leninization, cultural liberalization, and the rhetoric and beginnings of political democratization; and of course because of concurrent political and economic developments in East Central Europe itself.

An ancient dictum of Christian political theology has proven true: that peace is a matter of rightly ordered political community among nations. The negotiating process has succeeded for the present because of an altered relationship between Russia and the United States, which was in turn made possible by changed declaratory and on-the-ground policy by Russia. Change in weapons policy followed political change.

"The Challenge of Peace," in retrospect, appears to be more of a "weapons pastoral" than a "peace pastoral." And had it paid more attention to peace as a matter of political structure within and among nations, the Church in this country would also be in a better position to have a voice in the debate over the role of the United States in the democratic revolution in world politics. The democratic revolution, it may be argued, is the structural element of the human rights revolution which the Church had advocated and linked to the pursuit of peace since *Pacem et terris* in 1963.[37]

The democratic revolution also raised the issue of thematic linkages in the bishops' pastoral letter. That is, the moral debate about deterrence needs to address the issue of how to improve the economic and human-rights situations in both North-South and East-West contexts, and reduce the danger of nuclear war.

To maintain that the quest for international stability should be framed in terms of the political culture within and among nations is not to imply that weapons issues are insignificant. The 1990s are already witnessing a newly intensified effort at major conventional arms reduction in Europe. Here, also, weapons issues should be linked to those of political change within and among the countries of East Central Europe. Can the "nuclear ethics" debate, on both sides of the Atlantic, contribute to the fleshing out of the image of a "common European home?" This is currently a matter of conjecture. What is not is the knowledge that the challenge of peace still lies before us.

This book examines some critical moments in the history of religion and the transformation of what today would be called national traditions. Some of the essays articulate the complex relationship between various world religions and coexisting cultural, social, and political developments. They strive to concentrate on the universal, the specific, and the contextual elements of their subject.

The essays indicate that culture is not a totally or consistently articulated system or set of symbolic codes, but rather an evolving reality, influenced by "root paradigms," that is, by axiomatic frames or myths that propel and transform individuals and communities at critical moments. The nature of social order is that of a process often marked by a "dramatic" character.

Because of the episodic nature of social systems, the sociologist Kurt Lewin's image of society as "social fields," seems an apt one. Culture thus may be considered as a constantly negotiated set of meanings. The essays in this volume therefore mirror a shift in historical study away from notions such as structure, equilibrium, function, and system to an emphasis on process and indeterminacy, as embodied in "turning points" experienced in the history of religious communities.

---

[37]Cf. George Weigel, "Catholics and Peace: The Debate Ahead," *First Things* (April 1990).

The Destruction of the Temple and the Rise of Judaism

Baruch A. Brody

In this paper I present both a negative thesis and a positive thesis. The negative thesis attacks the widely held view that Judaism is the religion of the Old Testament much as Christianity is the religion of the New Testament. I think both those claims are false, but here I will just try to show why the first is false. The positive thesis will be an account of the origins of Judaism that does *not* identify it with the religion of the Old Testament. In saying all this I do not mean to suggest that there is no relationship between the Old Testament and Judaism, nor for that matter that there is no relationship between the New Testament and Christianity. I only intend to say that the religion of the Old Testament and New Testament cannot be identified with the religions that take them to be their sacred texts.

The Negative Thesis

The argument for the claim that the religion of the Old Testament is not the foundation and heart of Judaism as a religion is really very simple. If one asks what is the main religious institution of the Old Testament, it is clear that the answer to that question is the temple and its sacrificial cult. This should come as no surprise. Temples were the central institution of so many Near Eastern religions, and sacrificial cults were central to all of those temples.[1] Even a cursory review of the Old Testament establishes this point. The second half of the book of Exodus (chapters 25–31, 36–40) is devoted to a detailed description of the building of the temple and its sacred vessels. The book of Leviticus (chapters 1–10 and 12–16) gives an extensive account of the laws of sacrifices, and the laws of purity and impurity (which are connected to the temple as an institution, because the impure cannot enter the temple). The book of Numbers and to some degree even the book of Deuteronomy, continues this trend, with Deuteronomy

---

[1] Yehezkel Kaufmann, *The Religion of Israel, from Its Beginnings to the Babylonian Exile*, trans. and ed. Moshe Greenberg (London: George Allen and Unwin; Chicago: University of Chicago Press, 1960) 53–55.

(chapter 12) adding the thesis of the centrality of worship at one temple. The historical books of Joshua–Kings (and the later books of Chronicles, Ezra, and Nehemiah) place great emphasis on the cultic worship (including many chapters devoted to the building of the temple in Jerusalem) and upon this centrality of worship theme.

It is true that the prophets taught that the temple is not the whole of religion, that one ought to be concerned for other things as well, including justice.[2] But that does not mean the prophets opposed the temple. Ezekiel, for example, devoted many of his prophecies to describing what the future temple would be like (see chapters 40–48). It was not quite like the old temple, and that was a great problem for those who would canonize the book of his prophecies, but it clearly indicates that the prophets were not forsaking the temple as an institution. That is not surprising. They would not have been prophets of Old Testament religion if they had been opposed to the central institution of Old Testament religion.

For a very long time, Judaism has had little to do with animal sacrifices in a temple. Clearly, then, if Judaism is the religion of the Old Testament, there is a tremendous problem. It is not merely that the temple and animal sacrifices do not exist as institutions, but the hope for their restoration (while still present at least in traditional circles) hardly seems to be central to the thinking and practice of Judaism. That is one half of the argument for the negative thesis that Judaism is not the religion of the Old Testament: Judaism as it has been for a long time essentially leaves out the main institution of Old Testament religion.

The other half of the argument is that the main institutions of Judaism barely appear in the Old Testament. Consider, for example, the institution of the synagogue, which is, after all, a central institution in Judaism. Where are the references to the institution of the synagogue in the Old Testament? That is not to say that prayer does not get mentioned in the Old Testament. It certainly does. Even the idea of prayer three times daily gets referred to in the book of Daniel (6:10; see also Psalm 55:17). But none of the prayers are ones that will become central to Judaism. To be sure, the Shema (the Jewish "confession of faith") appears (Deuteronomy 6:4-9), but not as a prayer. Moreover, and most crucially, the synagogue as an institution does not appear in the Old Testament.[3] Or consider the Sabbath and the holidays, central institutions of Judaism. The Sabbath and the holidays are ushered in by the lighting of candles and by a benediction on wine which sanctifies the day. Where are the references to these institutions in

---

[2]See, as one example among many, Amos 5:22.

[3]Among the earliest clearcut references are those in Hellenistic authors such as Philo (*De Legatione ad Caium* 20) and Josephus (*The Antiquities of the Jews*, bk. 19), but the fact they feel no need to explain the institution attests to both its familiarity and antiquity.

the Old Testament? This is true of many of the other positive acts connected with the Sabbath and the holidays (with the exception of eating unleavened bread on Passover and sitting in a booth on the Festival of Sukkoth or Tabernacles, the Jewish harvest festival).[4] The idea of not doing work on these days is mentioned, but its elaboration is clearly a later development.

Some of the other major institutions present a mixed picture. The food laws are partially presented, because there is a clear representation of which species of animals, fish, and birds are permitted, but only an allusion to ritual slaughtering and a strange reference to not mixing meat and dairy products.[5] Marriage and divorce is presupposed, but only one passage (Deuteronomy 24:1-2) alludes in any way to the central practices connected to them. Finally, and most crucially, that central institution of Jewish life, the study of Jewish law, finds few if any references in the Old Testament.

In short, if you actually look at the major institutions and ceremonies of Jewish life and Judaism as it has existed for many centuries, you will find little of them in the Old Testament. This then is my argument that Judaism is not the religion of the Old Testament, nor is Old Testament religion Judaism. It is simply that the major institutions of the one are not the major institutions of the other. Again, this is not to say that there is no connection between the two, or that one does not grow out of the other in some way; it is only to say that we are not talking about the same religion.

The Positive Thesis

I want now to give an account of the origin of Judaism. It is an account that has to do with a group of people who have acquired a very bad reputation, the Pharisees. To describe someone as Pharisaic, at least according to my dictionary and most others, is not a compliment. How these people came to have such a reputation is an interesting story for another paper.

The Pharisees were a group of religious leaders in ancient Palestine, during the last two centuries BCE and the first two centuries CE, who identified themselves as a party in opposition to other religious parties, the most important of whom were the Sadducees. Most people recognize these names primarily from the New Testament account of the Pharisees and the Sadducees. In fact, there is a great difficulty here, because the Pharisees are often portrayed in the New Testament as teaching the opposite of what their own documents tell us they taught.[6] There are some extremely interesting and important scholarly questions: Who are the Pharisees being described in the New Testament, if they are not the

---

[4]See Deuteronomy 16:1-15.
[5]See Deuteronomy 14:3-21.
[6]See, e.g., Matthew 23.

Pharisees whose writings we have, since there is little relationship between the two? And what is the relation between that and the dictionary's insulting definition of "pharisaic"?

We have two accurate accounts of the Pharisees. One is a large body of sayings and opinions—legal, moral, philosophical—that are preserved in their later writings,[7] and the other is a smaller account in the writings of Josephus, the famous Jewish-Roman historian of the first century CE.[8]

What did the Pharisees teach, and how did they come to be the originators of the religion of Judaism as we know it today? Josephus tells us, and the writings of the Pharisees confirm, that the Pharisees were for the most part religious leaders drawn from the masses of the population. There were occasional priests in the temple who adhered to the Pharisaic party, but for the most part the priests in the temple and the larger wealthier landowners were Sadducees. The Pharisees tended to be drawn from the class of small landowners and from the working class.

In the Rabbinic literature, there is a very famous story of a Pharisee leader, Joshua, who had been in a fight with the head of the party, Gamaliel. Gamaliel came to make peace with Joshua and discovered that he was a charcoal maker and that his house was very dirty. Gamaliel said, "I see from the walls of your house that you a charcoal maker." Joshua quickly responded, "Woe unto the generation whose leaders do not know of the hardship of scholars" (*Berakot* 28a). That account is a reasonably good indication of the social strata from which the Pharisees were drawn. There were exceptions. The leader mentioned in the story, Gamaliel, was a man of great wealth, but he was truly an exception. For the most part, the Pharisees were drawn from the urban proletariat, if we can use that phrase, and from the rural less well-to-do landowners and agricultural workers. They were, in that respect, a party of the people, close to the people, to their religious concerns, and to their religious needs. That very important point needs to be kept in mind as we sketch our account of the origin of Judaism.

As a result of this social aspect of the Pharisaic movement,[9] the Pharisaic attitude towards religion and towards the religious needs of people tended to be rather flexible. Let me explain why I view flexibility as an outcome of socioeconomic factors.

What is the power of a priest? It is the power to perform the rituals. The power of the priest is that he claims to know the "right way" to get God's favor.

---

[7]The Mishna and the Halachik Midrashim.

[8]See, e.g., *The Jewish War* 2.162-66 (older editions: 1.5.2); *The Antiquities of the Jews* 13.171-73 and 18.11-17 (13.10.5 and 18.1.3).

[9]Cf. Louis Finkelstein, *The Pharisees* (Philadelphia: Jewish Publication Society, 1966).

That right way constitutes following the rituals that have been handed down, the mysterious secrets of how to stay in a good relationship with the gods. Those who draw their religious leadership from their priestly role are by their very nature conservatives on matters of religious innovation and religious ritual. We see this in our own time, but it is also an important historical truth. Not surprisingly, the priestly leaders who directed the cult of the temple in Jerusalem were great believers in the religious status quo, which meant performing the temple rituals in a fashion as close as possible to the actual description given them in the Old Testament. However, the people often develop new religious needs. Then, the priest may suddenly seem to be irrelevant, or at least the priestly rituals may suddenly seem not to speak to the religious needs of the people.

Let me give an ancient example.[10] It is not going to resonate with our religious sensitivities, but it is an example that is extremely important and that will help to clarify this point. The lack of an adequate water supply in Palestine is a very serious matter. Water falls only a few months a year, mostly from around early October until the end of January or February. If there is not enough water, especially in the early months, people may go hungry and even die. The greatest need of agricultural people was rain each year at the right time. (I am not talking about the wealthy landholders who would always have grain in their warehouses, but about the poor people, the working classes, the small farmers.) When people have a great need and they are religious, they turn to their religion to express that need. But nothing in the Old Testament talks about a ritual related to the need for water. The Sadducees felt that if there was not such a ritual in the Old Testament, then there was no need for one. If there had been such a need, God would have given it to man in the Old Testament. The Pharisees did not see it that way. They were master readers of the text. There is a biblical text that talks about a ritual for the pouring of wine on the altar of the temple during the harvest rituals, and there is a grammatical oddness with one of the phrases that almost makes it appear as if there were two pourings. The Pharisees developed an interpretation that one pouring was of wine, while the other was of water.[11] If water is needed in September, it goes without saying that is what the Bible intended.

I see the Pharisees as arguing as follows: The people need a religious ritual directed to saying to God, "Give us water so we can live." If the Old Testament does not explicitly have such a ritual, it must be there implicitly. So we need a new special form of exegesis.

Interestingly enough, although the Sadducees often controlled the temple, Josephus tells us that the water ritual was performed every year because it was

---

[10]Cited in ibid., 700-708.
[11]The "oddity" is the plural of "drink offerings" in Numbers 29:30, 31.

dangerous to be a high priest and not do so. In fact, one year the high priest attempted to leave out the water ritual and the people pelted him in the temple.

This is a rather archaic example, but it helps illustrate the sort of religious spirit that lay behind the Pharisees. It was an attempt to meet the religious needs felt by the common folk.

The objection might be raised: Were not the Pharisees the people who developed Talmudic law, and who believed that people are saved by following those laws? How could they be flexible and innovative, and at the same time so legalistic? Paul, who was trained by the Pharisees and who knew their teachings well,[12] knew that was what they believed. But what did they mean when they said that man is saved by law? And how does that relate to the notion of flexibility and innovation?

In twentieth-century America, we have a rather negative image of "law." Law is what highly trained technicians use as a tool to get things for their clients that they really should not have. Whether or not that is an accurate account of twentieth-century American law, it is certainly an attitude many people have towards the law. It is encouraged to some degree by the behavior of at least some attorneys.

The ancient Near East, and for that matter most of Western civilization, did not have that picture of law. It did not view law as a series of technical rules clever technicians could use and bend for their client's purposes. Instead, it viewed law as a divinely given gift to order relationships among people so justice and righteousness could be done. This view predates even the Old Testament. We find it among the Babylonian kings who gave us earlier codes of law. Even Hammurabi saw that it is the divinely ordained task of the king to be a legislator,[13] to lay down the law, because law is the tool that the gods have created so that justice can be done among people. Through most of the history of the West, this has been the dominant picture of law. Through most of the history of Western thought, those who believed in the idea of natural law have been dominant. They believed there is built into the order of the universe, the cosmos, not merely physical laws, but also laws governing relationships among people. Only those laws can be the true laws and any other law is not really a law at all. That is what the Pharisees believed, and that is why they thought that men were saved by two things, by the study of the law and by the performance of the law. You could hardly perform the law unless you had studied it. On the other hand, study had to lead to performance.

---

[12]See Acts 26:4-5.

[13]See *Code of Hammurabi* 5.12, in *Ancient Near Eastern Texts Relating to the Old Testament*, ed. James B. Pritchard (Princeton NJ: Princeton University Press, 1953) 165b.

So Paul was right. These very same people who believed in flexibility and innovation also believed that man was saved by living in a society governed by laws, laws governing the relationship among people and laws governing the relationship between people and God. But what about flexibility and innovation? The Pharisees saw that flexibility requires complicated laws. Laws are bad things to live by only when you have simple laws, laws that are too simple for a complex world. Hence, the many books of the Mishnah and of the Talmud.

We have seen so far three characteristics of the religion of the Pharisees: first, it was based in the people; second, it emphasized innovation and flexibility; and third, it elaborated the doctrine of salvation by law. Salvation from what? From death. The Pharisees taught the doctrine of the resurrection of the body[14]— not the immortality of the soul, whose roots are in Greek philosophical thought, but the resurrection of the body.

They gave a marvelous folk image[15] to explain why only the resurrection of the body was relevant. The image was a simple one: suppose you have a lame man and a blind man and they both want to get an apple down from a tree which does not belong to them. The lame man cannot walk and the blind man cannot see. To accomplish their goals, the blind man carries the lame man, who guides the blind man, and that is how they get the apple down. Who is to be blamed and who is to be punished? Or alternatively, who is to be praised and who rewarded? The lame man, the blind man, or the combination of the two? It does no good for God to reward or punish either the body or the soul, because human beings are both. Plato had taught in the *Phaedo* that human beings were a soul imprisoned in the body. The Pharisees denied that. Their view was that a human being was a composite of the two, and any hope we had of being saved and rewarded or punished had to be in an embodied fashion. So the Pharisees taught the doctrine of the resurrection of the body and not the immortality of soul. They built it into the daily prayers they instituted. The end of the second blessing of their daily prayer is "Blessed be you, God, who resurrects the dead."

The Sadducees did not teach that doctrine.[16] If you live a good comfortable life because you are a rich priest in Jerusalem or a wealthy landowner, then you might be happy with your rewards and punishments in this life. But if you are a poor struggling farmer, you will want salvation in some other life because this life has not worked out so well.

---

[14]Josephus, *War* 2:162-66; *Antiquities* 13:171-73 and 18:11-17; *Mishna Sanhedrin* 11.1.

[15]*Sanhedrin* 91b.

[16]See Josephus, *War* 2.162-66; *Antiquities* 13:171-73 and 18.11-17.

There is, I think, some connection between socioeconomic status and belief in some life after this life. The Wobblies,[17] an indigenous American socialist group in the early part of the twentieth century, used to make fun of this but they got the connection wrong. They had a song called "Pie in the Sky When You Die."[18] This was, of course, just the Wobblies' way of saying that this whole set of beliefs was being used by the wealthy to keep the poor satisfied. Do not worry about the fact that you are now poor and miserable and unhappy and exploited. You'll get your pie in the sky when you die. But the Wobblies were historically wrong. It was not the wealthy but the poor who originated such beliefs. Maybe it was self-delusion, but in any case it was not the deliberate attempt at repression the Wobblies thought it was.

The Pharisees, then, believed in the doctrine of the resurrection of the body. In fact, they went so far as to say that the only people who were cut off from salvation were those who denied the doctrine of the resurrection of the body.

A fifth and final crucial point about the Pharisees is that, although they elaborated a doctrine of the law and a doctrine of reward and punishment for obedience and disobedience to the law, they also taught that there was something deeper than the law. Let me give two important examples. One is an important teaching: "Do not be like a servant, who serves his master out of a desire for reward" (*Abot* 1.2). That is a very important thing to say while at the same time teaching a doctrine of law and of reward and punishment. It is a way of saying that while those who are of goodwill are to be rewarded and those who have sinned and done harm to their neighbors will be punished, it is also true that this is not what human beings ought to be attending to. What they ought to be attending to is the love of their master.

Even more important than this saying is the doctrine of going beyond what the law requires. There is a story of a Pharisee master who was required by another master to pay the salary of a worker who had negligently destroyed property and to not deduct the cost of the property. The first master asked, "Is this what the law requires of me?" The second master answered, "Of course, because it is written that thou shalt follow the paths of the righteous" (*Baba Metzia* 83a). That, too, is an interesting and important portion of Pharisaic tradition. The law sets down the view that there are higher standards of righteousness that go beyond the strict law but which we must aspire to follow.

---

[17]After "WOWs" or the Industrial Workers of the World.

[18]*Songs of the Workers* (Chicago: Industrial Workers of the World, 1927) 12-13. In fact, the title of the song was "The Preacher and the Slave," ostensibly written by Joe Hill (Joseph Hillstrom) and including these lines: "Work and pray, live on hay, / You'll get pie in the sky when you die."

Such was the teaching of the Pharisees, a group of religious teachers drawn from the people. In their conflict with the Sadducees, they won, but in a most peculiar fashion. In the year 70 CE, at the end of a three-year revolt of the Jewish people against Rome, the Romans conquered Jerusalem, sacked the city, burned the temple, slaughtered most of the inhabitants, and sold the rest into slavery. It was a difficult and long revolt. But the Romans did win and the temple was destroyed. The heart of the Sadducean party were the priests in Jerusalem, and they stayed in Jerusalem during the great revolt. So the Sadducean leadership and their only central institution were destroyed in the year 70 CE. If Judaism had been the Old Testament religion of the Sadducees, it, too, would have been destroyed in the year 70 CE. But shortly before the destruction of the temple, one of the Pharisees, Yochanan ben Zakkai, fled Jerusalem and made a deal with the Romans (*Gittin* 56a-b). Ben Zakkai promised obedience to Emperor Vespasian in return for three things, the most crucial of which was that he would be able to maintain an academy to teach the law at the small coastal town of Yavneh. The Romans, who were looking at that time for possibilities for making peace with these difficult rebels, viewed such a Jewish academy as a trivial gift. It was not trivial; it made all the difference in the world. Ben Zakkai gathered around him the remnants of the Pharisee leadership who then trained another generation of leaders. They became the founders of Judaism as we know it today. That, of course, is the positive thesis I argue for in this paper.

What brought about the rise of Judaism as we know it today was the survival of the Pharisees following the destruction of the temple. In short, around 70 CE, Yochanan ben Zakkai founded Judaism as we know it today.[19] That statement is of course an exaggeration, but it is a useful one.

---

[19]This view is similar to, but not identical with, the view expressed by Jacob Neusner in *From Politics to Piety* (Englewood Cliffs NJ: Prentice Hall, 1973) 11: "Judaism as it is now known begins with the Pharisees of the two centuries before the destruction of Jerusalem and the temple in 70 AD."

Conclusion

I have argued that Judaism as a religion is not the religion of the Old Testament because the main institutions of the two are not the same, and that Judaism as we know it today is the product of a party that arose during the last two centuries BCE, the Pharisees. The Pharisees grew out of the people; emphasized on the one hand the doctrine of salvation by law and on the other hand the doctrine of flexibility and innovation; proclaimed that people were saved from death by obedience to the law; and preached that people had to aspire even to transcend that law. The Pharisees won out over the Sadducees in part because of the merits of their teaching, but also because the core leadership of the opposition Sadducees, with the temple, was destroyed by the Romans in 70 CE.

Gnosis
and the Origins of Christianity

Werner H. Kelber

In the spring of 1947 a Bedouin shepherd looking for a goat that had wandered off from his herd sat down to rest among the rocky cliffs towering above the northwest corner of the Dead Sea. To amuse himself he threw rocks into a hole of the cliff face in front of him, and to his surprise the sound of something breaking came from the inside. He never found his goat. But he had hit upon a priceless collection of ancient manuscripts. Such was the beginning of the discovery of the Dead Sea Scrolls, an ancient library once in possession of a Jewish community that had seceded from the Jerusalem priestly establishment in a fierce struggle over power. The details of subsequent finds and their decipherment need not concern us here. Suffice it to say that a strange mixture of cooperation and competition marked all further relations between archaeologists and local Bedouins as they pressured each other into something of a scroll rush, which for many Bedouins turned into a veritable gold rush.

While competent scholars began the tedious and unglamorous business of deciphering and evaluation, the media sensed the makings of a big story, and promptly did their best to sensationalize the findings. Interest in the Dead Sea Scrolls is initially particularly lively in North America, and here in the academic, intellectual community. This was due to the writings of the prominent literary critic Edmund Wilson. In 1955, Wilson wrote an article for *The New Yorker* which he then revised and published as a book entitled *The Scrolls from the Dead Sea.*[1] The book enjoyed top ratings on bestseller charts for quite some time. One may plausibly contend that the popular success of Wilson's writings was due largely to his suggestions that the Scrolls had drastic ramifications for our understanding of Christian origins.

Notwithstanding continuing efforts to sensationalize these ancient scrolls, most scholars know that the discovery at the Dead Sea, while eminently signifi-

---

[1]Edmund Wilson, "The Scrolls from the Dead Sea," *The New Yorker* (14 May 1955): 45-121; *The Scrolls from the Dead Sea* (London: Oxford University Press, 1955).

cant for our understanding of ancient Judaism, has yielded precious little information about the beginnings of the Jesus movement. There is, however, a group
of manuscripts, discovered about the same time as the Dead Sea Scrolls, but
neglected by Edmund Wilson and the news media, that does cast fresh light on
Christian beginnings. These documents take us not to Israel, but to Egypt, and
away from the desert surrounding the Dead Sea to the valley of the Nile River.
The discovery is associated with Nag Hammadi, a small town in Upper Egypt,
approximately 370 miles south of Cairo and eighty miles north of Luxor. Nag
Hammadi itself is not the place of discovery, but the town nearest to the find.
Because Nag Hammadi served as base camp for scholars, antiquities dealers,
middlemen, representatives of museums, politically and economically influential
persons, and inevitably a host of crooks, this town became the address of the
discovery.[2]

I

The history of the finding of the Nag Hammadi documents, of their partial
destruction, of their discoverers, dealers, and profiteers, and of the painfully slow
process of their publication surpasses the imagination of most detective writers.[3]
Neither the date nor the place of the discovery is verifiable with absolute
certainty. The date is now estimated to have been December 1945. The probable
site is at the foot of the cliffs Jabal al Tarif (or Gebel et-Tarif) along the Nile
River, approximately six miles northeast of Nag Hammadi. It was there that
Egyptian peasants digging for "sabakh," a nitrate-rich gravel used as a low-grade
fertilizer, found the large clay jar containing the documents.

The general area of the discovery is deeply rural and virtually untouched by
urban, Egyptian culture. Peasants in this part of the world live in a preliterate
society, forever involved in blood feuds among each other and against neighboring villages, and not averse to taking the law into their own hands. Members of
the family who made the discovery were before and afterwards victims of brutal
murders. They were hacked to pieces limb by limb, their hearts cut out and
consumed by the murderers—the ultimate act of blood revenge. It is now
admitted that considerable damage and losses occurred as the manuscripts were
divided up by the Islamic natives who did not recognize their true significance.
Initially much of the material was stored in peasant houses, dumped next to

---

[2]One of the early Western explorers of the site, the French scholar Jean
Doresse, wanted to call the discovery after Chenoboskion, a nearby village and
early monastic center. But the name simply did not catch on.

[3]For a painstaking reconstruction of the history of the discovery, see James
M. Robinson, "The Discovery of the Nag Hammadi Codices," *Biblical Archeologist* 42 (1979): 206-24.

kitchen stoves, some of it used to clean floors, and some of it to make fires. It was, in short, not the kind of environment conducive to a safe and professional handling of ancient manuscripts.

Under the circumstances it is hardly surprising that the Nag Hammadi documents soon became embroiled in a succession of bargains and petty deals among outlaws and desperados, camel drivers and shepherds, peasants and ordinary villagers, all trying to get a few piasters or some cigarettes out of something whose significance and value they did not really understand. With time, some manuscripts attracted the attention of knowledgeable Coptic priests and teachers, proprietors of antiquities shops, and also scholars.[4]

At this point the story shifts from local pettiness to the world of high finance, politics, and, last but not least, fierce jealousies among ambitious scholars. Efforts to make the manuscripts available to the educated public were frequently frustrated. In part, this was because publishers, academicians, and national governments were locked in acrimonious contention over the rights to publication. It part, negotiations became entangled in the turbulent politics of the Middle East. The Egyptian revolution in 1952 and the Suez Crisis in 1956 further slowed the publication process by several years. Negotiations were interrupted once more by the Six-Day War between Egypt and Israel in 1967. During that war, on June 5, 1967, a bomb exploded across the street from the Coptic Museum in Cairo where the documents had found a permanent home. By 1970 only thirty-four percent of the Nag Hammadi material had been published in German or French, and only twenty-one percent in English. Though the political climate was now improving and the tempo of the publication process accelerating, the fact that within the first quarter of a century after the discovery only a third had been published at all, and only a fifth in English, left much to be desired.

The impasse was finally overcome by the intervention of UNESCO, the United Nations Educational, Scientific, and Cultural Organization. Working closely with the United Arab Republic, UNESCO managed to organize an international committee of scholarly experts. This committee subsequently received substantial financial aid from UNESCO. With support on such a grand scale, the publication project was at long last to become reality. Between 1972 and 1977 the codices were published (in ten volumes) by E. J. Brill, the world-renowned publishing house in Leiden; the *Cartonnage* volume followed in 1979 and the *Introduction* volume in 1984, completing the twelve-volume set. These volumes contain facsimile editions of all the Nag Hammadi texts.[5] In 1977, Brill and

---

[4]One of the first persons credited with recognizing the potential worth of the documents is a certain Raghib, a teacher of English and history who moved from village to village on a circuit of Coptic parochial schools.

[5]James M. Robinson et al., eds., *The Facsimile Edition of the Nag Hammadi*

Harper & Row published an English translation of the documents, followed in 1981 and 1984 by an inexpensive paperback edition (with some additions); the English translation was revised in 1988 and appeared in paperback in 1990.[6] The net result of this labyrinthine story is that twelve codices plus eight leaves of a thirteenth one, containing fifty-two writings in all (of which six are duplicates and six were previously known), have now been made available for the public readership.

In terms of physical format alone, the Nag Hammadi documents differ from the Dead Sea material. The latter was written on leather scrolls, which as a rule contain one text on one side of a sheet. The Nag Hammadi documents are written on papyri codices, which carry more than one text on both sides of the sheets. The Dead Sea Scrolls, in other words, predate the book format while the Nag Hammadi Codices help launch the period of the modern book format. Moreover, the Dead Sea Scrolls were written mostly in Hebrew, although some were in Aramaic, and a sprinkling even in Greek. The majority was written during the first century BCE, but some scrolls rely on textual versions that go as far back as the fifth century BCE. All Nag Hammadi texts are in Coptic (mostly in the Sahidic dialect), which was the Egyptian vernacular during the Hellenistic period. The date of their composition is now estimated to have been approximately 350–400 CE. Most codices, however, are on philological and ideological grounds assumed to be older, and thought often to be translations of an underlying Greek.

With respect to titles and content, the Nag Hammadi Codices manifest considerable diversity. Some titles appear to reflect merely an extension of the orthodox, catholic tradition: the *Gospel of Mary*, the *Dialogue of the Savior*, the *Gospel of Philip*, the *Apocalypse of Paul*, the *Treatise on the Resurrection*, the *Apocryphon of John*, the *Letter of Peter to Philip*, and of course, the famous *Gospel of Thomas*. But other titles appear strange to conventional Christian sensibilities: the *Three Steles of Seth*, *Zostrianos*, the *Thunder, Perfect Mind*, the *Paraphrase of Shem*, the *Thought of Norea*, the *Interpretation of Knowledge*, *On the Origin of the World*, the *Hypostasis of the Archons*, and so forth. Indeed, not all the texts are Christian. There is, for example, a fragment of Plato's *Republic*.

Codices, published under the auspices of the Department of Antiquities of the Arab Republic of Egypt in conjunction with UNESCO, 12 vols. (Leiden: E. J. Brill, 1972–1984).

[6]*The Nag Hammadi Library in English*, James M. Robinson, gen. ed., trans. by members of the Coptic Gnostic Library Project of the Institute for Antiquity and Christianity, Claremont, California, 3rd, completely rev. ed. (San Francisco: Harper; Leiden: E. J. Brill, 1988; pbk. 1990); henceforth referred to as NHL. The rev. ed. (1988, 1990) is cited here, but the 1st ed. (1977) is consulted and cited when appropriate to show an alternate translation.

There is material associated with the Egyptian god Hermes Trismegistos. There is also a prayer addressed to the healer god Asclepius.

Specialists in the history and literature of antiquity are not necessarily surprised by this heterogeneity. The situation is not unrelated to the processing of information in the ancient world. By modern standards the flow of information was slow and irregular, and subject to countless hazards. Whereas we moderns have nearly instantaneous access to systematically organized data and are used to operating with broadly agreed-upon intellectual conventions, the ancients lived with conflicting nomenclatures, chronologies, and maps, and in the absence of an organized body of knowledge. Standardization of knowledge was hard to come by, and hardly a desirable objective at this time. In this climate of cultural heterogeneity, early Christianity was more diffuse and more thoroughly devoid of ideological systematization than we care to imagine in our passion for intellectual tidiness. In its initial phase the early Christian movement exploded into multiple directions. Nag Hammadi represents one such direction, which is itself far from measuring up to the norms of modern, doctrinal exactness.

Given the religious diversity of the Nag Hammadi texts, one risks error in attempting to designate the collection with a single label. For this reason also, scholars are debating whether or not Nag Hammadi can justifiably be called "gnosis." James M. Robinson, for example, subscribes to the gnostic designation of the Nag Hammadi texts, but recognizes that their lack of homogeneity challenges the very concept of gnosis, or gnosticism:

> The library as a whole lacks a clear mythological or doctrinal unity—even the individual Gnostic texts do not fit nicely into the standard subdivisions of Gnosticism or, at times, into a proper definition of what we have understood as Gnosticism.[7]

Robert A. Kraft and Janet A. Timbie, on the other hand, regard the gnostic label as premature at best, and as arbitrary and misleading at worst. Impressed by the textual heterogeneity of the Nag Hammadi collection, they conclude that

> the designation "gnostic" loses its usefulness—the hint of homogeneity it suggests needs to be laid aside in favor of close attention to the varieties of perspective, tradition, and approach that clearly existed even within overtly "gnostic" circles, not to mention less clearly defined "dualistic" and/or "ascetic" groups.[8]

---

[7]James M. Robinson, "Introduction. What is the Nag Hammadi Library?" *Biblical Archeologist* 42 (1979): 204.

[8]Robert A. Kraft and Janet A. Timbie, review of the *Nag Hammadi Library in English*, in *Religious Studies Review* 8 (1982): 38.

Less skeptical, and perhaps more to the point, was one of the earliest scholarly assessments undertaken by Father Bernard Couroyer, the Coptologist at the École Biblique in Jerusalem. Upon studying the photographs of a number of pages from Codex I he wrote in January of 1947:

> One finds oneself on the border between orthodox theology and Gnosticism. In the case of the present manuscript I do not believe that one is in the presence of a purely Gnostic work.[9]

When allowance is made for internal Christian differences and developments, and when one recalls that many of the Nag Hammadi documents may hark back to the third, second, or even first centuries, it is possible to observe a gnosticizing direction. That is to say, on a broadly developmental scale, the bulk of the Egyptian writings appears to occupy a stage toward the full-blown gnostic systems of the third and fourth centuries. Nevertheless, the doubts of those who question a simple, gnostic designation for Nag Hammadi cannot entirely be dispelled. When in the following we proceed to single out conspicuously gnosticizing features, we do so in full knowledge of probably oversystematizing what for the ancients was a more diffuse, less organized experience.

II

In Genesis 1, God looks at his created world and finds it very good indeed. Christians of gnostic persuasion look at the world and find it very bad indeed. Based on their observation, they conclude that God was either mistaken in assuming perfection, or that he did not know any better. In either case, the God of Creation is considered inferior, and hence no real God at all. *The Hypostasis of the Archons* expresses a conviction widespread among the Nag Hammadi Christians when it calls the creator God arrogant, ignorant, and a God of the blind. When he said: "It is I who am God, and there is none other apart from me" (NHL, 167), he was sinning against Wholeness. This Wholeness, or Entirety, refers to another God that many gnostics assumed to exist apart from the evil creator God. This other God is the true God. He, or rather It, is a powerful being that exists far above the wicked God of creation. This true God is nonpersonal. It never took on personal attributes, nor can it properly be grasped in anthropomorphic terms. God is the undifferentiated Wholeness, the Unity, the Oneness, that existed prior to the mistaken creation of the cosmos and all the worlds within it.

In one sense, therefore, emergent gnosticizing Christianity was profoundly pessimistic about the universe and the human condition within it. Everything in

---

[9]Robinson, "The Discovery," 221.

the visible, created cosmos is poisoned, corrupt, and to all appearances beyond redemption. The true God is removed from our world by an infinitude of light years, and this world bears witness to the *absence* of God. Ours is in fact the *worst* of all possible worlds.

Christianity of gnostic persuasion shares this pessimistic view with many people in the ancient world. Historians and historians of religion have amply documented this spirit of late antiquity, a pervasive anxiety about the insoluble, irredeemable human condition.[10] It is connected with radical changes sweeping across the ancient world. Hellenization internationalized life, and in the process disrupted national governments and subverted ethnic identities. The monarchy, a prestigious form of government that had enjoyed a millennial history stretching back into the archaic past, had to yield to more democratically oriented city governments. Israel is annihilated, her temple burnt to the ground, and Jews throughout the Greek-speaking world ask painful questions about the presence of God. Last but not least, Greek literacy, the technology of alphabetic writing, spread rapidly and threatened longstanding habits of classical rhetoric and oral communication, not unlike the way in which our electronic media subtly undermine literacy and our literate modes of thought.[11]

Overwhelmed by change, and haunted by the experience of physical destruction and metaphysical absence, gnostic Christianity sought to account for the dilemma by tracing its roots to the creator God. He is held responsible for having created the worst of all possible worlds and a demonized universe. The problem of evil has thereby found an ingenious explanation. Evil is rooted metaphysically in the domain of a deity. But if one wonders why and how the creator God himself came into existence, no satisfactory answer is readily forthcoming. Orthodox Christianity and Judaism, on the other hand, insist on the goodness and wisdom of the creator God. But they, too, run into intellectual difficulties, as is well known. For theirs is the problem of how to reconcile a wise creator God with the existence of evil in the world.

---

[10]See, e.g., Eric Robertson Dodds, *Pagan and Christian in an Age of Anxiety. Some Aspects of Religious Experience from Marcus Aurelius to Constantine* (Cambridge, England: Cambridge University Press, 1965); Arthur Darby Nock, *Essays on Religion and the Ancient World*, 2 vols. (Cambridge MA: Harvard University Press, 1972); Peter Brown, *The World of Late Antiquity. From Marcus Aurelius to Mohammed* (London: Thames and Hudson, 1971); idem, "The Rise and Function of the Holy Man in Late Antiquity," *Journal of Roman Studies* 61 (1971): 80-101.

[11]See, e.g., Eric E. Havelock, *Preface to Plato* (Cambridge MA: Harvard University Press, 1963); idem, *The Literate Revolution in Greece and Its Cultural Consequences* (Princeton NJ: Princeton University Press, 1982).

Naturally, the Nag Hammadi Christians accepted Jesus as the figure of salvation, yet their version differs from that of the orthodox tradition. On this matter of Christology, the gnostic considerations are as follows. If the redeemer figure is to be effective in a world as thoroughly perverted as ours, he must abstain from worldly contact altogether. He can truly redeem the world only if he represents divine Wholeness without entering into the flesh of the human condition. The Jesus dramatized in gnostic writings is for this reason almost always the living Jesus, or the spiritual Christ, or the risen Lord, and not the earthly human person. The *Gospel of Thomas*, for example, introduces what it calls "the living Jesus" who speaks to the disciples and does very little else. By orthodox standards *Thomas* is not a gospel at all. It shows next to no interest in narrating the story of Jesus' life and death. All the emphasis is placed on his sayings and parables. In other words, the Jesus of the *Gospel of Thomas* is not an historicized figure of the past who once lived at a given period in history, but the "living Jesus" who through his words continues to speak to and remain alive in the present community of hearers. Similarly, the *Apocryphon of John* begins with John's experiencing Jesus as a luminous presence that addresses him by saying: "Do not [be] timid!—I am the one who is [with you (pl.)] always. . . . [I have come to teach you] what is [and what was] and what will come to [pass] . . . " (NHL, 105). The one speaking in this document throughout is the risen One who, in the orthodox gospels of Matthew, Luke, and John, speaks only at the end, and then very little.

What is remarkable about the Nag Hammadi texts is that none of these fifty-two documents comes even close to the genre of the orthodox gospels. The gospels of Mark, Matthew, Luke and John begin with baptism or birth and end with resurrection; the predominant style among the Nag Hammadi texts is to begin with the living, risen Christ. In other words, *the gnostic gospel begins precisely at the point where the orthodox gospel ends.*[12] This is significant for two reasons. First, we now have to reckon with two "gospel" forms in the early Christian tradition, the orthodox narrative gospel and the gnosticized sayings or dialogue gospel. These two forms are the outcome of two different concepts of Jesus and of redemption. The gnosticized gospel presents a living Jesus who, untainted by human flesh, redeems through words of wisdom; the orthodox gospel presents a Jesus who redeems by fully entering into the human condition. Second, we can no longer view the orthodox form of gospel as the self-evident expression of the Christian experience. The one form we have tended to take

---

[12]James M. Robinson, "On the Gattung of Mark (and John)," in *Jesus and Man's Hope*, vol. 1 (Pittsburgh: Pittsburgh Theological Seminary, 1970) 114; reprinted in *The Problem of History in Mark and other Marcan Studies* (Philadelphia: Fortress Press, 1982) 27.

most for granted cannot be taken for granted any more. We shall return to this issue below.

If the gnosticized gospel commences with the living Jesus, what was the significance of Jesus' crucifixion and death? To begin with, one must recognize that interest in this question is conditioned by the predilections of orthodoxy. Many Nag Hammadi writers did not deem it necessary to make any reference to Jesus' death and the circumstances surrounding it. After all, what mattered to them was the living Jesus, not the dead one. Those texts that do treat the crucifixion frequently offer an interpretation that conflicts with the orthodox version. In the *Second Treatise of the Great Seth*, for example, Jesus suggests that

> I was not afflicted at all. Those who were there punished me. And I did not die in reality but in appearance. . . . For my death which they think happened, (happened) to them in their error and blindness. . . . it was another, Simon, who bore the cross on his shoulder. It was another upon whom they placed the crown of thorns. . . . And I was laughing at their ignorance. (NHL, 365)

The understanding here is that Jesus was represented at crucifixion by a substitute, presumably Simon of Cyrene. The execution, therefore, was a sham, because it tricked the adversaries into believing they had put Jesus to death. What adds a comic touch to the scene is Jesus standing vis-à-vis his assumed execution, watching it from afar, and getting the laugh of his life at the people's ignorance. This is the gnostic motif of the laughing savior who rejoices over the lack of understanding and blindness of those who thought they had put an end to him.[13]

Similarly, in the Nag Hammadi *First Apocalypse of James*, the exalted Christ consoles James who is grieved over the suffering of the Lord:

> James, do not be concerned for me or for this people. I am he who was within me. Never have I suffered in any way, nor have I been distressed. And this people has done me no harm. (NHL, 265)

The conviction here is that Jesus' *body* was killed, a body he had taken on to conceal his spiritual self. Insofar as the redeemer has assumed the appearance of a human being, whereas in truth he remained uncontaminated by human flesh, his execution did not affect his true being. The crucifixion did not bring about his death any more than it brought about the salvation of the world. It did, however, bear testimony to the blindness of the powers of the world.

Strictly speaking, therefore, gnostic Christianity by and large did not believe in Jesus' resurrection, if resurrection is perceived to be the resuscitation of a

---

[13]John Dart, *The Laughing Savior. The Discovery and Significance of the Nag Hammadi Gnostic Library* (New York: Harper & Row, 1976).

body whose life had come to an end. Dead bodies do not, cannot, and indeed never should rise, according to gnostic convictions. It is worth remembering that those who objected to literal resurrection faith were Christian believers whose sincerity should not be in doubt. They were utterly persuaded both of the imperishability of the Spirit, and of the redeemer's spiritual nature. It could thus not have been within the powers of Jesus' murderers to touch the core of his person. And if the living Jesus in effect never died, he could not very well have risen from the dead.

What, then, is the fate of the world and of human beings in it? This world, gnostic faith suggests, is the worst of all possible worlds because it is furthest removed from divine Wholeness. It provides a hostile, alien environment for all those living in it, and it is as little our natural habitat as is the body our natural place to dwell. Hence, Jesus did not come to save the world.

> Men think, perhaps, that it is peace which I have come to cast upon the world. They do not know that it is dissension which I have come to cast upon the earth: fire, sword, and war. (#16: NHL, 128)

One aspect of discipleship, therefore, is to encourage alienation and withdrawal from the world.

> Whoever finds the world and becomes rich, let him renounce the world. (#110: NHL, 138)

Despite such deeply pessimistic views, Christian gnosis is by no means a religion of all-out despondency. After all, its followers embrace a redeemer in the conviction that redemption remains possible. Not only is there a redeemer, but his effectiveness is enhanced by the fact that humans bear within themselves the potential of their salvation. This human potential is variously called inner light, divine spark, or the Spirit. It resides in wretched, mortal bodies, and supplies the vital link to the divine Wholeness. Given the condition of incarceration in an alien world and in alien bodies, people have remained ignorant of the immortal core within themselves. They are, in gnostic terminology, drunk or asleep with respect to their true situation.

It is this situation of drunkenness or slumber that the Redeemer seeks to correct by offering gnosis, that is, knowledge. He comes to awaken people to their real identity by conveying knowledge of their origin and destiny. As individuals find self-realization, they awaken to the Kingdom and live in the fullness of the Spirit. They have transcended the laws of this world, and death holds no power over them. Hence the injunction of Jesus' first, programmatic saying in the *Gospel of Thomas*:

> Whoever finds the interpretation of these sayings will not experience death. (#1: NHL, 126)

Gnostic redemption is thus a process more of seeking and finding than of believing. The truth to be discovered is the image of God within ourselves, and the objective is full life here and now.

Again, the history of early Christianity can reasonably be said to bifurcate into a gnosticizing and an orthodox trajectory. The orthodox direction, led on by Paul the apostle, strenuously objected to the notion that humans bear within themselves the potential of their own salvation. Individuals do not *have* the Spirit as a natural given, but they may well *receive* it (compare 1 Corinthians 4:7). The difference is between discovering what one already possesses (in gnostic Christianity) and receiving what one did not have (in orthodox Christianity). In the latter case, the Redeemer does not deliver knowledge of something already in possession of human beings, but rather inspires faith in Himself who may grant us what we are lacking.

Further differences between the gnostic and orthodox position are apparent in their respective explanations of the human plight. For gnostic Christians, the principal flaw is ignorance or lack of knowledge pertaining to the human condition. Orthodox Christians define the cardinal fault as "sin," most commonly understood in terms of willful departure from divine commandments.

Last but not least, redemption in the orthodox tradition extends not merely to the spiritual core, but rather to the wholeness of persons. In Pauline terms, redemption entails a transformation of our bodily selves, a process never completed during our earthly lives. Eternal life, while presently realized in the gnostic tradition, is more or less a promise of the future in orthodox Christianity.

III

We have, of course, long known of the gnostic version in the early Christian tradition. Our knowledge stemmed from the orthodox authorities who produced extensive writings in condemnation of gnosis. With Nag Hammadi, however, the gnosticizing tradition has been permitted to speak with its own voice and on its own behalf. Little wonder that the discovery has aroused renewed interest in what was once condemned as heresy. Since 1945 approximately 5,000 books, articles, and reviews have appeared in print. One of the intriguing aspects of this upsurge in gnostic scholarship is the role played by women scholars. An unusually large number of women, mostly Harvard trained, are presently playing leadership roles in gnostic research. Women, one ventures to speculate, have traditionally shown much loyalty to the orthodox tradition, but they have also traditionally been barred from full participation. This peculiarly ambiguous experience may well have prepared them to be exceptionally sensitive to a version of Christianity that in some of its documents exhibits greater sympathy for the status and rights of women.[14] In the *Gospel of Mary*, for example, Mary alone is in possession of secret words of Jesus.

> Peter said to Mary, "Sister, we know that the Savior loved you more than the rest of women. Tell us the words of the Savior which you remember—which you know (but) we do not, nor have we heard them." Mary answered and said, "What is hidden from you I will proclaim to you." (NHL, 525)

But Mary's teachings are greeted with disbelief by Andrew and Peter who question whether the Savior could have favored her over them. The gospel continues:

> Then Mary wept and said to Peter, "My brother Peter, what do you think? Do you think that I thought this up myself in my heart, or that I am lying about the Savior?" Levi answered and said to Peter, "Peter, you have always been hot-tempered. Now I see you contending against the woman like the adversaries. But if the Savior made her worthy, who are you indeed to reject her? Surely the Savior knows her very well. That is why he loved her more than us." (NHL, 526-27)

In *Pistis Sophia*, a document not found at Nag Hammadi but belonging to the same gnosticizing religiosity, Mary takes Jesus into confidence, admitting that she hardly dares speak to Peter because, in her words, "Peter makes me hesitate. I am afraid of him because he hates the female race" (*Pistis Sophia* 36.71). Or again, one reads in the *Dialogue of the Savior*, a Nag Hammadi text, that Mary is praised by Jesus above all male disciples because "she spoke as a woman who knew the All" (NHL [1977], 235) or "who understood completely" (NHL [1988], 252). The "All" is gnostic reference to divine transcendence. What one observes in these and other documents is Mary rising to the status of a privileged apostle, in conflict with Peter, but upheld over and above him.

As for Mary's relationship to Jesus, it is a matter of considerable sensitivity. The *Gospel of Philip* struggles with the delicate issue of her being the Savior's preferred companion.

> There were three who always walked with the Lord: Mary his mother and her sister and Magdalene, the one who was called his companion. (NHL, 145)

---

[14]For a study of the Nag Hammadi texts from a feminist perspective, see Elaine H. Pagels, *The Gnostic Gospels* (New York: Random House, 1979; repr. New York: Vintage Books, 1981).

In the Coptic text the word "companion" is rendered with the Greek loanword *koinōnos* which suggests intimate companionship. Farther on in the same gospel a badly mutilated passage reads as follows:

> And the companion of the [Savior? is] Mary Magdalene. [But Christ? loved] her more than [all] the disciples [and used to] kiss her [often] on her [mouth?]. The rest of [the disciples were offended?]. They said to him, "Why do you love her more than all of us?" The Savior answered and said to them, "Why do I not love you like her?" (Cf. NHL [1977], 138, and NHL [1988], 148)

Undoubtedly, texts that confer special privileges upon a woman will have inspired their readers to advance the religious and social rights of women. Inasmuch as Peter's authority came to serve as model for orthodox Christianity, Mary Magdalene provided for at least some gnostic groups a counterbalance to male dominance.

It must be admitted, however, that the gnosticizing tradition was by no means universally sympathetic toward women. Some gnostic texts are decidedly unfriendly or even hostile toward women. In the *Dialogue of the Savior*, for example, Matthew the disciple reports the following two dominical sayings.

> The Lord said, "Pray in the place where there is [no] woman. . . . meaning, "Destroy the works of womanhood." (##91-92: NHL, 254)

One of the more notorious antifemale statements forms the conclusion to the *Gospel of Thomas*. First, Peter brazenly suggests:

> "Let Mary leave us, for women are not worthy of Life." (#114a: NHL, 138)

Next, Jesus responds:

> "I myself shall lead her in order to make her male, so that she too may become a living spirit resembling you males. For every woman who will make herself male will enter the kingdom of heaven." (#114b: NHL, 138)

What is recommended here is not abolition of male and female roles according to the motto "neither male nor female" (Galatians 3:28), but rather a transformation of female into male identity. Female sexuality is perceived to be corrupted and redeemable only through an exchange of sexual roles.

IV

If in the light of the Nag Hammadi codices we can discern more clearly two modes of Christianity emerging, how does this affect our understanding of the New Testament and the beginnings of the Jesus movement? In general terms, the Nag Hammadi codices help us read parts of the New Testament from a fresh perspective. Once we have familiarized ourselves with the gnosticized tradition, a good number of New Testament texts appear to be both influenced by and set against that type of religiosity. If we remind ourselves that the bulk of the New Testament was written roughly between 50 and 120 CE, we must admit that already in the first century Christian traditions existed side by side and in conflict with each other. Christianity, it becomes increasingly clear, was from very early on diverging in different directions. A few examples are sufficient to demonstrate this drama of traditions in conflict.

Already in the oldest extant Christian texts, Paul's correspondence addressed to Christians in Thessalonica, written as early as 48 or 49 CE, the apostle objects to tendencies that contain the germ of gnosticizing developments. Death has occurred in the community and people are in shock, not merely in mourning, for they had not expected their friends to die. Moreover, Paul admonishes the people to show respect toward those in charge over them, to abide by the rules of monogamy, and to appreciate the value of work. These items allow us a fascinating glimpse into a very early Christian situation. We see Christian converts defying the fundamentals of the human condition: death, authority, marriage, and work. When pressed for justification, they volunteer the statement that "The Day of the Lord has already Come" (2 Thessalonians 2:2). One must conclude that Paul objects to people who lived in full realization of their spiritual selves.[15]

A far more developed and better-known picture of gnosticizing tendencies emerges from Paul's first letter to the Corinthians. Writing about 51 or 52 CE, the apostle criticizes the spirituality of those who are proud of their newly gained knowledge. As possessors of the Spirit they already live a life in resurrection. They curse the early Jesus in favor of the heavenly Lord (1 Corinthians 12:3). All things are permissible to them because they have transcended the biological and cosmological errors that block our path to spiritual perfection. An enthusiastic exercise of freedom characterizes the life of the congregation, and women fully participate in it. This casts fresh light on some of Paul's most antifemale statements that occur in 1 Corinthians. Although these proved damaging to the status of women in Western culture, they remain of interest to the historian of religion. For Paul's objection to women's rights and affirmations in 1 Corinthians, a letter written in repudiation of gnostic tendencies, amounts to an admission of gnosticism's success among women. The history of gnostic Christianity (or parts thereof) as a liberation movement for women in late antiquity still remains to be written.

---

[15]Cf. Robert Jewett, "Enthusiastic Radicalism and the Thessalonian Correspondence," *SBL Seminar Papers* 1 (Missoula MT: Scholars Press, 1972); Jewett, *The Thessalonian Correspondence. Pauline Rhetoric and Millenarian Piety* (Philadelphia: Fortress Press, 1986).

The letter to the Colossians (ca. 80 CE), written in all probability not by Paul himself but by a member of the Pauline tradition, debates a radical form of gnosticism, while itself being under the influence of a moderate form of it. Attention must further be drawn to such orthodox documents as the Johannine epistles (ca. 100 CE), the letter of Jude (ca. 100 CE), and the so-called Pastorals (ca. 110 CE), all of which attack early Christian teachers and prophets for representing gnosticizing versions of the gospel.

In addition to the epistolary literature, some of the orthodox gospels likewise appear to be responding to gnosticizing manifestations. The Gospel of John, by far the most popular gospel, holds a precarious borderline position between orthodox and gnostic interests. In its gnostic proclivities it expresses both utter pessimism about the world and an almost total sense of redemption from it. What rescues the gospel from full-blown gnosis is the incarnation of the redeemer and a narration of his earthly career. The Gospel of Mark, probably the least popular gospel, is also the most overtly antignostic gospel. It narrates Jesus' earthly career minus a resurrection appearance story. The living, resurrected Jesus never makes an appearance and never speaks in this gospel.[16] Consequently, the full narrative climax has come to be placed on Jesus' death. Paradoxically, he becomes Son of God at crucifixion. If one remembers that gnostic Christianity focuses on the living Christ while disregarding his earthly career and his death, the Markan gospel, which set the norm for the gospel genre in the orthodox tradition, appears to have come into existence in direct conflict with gnosticizing proclivities.[17]

Experts are widely agreed today that Nag Hammadi has acutely raised our consciousness about the gnosticizing climate surrounding Christian origins. Many, although by no means all, of the twenty-seven New Testament documents appear to interact in various ways with gnosticizing traditions. Gnostic tendencies intermingled more thoroughly with the genesis of Christianity than most of us might dare admit. Indeed, when in case after case one observes orthodoxy reacting to more or less flourishing gnostic interpretations, we may wonder: Which came first, the gnostic or the orthodox version? This question brings us finally to the crucial test case, the *Gospel of Thomas*.

Of all the Nag Hammadi documents, none is more revealing with regard to early Christian origins than the *Gospel of Thomas*. It consists of 114 sayings that

---

[16]Both substantial manuscript evidence and the logic of the narrative point to Mark 16:8 as the original ending of the gospel.

[17]For a suggestion that the orthodox narrative gospel arose by way of repudiating a gnosticizing sayings gospel, see Werner H. Kelber, *The Oral and the Written Gospel. The Hermeneutics of Speaking and Writing in the Synoptic Tradition, Mark, Paul, and Q* (Philadelphia: Fortress Press, 1983).

are attributed to "the living Jesus." Technically, *Thomas* is a sayings collection, lacking a coherent narrative frame in the style of the orthodox gospels. Until recently it was common practice to date the underlying Greek version of the Coptic *Gospel of Thomas* around 130–150 CE, a date I had accepted and taught my students for more than a decade. This second-century date suggested that a large part of the *Thomas* sayings was a gnosticizing development of sayings we find embedded in the orthodox gospels. It was an assumption clearly based on the model given to us by the early church fathers according to which the gnosticizing trajectory was a deviation from orthodoxy.

Thomas research, however, carried out mostly at Harvard Divinity School and at the Institute for Antiquity and Christianity at Claremont, has increasingly cast doubt on the second-century dating of the gospel. A growing number of scholars are now persuaded that the Greek *Thomas* belongs in the first century, that it even predated the orthodox gospels, and must be dated around 50 CE. The exceedingly complicated discussion can be broken down into three arguments in favor of the early dating of *Thomas*.

There is first the argument of composition. It has long been known that collections of sayings must have preceded the formation of Mark, Matthew, Luke, and John. Indeed, one such collection that goes under the label of Q has been reconstructed by biblical scholars. This Q collection is understood to have been utilized by Matthew and Luke in constructing their respective gospels. But while Q has already achieved some sense of compositional order and thematic progression, *Thomas* is a random collection, lacking, as far as we can see, organizational principles. *Thomas* clearly displays a more primitive character.

There is second the argument of sequentiality. The sequence of the *Thomas* sayings does not match the order in which sayings are arranged in any of the four orthodox gospels. Moreover, the order in *Thomas* does not appear to be a revision of the compositional sequences of any of the orthodox gospels either. As far as sequential order is concerned, *Thomas* is apparently independent of the orthodox gospel tradition.

There is thirdly the argument of adjustment features. The canonical gospels tend to adjust their sayings to make them fit their respective gospel projects. But not one of the *Thomas* sayings demonstrates known Matthean, Markan, Lukan, or Johannine adjustment features. There is no evidence, then, that Thomas constitutes a further development of the sayings embedded in the canonical gospels.

The cumulative weight of these arguments is impressive. Barring any evidence to the contrary, I am inclined to join those scholars who place the *Gospel of Thomas* in a period prior to the orthodox gospels. Since Q is a hypothetical reconstruction, Thomas is therefore our first hard evidence of one of the earliest mechanisms of data gathering in the Christian tradition, the clustering of sayings. In efforts to reconstruct the history of the transmission of Christian traditions we must henceforth work with two sayings sources, the Thomas collection and the Q collection.

Whereas, through Matthew and Luke, Q was accepted into the mainstream of orthodoxy, Thomas was not. What is more, Thomas eventually turned up in the gnostic, heretical Christianity of Nag Hammadi. This is connected with the theological framework into which Q and Thomas each have cast their sayings materials. The Q sayings emphasize the imminent coming of the Son of Man, and the consummation of the Kingdom in the future. Historically, Q's faithful orientation toward the future represents an apocalyptic outlook. In Thomas, the Kingdom is entirely present. It is a matter of seeking and finding what is within ourselves, rather than a matter of faithful waiting for the coming of the Son of Man. Historically, Thomas's religion of wisdom and knowledge represents a gnosticizing outlook. In the end, Q's position was more acceptable; Thomas's position was suppressed.

Recognition of the tradition's early divergence into two theologically distinct trajectories inevitably forces the question: Which one is more closely representative of the outlook of the historical Jesus? Surprisingly, scholars have been reluctant to settle for the orthodox Q tradition, and Helmut Koester of Harvard has invited us to think of the *Gospel of Thomas* as a type of proclamation that may be in continuity with the historical Jesus:

> Why is it unlikely that the tradition of Jesus as a teacher of wisdom in the *Gospel of Thomas* is a direct continuation of the teaching of the historical Jesus?[18]

In other words, when one arrives at the earliest recoverable bifurcation in the tradition, Koester claims it was the gnosticizing direction that preserved the thrust of Jesus' proclamation more faithfully. This takes us to the edge of contemporary gnostic scholarship, and deep into the heart of the problem of Christian origins.

Conclusion

The single most important conclusion to be drawn from the Nag Hammadi discovery is the need for reconstructing early Christianity in its historical fullness, not merely from its orthodox perspective. There is both a moral obligation and a historical necessity. In listening to the orthodox church father Tertullian

---

[18]Helmut Koester, *"The Historical Jesus*: Some Comments and Thoughts on Norman Perrin's *Rediscovering the Teaching of Jesus,"* in *Christology and a Modern Pilgrimage. A Discussion with Norman Perrin*, ed. Hans Dieter Betz (Claremont CA: The New Testament Colloquim, 1971) 129-30; see also Koester, "One Jesus and Four Primitive Gospels," in *Trajectories through Early Christianity* (Philadelphia: Fortress Press, 1971) 158-204.

and his plea for "the prosecution against the heretics,"[19] and to Irenaeus's call "not only to expose but also from every side to wound the beast,"[20] one must wonder about the fairness of their procedure. All too often orthodoxy spoke the language of barely concealed violence, compacted with raw ambition. It was the kind of language that inspired expulsion of people and the burning of books. It is little wonder so very few of the gnostic documents have come down to us. The vehemence with which gnostic Christians were once rejected must not obscure the fact that they raised profound issues about God and the cosmos, Christ and the human condition, and also about afterlife. Indeed, a number of gnostic ideas have persisted way into contemporary Christianity, and some even been embraced by orthodox theologians.

If we learn to see gnostic Christianity not as wicked heresy, but as an alternative interpretation of the gospel, and if we learn to see this alternative gospel as an essential part of the whole complex of early Christianity, we will have made progress in coming to terms with the origin and meaning of an important part of our Western heritage.

---

[19]Tertullian, *De praescriptione haereticorum.*
[20]Irenaeus, *Adversus haereses* 1.31.4.

Buddhism and the "Great Persecution" in China

Richard J. Smith

Charting the course of religious change in any society can be a hazardous under-taking. In the first place, the process of transformation is often masked by the apparent "timelessness" of sacred symbols. The outward expression of religious concepts, in other words, can remain the same while their content and substantive meaning may change, sometimes radically. Another problem arises from the fact that the way in which religious concepts are generally held and expressed leaves them inherently ambiguous, if not also somewhat ambivalent. This interpretive problem is often magnified by the difficulty of finding linguistic equivalents for religious terms and expressions when the tradition under consideration is not one's own. A further problem, of course, is understanding the enormously complex process by which religion as a "cultural system" interacts with its larger political and social environment.[1] For these and other reasons, scholars of religious history should always have a healthy respect for the dangers of running aground in the midst of their investigations.

Let us, however, accept the risks and venture forth to explore a large and significant topic: the history of Buddhism in China. Our particular concern will be the massive purge of the Buddhist religious establishment during the years 841–845 CE. Historians have long viewed this event as a "turning point" in the religious history of China. J. J. M. de Groot, author of a classic two-volume his-tory on religious persecution in China, maintains that as a result of the purge "Buddha's church received a blow from which it was never to recover." In a similar view, the modern Chinese historian Kenneth Ch'en observes that the year 845 was "a pivotal date, marking the end of the apogee and the beginning of the decline of the [Buddhist] religion." E. O. Reischauer asserts that "The 845 perse-

---

[1]On the above points, consult William Lessa and Evon Vogt, eds., *Reader in Comparative Religion*, 4th ed. (New York: Harper & Row, 1979) ch. 9, "Dy-namics in Religion," esp. 413-15.

Note: In the interest of clarity and consistency, I have modified some translations from the secondary sources cited below.

cution permanently crippled Buddhism and virtually wiped out the other foreign religions then extant in China."[2] It is important to remember, however, that the so-called Hui-ch'ang suppression was only one of several such persecutions in early Chinese history. What were the distinguishing features of this particular event, and in what specific respects can it be considered a turning point?

Before examining the purge itself, let us briefly sketch the history of Buddhism in China up to the middle of the T'ang dynasty (618–907). As is well known, Buddhism arose in India during the same general period that Confucianism emerged in China—between the sixth and fifth centuries BCE. Over time, it developed from a stark and rather pessimistic view of the world into a highly sophisticated universal religion, with colorful rituals, numerous sectarian distinctions, an elaborate cosmology, and a highly refined monastic structure. Sometime in the first century CE, during the so-called Eastern Han period (25–222 CE), Buddhism found its way to China.[3]

In China, Buddhism encountered a culture based on principles quite different from those of its Indic homeland. The classical Chinese language, for example, was uninflected, lographic, largely monosyllabic, and devoid of a systematic grammar. The major Indic languages, on the other hand, were highly inflected, alphabetic, polysyllabic, and possessed of a clearly articulated grammatical structure. Chinese writing was terse and concrete; Indian literature was discursive and abstract. Indian philosophical attitudes also differed substantially from those of the Chinese. For example, India had a science of psychological analysis almost completely alien to China. The Chinese, for their part, tended to view time and space as finite and closely linked to terrestrial concerns, while Indian philosophers considered time and space to be endless. Perhaps most important, Chinese Confucianism was based on the primacy of the family, on particularistic values ("love with distinctions," *ai yu ch'a-teng*), and on the ideal of service to society (*ching-shih*, "managing the world"), whereas Indian Buddhism focused on individual salvation, a universalistic ethic, and otherworldly concerns (in Chinese, *ch'u-shih*, "withdrawing from the world").[4]

---

[2]J. J. M. De Groot, *Sectarianism and Religious Persecution in China* (repr. Taipei, Taiwan: Literature House, 1963; orig. 1903) 67; Kenneth Ch'en, *Buddhism in China* (Princeton: Princeton University Press, 1964) 232.

[3]For a detailed English-language analysis of the early history of Buddhism in China, see Erik Zurcher, *The Buddhist Conquest of China*, 2 vols. (Leiden: E. J. Brill, 1959). Since the essays in the present volume are designed primarily for nonspecialists, I have not cited any Chinese or Japanese language works on Buddhism except those available in translation.

[4]These differences are discussed in Hajime Nakamura, *Ways of Thinking of Asian Peoples* (Honolulu: East-West Center Press, 1971); see also Richard J.

In light of these radical differences, it is hardly surprising that Buddhism made little initial headway in China—particularly during the Confucian "restoration" of the Eastern Han dynasty. By the end of that dynasty in 222 CE, however, Buddhism's popularity began to grow rapidly, as did the naturalistic and essentially escapist indigenous philosophy of Taoism, which by later Han times had become ever more mystical and directed more toward the attainment of personal immortality by various meditative, alchemical, and magical means than toward a return to the pristine simplicity of nature. The popularity of Buddhism and so-called Religious Taoism during the Six Dynasties period (222–589 CE) can be explained primarily by the turmoil of the time, and the quest by both individuals and groups for some kind of solace or release from suffering and misery.[5]

Taoism enjoyed the advantage of its indigenous origins and an attractive body of playful and poetic literature, but Buddhism boasted its own great literary tradition, as well as a rich artistic and musical heritage. Furthermore, Buddhism had a sophisticated ritual apparatus and an elaborate institutional structure for which there was no orthodox Taoist counterpart. Organized Taoism was associated more often than not with popular uprisings during the Han period, and in fact the demise of the dynasty was hastened by Taoist-inspired rebellions.[6] Thus Buddhism found itself in a strategic position to challenge Confucianism for ideological supremacy in China.

Although the fall of the Han had stigmatized Confucianism as state orthodoxy, long-standing Confucian social values, no less than the enormous prestige of the classical Chinese language (learned largely from the rote memorization of Confucian texts), placed formidable obstacles in the way of Buddhist missionaries and translators. The famous Indian translator Kumarajiva (344–413), after long experience in rendering Sanskrit texts into Chinese, compared the process to chewing rice and then giving it to someone else to eat. "When one translates the Indian [originals] into Chinese," he wrote, "they lose their literary elegance. Though one may understand the general idea, he entirely misses the style."[7]

Smith, *China's Cultural Heritage* (Boulder CO: Westview Press, 1983) chs. 5–7.

[5]On Taoism in imperial times (i.e., 221 BCE–1912 CE), consult W. T. de Bary et al., eds., *Sources of Chinese Tradition*, 2 vols. (New York: Columbia University Press, 1964) 1:240-65.

[6]See R. A. Stein, "Remarques sur les mouvements du taoisme politico religieux au 11° siècle ap. J. C.," *T'oung Pao* 50 (1963).

[7]Cited by Arthur Wright in "The Chinese Language and Foreign Ideas," *Studies in Chinese Thought*, ed. Arthur Wright (Chicago: University of Chicago Press, 1953) 287.

As a result, translators made many compromises. When Buddhist texts were first introduced into China, for example, the term *dharma* ("law" or "teaching") was customarily rendered *tao*, ("the way"), a concept heavily laden with both Confucian and Taoist overtones. Similarly, the elusive Sanskrit term *nirvana* ("extinction") often appeared in Chinese translation as *wu-wei* ("do nothing"), a rather mundane expression with connotations in both Confucian and Taoist classical discourse of "not overdoing." The general and abstract Buddhist term for morality (Sanskrit: *sila*) appeared as *hsiao-hsun* ("filial piety and obedience"), a pivotal doctrine of family-centered Confucianism.[8]

Translators also sought to establish analogies between Chinese and Indian concepts. Thus the Indian notion of the "four elements" became identified with the Chinese idea of the "five elements" or "activities," just as the "five constant virtues" of Confucianism were equated with the five major precepts of behavior for Buddhist lay adherents. This "matching of concepts" (*ko-i*), was often artificial and misleading, but even more misleading was the deliberate distortion of texts. Perhaps the most striking example of this phenomenon appears in the famous Buddhist text on lay morality known as the "Address to Sigala," in which the original Sanskrit line "Husbands should respect their wives" appears in Chinese as "Husbands should control their wives"—an obvious concession to male chauvinism in China.[9] Over time, despite the development of a new technical vocabulary that helped minimize the problems of false analogies and imperfect conceptual equivalents, Buddhism became heavily sinicized.[10]

Viewed from this perspective, it is hardly surprising that the most popular form of Buddhism in China was Mahayana (Chinese: *Ta-ch'eng* "The Great Vehicle"), an eclectic school of Indian Buddhism that developed in reaction to the austere and rather exclusive early school known as Theravada or the Way of the Elders. Although the Mahayana school considered its teaching to represent the highest truths of Buddhism, it could tolerate other belief systems—including Theravada and even Confucianism and Taoism—as "lesser truths," valid in some sense but ultimately inferior. This relativistic emphasis, a matter of expedience, proved to be quite compatible with the syncretic tendencies of traditional Chinese

---

[8]Arthur Wright, *Buddhism in Chinese History* (New York: Atheneum, 1968) 36.

[9]On "the matching of concepts," consult Whalen Lai, "Limits and Failure of *Ko-i* (Concept-Matching) Buddhism," *History of Religions* 18/3 (February 1979). For examples of deliberate distortion, see Hajime Nakamura, "The Influence of Confucian Ethics on the Chinese Translations of Buddhist Sutras," *Sino-Indian Studies* (Visva Vharati, Santiniketan, 1957).

[10]For a full treatment of this theme, consult Kenneth Ch'en, *The Chinese Transformation of Buddhism* (Princeton NJ: Princeton University Press, 1971).

thought. And while both major schools of Buddhism held the same fundamental views regarding causality, the nature of the phenomenal world, ultimate reality, and the proper path of mental and moral discipline, Mahayana was more compassionate and other-oriented than Theravada. It also had a more sophisticated ritual apparatus and a far more elaborate metaphysical system—one that included the idea of a myriad of gods, all manifestations of the Buddha spirit or nature. Thus, in its eclecticism, social outlook, ritual, and polytheism, Mahayana fit comparatively well into the preexisting Chinese social landscape.[11]

Four major Mahayana schools formed the "spirit and substance" of Chinese Buddhism: (1) the T'ien-t'ai or Lotus (Fa-hua) School; (2) the Hua-yen ("Flowery Splendor") School; (3) the Pure Land School; and (4) the Ch'an or Meditation School (known more commonly as Zen, the Japanese pronunciation of the Chinese character for Ch'an). Of these four, only T'ien-t'ai had no Indian equivalent, but each developed along characteristically Chinese lines. Indicative of both the syncretic capacity of traditional Chinese thought and the accommodating outlook of Mahayana Buddhism, the Chinese had a common saying: "The "T'ien-t'ai and Hua-yen Schools for doctrine and the Pure Land and Ch'an Schools for practice."[12]

Although heavily sinicized, Buddhism exerted a profound influence on Chinese cultural life. In the realm of thought, for example, it introduced new concepts such as reincarnation, *dharma* (here meaning "psychosomatic elements of existence"), the retribution of *karma*, and the ultimate release of *nirvana*. Furthermore, it inspired a huge number of indigenous Chinese writings to supplement the massive original Buddhist corpus known as the *Tripitaka*. It introduced the idea of monastic discipline, and gave a formal structure to the previously rather inchoate Chinese spiritual world. Wing-tsit Chan goes so far as to say that Religious Taoism became "a wholesale imitation of Buddhism, notably in its clergy, temples, images, ceremonies, and canon."[13]

The impact of Buddhism was equally great in the realm of material culture. By some accounts, printing was a Chinese-Buddhist invention—although recent research on the mainland suggests a secular inspiration for Chinese block printing, perhaps as early as the Sui dynasty (589–618 CE). The earliest known printed book, dated 868 CE, is an exquisite edition of the famous Buddhist text known as the *Diamond Sutra*, written in elegant classical Chinese. Buddhist iconography established a new art form in China, while Buddhist-inspired changes in painting included new styles, line and shading techniques, and types of ornamentation. The Chinese pagoda provides a vivid illustration of the creative

---

[11]See Smith, *China's Cultural Heritage*, ch. 7.
[12]Ibid., 138.
[13]Wing-tsit Chan, *Neo-Confucianism, Etc.* (Hanover NH, 1969) 419.

blending of Indic and Chinese architectural influences, a process also evident in the evolution of Chinese religious music.[14]

Despite its world-denying orientation, Buddhism played an active social and political role in China from the early Six Dynasties period through much of the T'ang. This role can be explained in part by the strong emphasis on charity in Mahayana Buddhism; but it was made possible primarily by means of imperial and official patronage. The best-known early patron of Buddhism in China was Emperor Wu of the Liang Dynasty (reigned 502–549), who not only took his own Buddhist vows, but also periodically gave himself to a Buddhist temple so that his ministers would have to "ransom" him back with huge gifts to the temple.[15] Yet even during the height of Buddhist political power, religious institutions remained distinctly subordinate to the secular state. No Buddhist "pope" emerged to challenge the authority of the emperor in any sphere of Chinese life at any time.

The financial power of Buddhist monasteries and temples, many of them tax-exempt, came largely from imperial and official grants of land and money. This wealth, amplified by land rental, moneylending, and slaveholding, made possible a wide range of social services. Throughout China, Buddhist monks established schools, hospitals, and orphanages; they lectured in local communities, sponsored feasts, and observed a number of public festivals. The almost universal acceptance of Buddhism in China by the sixth century CE was assuredly a function not only of its successful adaptation to the Chinese cultural environment, but also its valuable social role.[16]

Despite its sinicization and manifold contributions to Chinese society and culture, Buddhism was not without its critics. One relentless criticism had to do with the alien origins of this religious teaching. Although China's cultural development was profoundly affected by foreign influences throughout much of its history, the Chinese continued to maintain an attitude of sublime superiority to all things foreign. This Sinocentric, "Middle Kingdom" mentality was based on the longstanding assumption that the attractiveness of Chinese culture would transform the "barbarians" (*yung-Hsia pien-i*), rather than the reverse.[17] Thus,

---

[14]See, e.g., Wright, *Buddhism in Chinese History*, 70ff.

[15]Ibid., 51.

[16]See Ch'en, *Buddhism in China*, 258-96; also see L. S. Yang, "Buddhist Monasteries and Four Money-Raising Institutions in Chinese History," *Harvard Journal of Asiatic Studies* 13 (1950); Edwin O. Reischauer, *Ennin's Travels in T'ang China* (New York: Ronald Press, 1955) passim.

[17]This theme is discussed in Richard J. Smith, "The Employment of Foreign Military Talent," *Journal of the Hong Kong Branch of the Royal Asiatic Society* 15 (1975); see also Smith, *China's Cultural Heritage*, 106-107.

from the very beginning of its spread into China, Buddhism aroused a certain culturally inspired resentment. The fifth-century scholar Ku Huan, for example, argued that "Buddhism originated in the land of the barbarians, is that not because the customs of the barbarians were originally evil? The Tao [Way] originated in China, is that not because the habits of the Chinese were originally good?"[18]

Other scholars launched attacks based on more specific cultural grounds. The sixth-century Confucian Fan Chen, for example, assailed Buddhism for undermining the foundations of imperial rule, and for corrupting popular customs. Buddhist monks, he maintained, deluded the people into "exhausting their fortunes . . . and going bankrupt in flattering the Buddha." By frightening individuals with the miseries of hell and enticing them with the delights of heaven, the monks had succeeded, Fan asserted, in causing families to "abandon their dear and loved ones and terminate their line of descendants."[19] Buddhism, in other words, encouraged unfilial behavior by promoting a false and beguiling metaphysic.

These and other such attacks from Chinese scholars in the south were largely confined to words; but in north China during the same period there were two actual persecutions of Buddhism—one in 446 CE and one in 574 CE. Both were inspired by intellectual rivals of Buddhism (Taoists or Confucians), but in each case the rationale for attempting to suppress Buddhism was less ideological than practical. At issue were such problems as abuses of clerical privilege, the mass retreat of peasants into holy orders so as to escape corvée and taxation, and the fraudulent transfer of land to temples and monasteries. Chinese officials argued with growing conviction that the Buddhist church was parasitic, anomalous, and potentially subversive. As a result, the northern emperors attempted to confiscate the wealth of Buddhist temples and monasteries, and ordered the clergy to return to lay life.[20]

There were no burnings, tortures, or massacres of the faithful, however, much less religious wars against the "infidels." To think of Buddhist persecutions in China in terms of either the relentless conflict between Christians and Muslims in the West, or of the fratricidal strife and inquisitions within Christianity itself, would be quite misleading. Moreover, in the case of China, the Buddhist persecutions were soon followed by general amnesties, and dramatic expiatory acts on the part of subsequent rulers. By the time of the Sui and early T'ang dynasties, Buddhism had fully reasserted itself in Chinese political, social, and intellectual life. Indeed, a number of scholars attribute the reunification of the

---

[18]Cited in Ch'en, *Buddhism in China*, 137.
[19]Ibid., 140-41.
[20]Ibid., 147ff.

empire in 589 CE at least in part to the spread of Buddhist culture in the latter part of the Six Dynasties period.[21]

Reunification under the Sui brought not only empire-wide state patronage of Buddhism but also the selective revival of Confucianism. In Arthur Wright's well-chosen words:

> Its [Confucianism's] ritual-symbolic procedures were refurbished for use in the court and countryside to give the Sui an aura of legitimacy and to demonstrate that the Sui was reviving the ecumenical empire of the Han. The civil virtues of Confucianism were proclaimed as norms for all the people, and knowledge of the Confucian classics was decreed as the basis for a revived examination and selection system. Despite its eclipse, the Confucian tradition had a monopoly of certain resources, notably in political theories and in techniques for political and social control, which neither of its rivals [Buddhism and Taoism] had come close to matching.[22]

Furthermore, the Sui and T'ang rulers took special steps to control the growth and influence of the Buddhist church through a clerical bureaucracy and an elaborate set of imperially imposed rules and regulations. Of special concern to the government was the subversive potential of religious societies inspired by the idea of a Buddha of the future (Indian: *Maitreya*; Chinese: *Mi-lo Fo*) who would inaugurate a new utopian age on earth.[23]

Buddhism thus occupied a somewhat ambivalent position in Sui and early T'ang China. On the one hand, its canons were revered, its spiritual truths were virtually unquestioned, and its cultural influence was evident at all levels of Chinese society. Temples and monasteries dotted the countryside, Buddhist art, architecture, music, and ritual were deeply woven into the daily life of the Chinese people, and even the great T'ang poets found inspiration in Buddhist ideas and themes. On the other hand, the state subjected the Buddhist religious

---

[21]See, e.g., Arthur Wright, *The Sui Dynasty* (New York: Knopf, 1978).

[22]Ibid., 66.

[23]The T'ang government's concern is reflected in an edict of 715, which reads in part:

> Now there are those with white clothing and long hair, who falsely claim that Maitreya has descended to be born. By means of supernatural and deceitful actions they have gathered followers from a wide area. They say they understand Buddhist concepts, and irresponsibly speak of good and bad omens. They have written short sutras which they falsely claim were spoken by the Buddha himself. They collect disciples and call themselves monks. They do not marry. They mislead and confuse the villagers and cause great trouble for the government.

Cited by Daniel Overmeyer in his *Folk Buddhist Religion* (Cambridge: Harvard University Press, 1976) 25-26.

establishment to relentless and systematic bureaucratic supervision, and continued, even in the midst of its own patronage, to look upon Buddhism as a potential challenge to the existing political order.

By the ninth century, changes had begun to take place that would fundamentally alter the position of Buddhism in China. One, of course, was the decline of Buddhism in India. Over time, this led to a diminished flow of new ideas into China, a trickle that ceased altogether by the eleventh century CE. Another change was the growth of Chinese antiforeignism after the rebellion of An Lu-shan (755–763). This outbreak was not only precipitated by a "half-breed" barbarian, but its suppression involved the use of the Turkic Uighur and other foreign allies, who proved to be almost as troublesome as the insurgents themselves. In time, the cosmopolitan self-confidence of the early T'ang power and the breakdown of its sophisticated system of taxation and militia service after the rebellion of An Lu-shan created a financial crisis that made it much more difficult for the state to bear the cost of an essentially tax-free Buddhist establishment.[24]

Meanwhile, Confucianism had begun to reassert itself, inspired in large measure by the intellectual challenge of Buddhism. The beginnings of this so-called neo-Confucian revival are often traced to a T'ang official named Han Yü (or Han Wen-kung, 768–824), whose passionate "Memorial on the Bone of Buddha" is one of the most famous documents in the history of Chinese Buddhism. It is worth quoting at some length:

> Now Buddha was a man of the barbarians who did not speak the language of China and wore clothes of a different fashion. His sayings did not concern the ways of our ancient kings, nor did his manner of dress conform to their laws. He understood neither the duties that bind sovereign and subject, nor the affections of father and son. If he were still alive today and came to our court by order of his ruler, your Majesty might condescend to receive him [in an audience, but] he would subsequently be escorted to the borders of the country, dismissed, and not allowed to delude the masses. How, then, when he has long been dead, could his rotten bones, the foul and unlucky remains of his body, be rightly admitted to the palace [to be worshipped]. [. . .] Your servant is deeply shamed and begs that this [Buddha's finger] bone be cast into fire and water, that this evil may be rooted out, the world freed from its error, and later generations spared this delusion. [. . .] Should the Buddha indeed have supernatural power to send down

---

[24]On the rebellion of An Lu-shan and the rise of Chinese antiforeignism, consult Smith, "The Employment of Foreign Military Talent." On the T'ang financial situation, see Kenneth Ch'en, "The Economic Background of the Hui-ch'ang Suppression of Buddhism," *Harvard Journal of Asiatic Studies* 19 (June 1956).

curses and calamities, may they fall only upon the person of your servant, who calls upon High Heaven to witness that he does not regret his words.[25]

Han Yü's memorial so enraged the emperor that Han narrowly escaped execution, and was later banished to the far southern reaches of the empire. Nonetheless, Han had made his mark on Chinese history. Although known more as a polemicist and prose stylist than as a formal philosopher, his writings were "rediscovered" in the tenth century, and he became a virtual patron saint of the Sung dynasty's (960–1279 CE) neo-Confucian revival. Sung neo-Confucianism not only buttressed traditional Confucian moral and political values with cosmological and metaphysical conceptions adapted from Buddhism and Taoism, but also undercut otherworldly Buddhism and escapist Taoism by reaffirming the positivistic, optimistic doctrine that human fulfillment is to be found only in the here and now, and that everyone has the potential to achieve this fulfillment and become a sage.[26]

Without these changes, it is doubtful that the "Great Persecution" of 841–845 would have been as historically significant as it now appears to be. In other words, one may justifiably argue that the significance of the Hui-ch'ang suppression is more symbolic than substantive—that the event itself did not alter the status of Buddhism in China so much as it reflected and, in a sense, presaged a number of other events and trends which together produced long-term effects on both the theory and the practice of Chinese Buddhism.

Still, the event is worth examining for several reasons. One is that it was unquestionably the largest persecution of its kind in early Chinese history. Although the Chinese, with their extreme love of classification, refer to the major Buddhist suppressions of the imperial era as the "Three Wu" (*san-Wu*; a reference to the character for "martial" in the posthumous titles of each of the three emperors involved), the T'ang persecution was by far the most widespread and severe. It is also interesting because we can see it in relatively full detail through the eyes of a contemporary witness, the famous Japanese pilgrim Ennin (793–864), who traveled throughout China from 838 to 847 and recorded his impressions and observations in a diary.[27] Finally, it provides a rare and revealing look at the relationship between T'ang factional politics and religious issues.

---

[25]Cited in de Bary et al., *Sources of Chinese Tradition*, 1:372-74 (slightly modified); see also Han's essay on "The True Way" (*Yuan Tao*) ibid., 1:276-379.

[26]One of many excellent works on the Sung neo-Confucian revival is Hoyt Tillman, *Utilitarian Confucianism* (Cambridge MA: Harvard University Press, 1982). Tillman's bibliography cites most other relevant studies. For an overview of neo-Confucianism, consult Smith, *China's Cultural Heritage*, ch. 6.

[27]*Ennin's Diary*, trans. Edwin O. Reischauer (New York: Ronald Press, 1955).

The Chinese official histories of the T'ang period say very little about the persecution of 841–845. The first T'ang history (*Chiu T'ang-shu*), compiled in the middle of the tenth century, contains but a few brief references to the event; and the second (*Hsin T'ang-shu*), written about a century later, states only that "There was a great destruction of Buddhist monasteries, and the monks and nuns were made back into commoners."[28] The brevity of these official accounts, indicative of the contempt most Chinese intellectuals had for Buddhism in the immediate post-T'ang era, makes the historian's task of reconstructing and explaining events especially difficult. For additional material on the persecution, therefore, we must turn to documents not included in the orthodox dynastic histories. One such source, of course, is Ennin's diary.

Although, as a Buddhist monk, Ennin was by no means a neutral observer of events in China, his diary provides a basically reliable and often quite illuminating account of his sojourn to the Middle Kingdom. According to Ennin, and undoubtedly in fact, the Wu-tsung emperor's personal attachment to Religious Taoism was a major factor behind the persecution of Buddhism during the Hui-ch'ang era. Ennin indicates, for example, that in the period 841–845, the emperor supplanted a number of state-approved Buddhist rituals with Taoist rituals, replaced established Buddhist icons at the capital with Taoist images, and even went so far as to order scholars of the court to "read Taoist scriptures and practice Taoist arts." He notes, however, that Chinese scholars were disinclined to follow the throne's directive to embrace Taoism.[29]

In late 842 the Wu-tsung emperor launched his first major attack on Buddhism. Ennin informs us that:

On the ninth day of the tenth month [November 14, 842] an Imperial edict was issued [to the effect that] all the monks and nuns of the empire who understand alchemy, the art of incantations, and the black arts [magical practices, including self-mutilation], who have fled from the army, who have on their bodies the scars of flagellations and tattoo marks [for former offenses, or who have been condemned to] various forms of labor, who have formerly committed sexual offenses, . . . [who now] maintain wives, or who do not observe the Buddhist rules, should all be forced to return to lay life. If monks and nuns have money, grain, fields, or estates, these should be surrendered to the government. If they regret [the loss of] their wealth and wish to return to lay life [in order to retain it], in accordance with their wishes they are to be forced to return to lay life and are to pay the "double tax" [*liang-shui*] and to perform the corvée.

Ennin goes on to state that

---

[28]Reischauer, *Ennin's Travels in T'ang China*, 224-25.
[29]See esp. *Ennin's Diary*, 340-48.

The Commissioners of Good Works for the Streets of the Left and the Right have notified the monasteries, investigated the monks and nuns and their wealth, and regulated them in accordance with the Imperial edict.

Significantly, however, we are told that the Army Inspector (*kuan-chün jung-shih*) Ch'iu Shih-liang opposed the Imperial edict and did not wish to regulate the clergy. Although Ch'iu was not successful in reversing the emperor's decision altogether, he was allowed to request a stay of one hundred days, whereupon he immediately notified the monasteries not to allow their monks and nuns to leave.[30]

From this remark and other evidence, it is clear that factional politics played an important role in the Hui-ch'ang persecution. Apparently, the Wu-tsung emperor's principal political adversaries were a powerful group of Buddhist-inclined palace eunuchs—led initially by Ch'iu Shih-liang, who, ironically, had once helped place the Wu-tsung emperor on the throne. The emperor's primary ally in this factional struggle was his able minister Li Te-yü, who, together with other Confucian scholar-bureaucrats, attempted to undermine the influence of the eunuchs. Li was not a fanatical hater of Buddhism, and was even tolerant enough of "barbarian influences" to write the preface for a book on loyal foreign employees in the Chinese service. But his antipathy for Ch'iu's faction ran deep indeed. During Ch'iu's lifetime, the eunuch's personal power was too great to challenge directly, but almost immediately after his death in mid-843, at least four of his principal henchmen were executed, and about a year later his son was killed by the sovereign himself after boasting in a drunken stupor that "Although the emperor is revered and noble, it was my father who set him up."[31]

Not surprisingly, Ch'iu Shih-liang's demise led to the rapid intensification of Wu-tsung's anti-Buddhist purge. Ennin's diary tells us that in early 844 an imperial edict was issued forbidding offerings to the teeth of the Buddha. Another edict banned offerings and pilgrimages to several prominent Buddhist shrines. Ennin recorded:

If someone presents a single cash,[32] he is to receive twenty strokes of the cane on the back, and, if a monk or nun accepts a single cash, he [or she] is to receive twenty strokes of the cane on the back. If in the various provinces, prefectures, and subprefectures there should be those who make offerings, they are to be seized on the spot and given twenty strokes of the cane

---

[30]Ibid., 350-51. Reischauer, *Ennin's Travels* 231-37 discusses T'ang factionalism.

[31]*Ennin's Diary*, 351-52.

[32]A *cash* is a small-value, usually copper alloy Chinese coin with a square hole in the middle—so, *any* offering, no matter how small.

on the back. Because of this, no one comes to these four holy areas or makes offerings. In accordance with the imperial edict, the monks of these places were questioned, and those lacking official credentials were all executed on the spot.

Other diary entries document the Wu-tsung emperor's growing hostility toward the Buddhist establishment and his increasing patronage of Religious Taoism.[33]

During late 844, the emperor embarked on a gigantic construction project that marked a new phase in the assault on Buddhism. The project was suggested by a Taoist priest named Chao Kuei-chen, who wrote a xenophobic memorial stating:

The Buddha was born among the Western barbarians and taught "non-birth." "Non-birth" is simply death. He converted men to Nirvana, but Nirvana is death. He talked much about impermanence, pain, and emptiness, which are particularly strange [doctrines]. He did not understand the [Taoist] principles of spontaneity and immortality.

Chao's idea was to build a "terrace of immortals" in honor of the native Taoist philosopher Lao-tzu, where "we may purify our bodies and mount to the heavenly mists [like Lao-tzu], and . . . preserve the pleasures of immortality."[34]

While work progressed on the terrace, an edict ordered the destruction of "the small monasteries of the land." According to Ennin:

Their scriptures and images were taken to the large monasteries, and their bells were sent to the Taoist monasteries. Those monks and nuns of the destroyed monasteries who were unrefined in their conduct or did not observe the rules, regardless of their age, were all forced to return to lay life, were sent back to their places of origin, and were made to perform the local corvée. Those who were old and observed the rules were assigned to the great monasteries, but those who were young, even though they observed the rules, were all forced to return to lay life. Upon completion of the terrace project in early 845, the emperor was reportedly overjoyed, and immediately ordered seven Taoist priests to concoct an elixir and to seek immortality on the terrace.

By this time, according to Ennin, the Wu-tsung emperor's behavior had become increasingly irrational and unpredictable. By contrast, the policies of his ministers—at least those policies pertaining to Buddhism—had become ever more regular and radical. Previously, the object of Wu-tsung's purge had been simply to weed out the "irregular" native clergy and to confiscate the private wealth of monks and nuns. Now, however, a series of edicts issued in the

---

[33]Ibid., 354-59.
[34]Ibid., 321-25.

emperor's name ordered the systematic destruction of all Buddhist temples, shrines, and monuments, as well as the confiscation of Buddhist land and other property. Ennin records a directive issued to the monasteries of the land "prohibiting them from establishing estates and also ordering that an inventory be made of the number of slaves of the monasteries . . . and their money, grain, and textile [holdings]."[35] These resources were all to be handed over to the state as a means of relieving the government's crushing financial burden.

At the same time, Wu-tsung's ministers embarked on a comprehensive campaign to rid the Buddhist establishment of its remaining regular clergy. The first step at the capital of Ch'ang-an was the defrocking of all monks and nuns under forty years of age—reportedly at the rate of three hundred clerics a day. Then came the return to lay life of monks and nuns under the age of fifty; and finally the purge of all those over the age of fifty. Similar procedures were followed in the provinces.[36]

An imperial edict issued in the latter part of 845 summarizes the scope of the persecution:

> More than 4,600 monasteries have been destroyed throughout the empire; more than 260,000 monks and nuns have been returned to lay life; . . . more than 40,000 privately established temples and shrines have been destroyed; thirty or forty million *ch'ing* [i.e. several hundred million acres] of fertile lands and fine fields have been confiscated; and 150,000 slaves have been transformed into regular taxpayers. [. . .] We have driven away the lazy and idle people to a number of more than ten million. We have done away with no less than ten thousand gorgeous but useless [Buddhist] buildings.[37]

Predictably, despite the Taoist inclinations of the Wu-tsung emperor, the edict cited above offers a quintessentially Confucian rationale for the eradication of Buddhism:

> We have heard that up through the Three Dynasties [Hsia, Shang, and Chou] the Buddha was never spoken of. It was only from the Han and Wei dynasties on that the religion of idols gradually came into prominence. So in this latter age it has transmitted its strange ways, instilling its infection with every opportunity, spreading like a luxuriant vine, until it has poisoned the customs of our land; gradually before anyone was aware, it beguiled and confounded men's minds so that the multitude have been increasingly led

---

[35]Ibid., 347-56; see also 373, 384-85, 388, and 390.
[36]Ibid., 357-58; 361-62.
[37]Cited in Reischauer, *Ennin's Travels*, 225-27. Cf. de Bary, et al., *Sources of Chinese Tradition*, 1:380-82.

astray. It has spread to the hills and plains of all the nine provinces and through the walls and towers of our two capitals.

[. . .] It wears out the strength of the people with constructions of earth and wood, pilfers their wealth for ornaments of gold and precious objects, causes men to abandon their rulers and parents for the company of [Buddhist] teachers, and severs man and wife with its monastic decrees. In destroying law and injuring mankind, nothing is worse than this doctrine. [. . .] Presented with an opportunity to suppress this age-old evil and fulfill the laws and institutions of the ancient kings, to aid mankind and bring profit to the multitude, how could We forbear to act?

Ennin did not record this document in his diary, perhaps because he had already left Ch-ang-an. We know from his other entries, however, that the policies proclaimed at the capital were, for the most part, carried out in the provinces. In both sympathy and sadness he wrote at one point:

The monks and nuns of China are naturally poor. Throughout the land they have all been returned to lay life, and now that they have been secularized, they lack clothes to wear and food to eat. Their hardships are extreme, and they cannot assuage their cold or hunger, so they enter towns and villages, and steal the property of others.[38]

Ennin's misery over this sorry state of affairs was undoubtedly heightened by the fact that he and a number of other foreign monks had been ordered by the throne to return home since they lacked official documents from the Bureau of Sacrifices.

Before leaving China, however, Ennin had the satisfaction of learning that the Wu-tsung emperor had died in the third month of 846—perhaps from the ill effects of taking too many Taoist "elixirs of immortality"! His successor, the Hsuan-tsung emperor, almost immediately began undoing the work of his deranged predecessor. In the fifth month the new ruler proclaimed a "great amnesty," which, according to Ennin, was accompanied by an edict stating that each prefecture in China was to build two monasteries and that regional commanderies were permitted to build three. Each monastery could have up to fifty monks, and monks over fifty years of age who had been returned to lay life during the previous year were allowed to take Buddhist orders again.[39]

Yet despite this renewal of imperial toleration—which followed the general pattern of previous religious persecutions—Buddhism never again enjoyed the kind of institutional power and intellectual appeal it had experienced prior to the ninth century. Most Chinese and Western works on Buddhism agree that the post-T'ang era represents a period of general decline in the faith, or in Buddhist

---

[38]*Ennin's Diary*, 386.
[39]Ibid., 391-92.

terms, a "decay of the dharma" (*mo-fa*). Certainly it is true that in late imperial times no new sutras of any importance were translated, no new sects were established, no new doctrines were formulated, and no Buddhist masters of great originality and brilliance emerged. In intellectual life, the rise of state-sponsored neo-Confucianism tended to overshadow Buddhism, just as the growth of the Chinese clan system in post-T'ang times made the social role of monasteries seem less important than it once had been. On the whole, institutional Buddhism fell steadily into disrepute.[40]

Meanwhile, the emergence in Sung times (960–1279) of folk Buddhist sects combining "piety with politics and rebellion" cast further suspicion on the Buddhist faith and led to further state restrictions on the Buddhist establishment. It is true, of course, that references to associations of "rebel monks" in China can be found as early as the fifth century CE; and we have already seen how the regulation of Buddhism in T'ang times was inspired in part by the seditious potential of at least some Buddhist organizations. But the Sung period witnessed a proliferation of folk religious sects as part of a general trend toward the establishment of new forms of voluntary association in the midst of rapid urban growth, increasing social differentiation, and economic specialization.[41] Of these religious sects, the eclectic White Lotus Society (*Pai-lien hui*)—which drew upon Taoism and Manicheanism, as well as elements of Maitreya and Pure Land Buddhism—played a particularly active political role from the twelfth to the nineteenth centuries in China.[42]

It would be wrong, however, to dismiss Buddhism in late imperial times as either a degenerate or an essentially moribund faith. In the first place, Buddhist festivals and common fasts, as well as pious practices such as the release of animals and the recitation of the Buddha's name (*nien-Fo*) remained extremely popular among the Chinese masses throughout the imperial era. Buddhist mourning rituals were widely observed as an integral part of ancestor worship, not only by commoners, but also by many members of the Chinese elite. Even "agnostic" Confucian households were not above hiring Buddhist clergy to say prayers for the deceased as a kind of "filial insurance" in case the Buddhist version of the afterlife happened to be correct. And at the highest levels of Chinese society, into the twentieth century, Buddhism continued to play a

---

[40]See, e.g., Ch'en, *Buddhism in China*, esp. ch. 16, "Recession and Decline"; cf. Chun-fang Yü, *The Renewal of Buddhism in China* (New York: Columbia University Press, 1981) esp. 4-5.

[41]See Overmyer, *Folk Buddhist Religion*, ch. 5, esp. 89-90.

[42]Ibid, passim.

significant role, since many Chinese emperors patronized Buddhism and called upon the Buddhist clergy to say prayers on behalf of the Confucian state.[43]

Furthermore, during the Ming dynasty (1368–1644), which was founded by a Buddhist monk (Chu Yüan-chang), the Religious Taoist concept of merits and demerits found its way into Chinese Buddhism. This doctrine, although similar in some respects to the idea of *karma*, was based on the notion that good deeds would prolong one's life and bad deeds would shorten it. Certain deeds counted for a certain number of points, and the net balance would determine one's fate. The emphasis was clearly this-worldly, but of wide appeal, especially in the late Ming period.[44]

Recent research has shown that, by late Ming times and during much of the Ch'ing (1644–1912), after centuries of "relative obscurity," Buddhism experienced a revival not unlike the neo-Confucian revival it had helped to stimulate in the Sung era. This revitalization was part of a general burst of Chinese intellectual activity in the late sixteenth and early seventeenth centuries, as well as a product of the individual efforts of several dedicated Buddhist monks—notably Yun-ch'i Chu-hung (1535–1615) and Han-shan Te-ch'ing (1546–1623).[45] Chu-hung, in particular, is known for adapting and popularizing the Religious Taoist system of merits and demerits mentioned above.

But the revival of Buddhism in the late Ming and early Ch'ing dynasties did not lead by any means to the eclipse of Confucianism as an intellectual force. On the contrary, one of the most characteristic features of Ming-Ch'ing Buddhism was its fundamental compatibility with neo-Confucian ideas and practices. Lay Buddhism, in particular, flourished precisely because it did not demand a radical break from the cultural system in which it existed. It was, in Chun-fang Yü's well-chosen words, "more activist than contemplative, more moralistic than theological, more world-affirming than world rejecting."[46]

Even institutional Buddhism made compromises. Perhaps no more vivid illustration of Buddhism's successful adaptation to the Chinese environment in late imperial times could be found than the common use of names such as Pao-chung ssu (Monastery for Honoring Loyalty [to the State]) or Hu-kuo ssu

---

[43]On the multifaceted role of Buddhism in late imperial China, see Smith, *China's Cultural Heritage*, chs. 3, 4, 7, and 10.

[44]For perspectives on the late Ming Buddhist revival, and two excellent studies of the monks mentioned in the text, consult Yü, *The Renewal of Buddhism in China*, and Sung-peng Hsu, *A Buddhist Leader in Ming China* (University Park: Pennsylvania State University Press, 1979).

[45]Yü, *The Renewal of Buddhism in China*, 228.

[46]Smith, *China's Cultural Heritage*, 135.

(Monastery of the kinship-renouncing doctrine of Buddhism was the common designation Kuang-hsiao ssu (Monastery for the Glorification of Filial Piety).[47]

In short, by the late seventeenth century, Chinese Buddhism had become fully sinicized—part of an expansive and syncretic philosophical outlook now vividly expressed in the popular slogan "The three teachings [Confucianism, Buddhism, and Taoism] are united into one" (*san-chiao ho-i*). This Buddhism was not degenerate, just different. No longer was it necessary for an individual to renounce social and family ties in order to become a Buddhist in China:

> To be a filial son and a loyal subject did not bar one from enlightenment. On the contrary, if one failed to be a filial son and a loyal subject, one also failed to be a true Buddhist.[48]

By harmonizing itself with China's evolving social and intellectual environment, Buddhism eventually recovered its vitality without sacrificing either its moral vision or its metaphysic. Perhaps this adaptability helps to explain the success of Buddhism in facing the challenges of China's post-imperial period, including those posed by iconoclastic intellectuals and political parties in the twentieth century.[49]

---

[47]Yü, *The Renewal of Buddhism in China*, 227-28.

[48]Ibid.

[49]On the fascinating history of Buddhism in twentieth-century China, see the 3 fine vols. by Holmes Welch, entitled *The Practice of Chinese Buddhism, 1900–1950, The Buddhist Revival in China*, and *Buddhism Under Mao* (Cambridge MA: Harvard University Press, 1966, 1967, and 1972 respectively). At present, under the comparatively "liberal" policies of the post-Mao era, Buddhism has once again begun to flourish on the Mainland. The acting president of the Chinese Buddhist Association asserted in 1979, for example, that the number of Buddhist lay believers in the People's Republic could be as high as one hundred million or more. Roger Garside, *Coming Alive* (New York: McGraw-Hill, 1981) 410.

Conquest or Inculturation: Ways of Ministry in the Early Jesuit Missions

Clement J. McNaspy, S.J.

I

In the year 635, almost a thousand years before the Italian missioner Matteo Ricci reached Beijing, the Syrian missioner Alopen reached a different Chinese capital 500 miles to the southwest, Chang-an (now Sian or Xian), then the largest city on earth, and was honorably received by Emperor T'ai-tsung (Li Shih-min) of the T'ang dynasty. Alopen belonged to the Christian sect known as Nestorians, and in a relatively short time Nestorian communities sprang up in the Middle Kingdom.[1]

Nestorian Christianity in China became known as the "Luminous Religion." Nonetheless it was wiped out a bare two centuries later, and other missioners returning in the thirteenth century achieved no lasting results either. Yet in that same century Europeans set out for the fabled kingdom in search of "spices and souls," as the phrase went; such dauntless travelers as Marco Polo and Giovanni da Pian del Carpini, and Franciscans like Giovanni de Montecorvino, soon to be consecrated first archbishop of what we now call Beijing. This new opening took place under the cosmopolitan Yüan or Mongol dynasty (1234–1368).

But with the advent of the Ming dynasty in 1368, China took a rather isolationist posture, while the first Ming emperor Hung-wu (Chu Yüan-chang) required every family of that highly literate nation to own a volume of his thoughts, thus making himself for a time (rather like Mao centuries later) the most widely read author on earth. It was under the same dynasty that Portugal began exploring the Orient, though any effort at Christian missionary activity in China was already effectively cut off. Meanwhile China's cultural influence was of course still dominant in what we call the Far East, having long since made its

---

[1]Joseph S. Sebes, "China's Jesuit Century," *Wilson Quarterly* (Winter 1978): 170-83. I use Sebes's article frequently in the Chinese portion of this essay.

way into Japan by way of Korea. The later Jesuit Francis Xavier, first missioner of his Order, became painfully aware that he must first evangelize China before he could be at all effective in Japan. He was to die on a tiny island just off the China coast in 1552, before realizing his ambition.

It was an Italian, Alessandro Valignano, who twenty-one years after Xavier's death was appointed director of all Jesuit missions in the Far East, and who devised a new, enlightened approach. Knowing something of the heights of Chinese culture, he realized better than most of his contemporaries that preaching was not enough, and that a more appropriate approach in China should not be vertical, as though from above, but horizontal, not looking down on the Chinese but honestly treating them as equals. In Valignano's view, the first and best things for prospective missioners to do would be to master the difficult Chinese language and dig deep into the ancient Confucian classics.

This was a radically new idea, exceedingly hard for smug Europeans to cope with, flushed as they were with a sense of Renaissance glory and perhaps more ethnocentric than ever. Michelangelo was still alive when Valignano was born, and Titian was to die three years after Valignano's appointment as religious superior of all Jesuits in the Far East. This was hardly a moment for Europeans to want to treat other cultures as equal. If Giorgio Vasari was then enlightening the West as to the superiority of the Italian Renaissance to the art of the belittled medieval Gothic, what would he have thought of Chinese or other oriental art?

Not all superiors of Jesuit missions were as open-minded as Valignano. Francisco Cabral, his predecessor in Japan, for example, disagreed vigorously and took positive steps to prevent the implementation of Valignano's ideas. Showing no understanding of Japanese culture, Cabral went so far as to discourage missioners from learning the language, satisfied to work through interpreters. Doubtless Cabral never learned that the Japanese nickname for Westerners was "Nanban" ("Southern Barbarians"), since they came in by the southern port of Nagasaki.

Valignano worked to change all this and directed that "To speak or write Japanese incorrectly is impolite and invites ridicule, like speaking Latin backwards with many mistakes."[2] Further, to encourage the correct use of that elegant language, he urged newcomers from Europe to spend at least eighteen months in intensive study. On his second trip to Japan Valignano even brought along a printing press, which proved to be the first in Japan to use movable metal type. Japanese Jesuit brothers taught the language to new arrivals, and textbooks for that purpose were soon printed on Valignano's press. One of the most astonish-

---

[2]Arimichi Ebisawa, "The Meetings of Cultures," in *The Southern Barbarians: The First Europeans in Japan*, ed. Michael Cooper (Tokyo: Kodansha, 1971) 126-27.

ing intercultural achievements of the epoch was the compilation and printing of the first Japanese dictionary ever to be published, the work of a committee of Japanese and European Jesuits, the *Vocabulario da Lingoa de Iapam* (1604). This was followed four years later by Father João Rodrigues's *Arte da Lingoa de Iapam*, the first Japanese grammar ever done. "It was a century before any comparable work was done by the Japanese themselves," we are informed by Japanese historian Arimichi Ebisawa. These volumes were among the first of a stream of works on linguistics done by Jesuit missioners in Asia, Africa, and the Americas. It was all part of a mammoth process of what we would call today inculturation or acculturation.

But adaptation in language was not Valignano's only emphasis. He wrote a treatise for the missioners on good manners in their dealings with the Japanese, stressing the importance of self-control and quiet demeanor. In this he focused too on liturgical style and urged his missioners to conduct their religious ceremonies with as much decorum and reverence "as the Buddhist bonzes [monks]" show, a somewhat unusual liturgical rubric. Mission residences were to be constructed in Japanese style, with a tearoom and provision for the traditional *sakuzuki* ("goblet," later the word for the chalice at Mass), while directives were specially laid out for the appropriate etiquette.

Another Italian missioner, Organtino Gnecchi-Soldo, perhaps outdid Valignano in his admiration for the Japanese. In a letter to Rome in 1577 he asserted:

> Here in Japan, scholarship, learning, and culture are held in greater account than elsewhere. You should not think that they are barbarians, for apart from our religion we ourselves are greatly inferior to them. . . . However prudent we may believe we are, we are great barbarians compared with them.[3]

The Portuguese Jesuit Luis Frois rivaled Organtino in his fascination with Japan. One of his letters written in 1565 was published eleven years later and contains the earliest account of Japan to be printed in English. In it Frois described Buddhist temples, funeral ceremonies, religious suicide, and the mysterious island of Yezo (modern Hokkaido), and the Ainu natives described as "savage men, clothed in beastes skynnes, rough bodyed with huge beardes and monstruous muchaches, the which they hold up with little forkes as they drynke"![4] But it is João Rodrigues who gives us most vividly the flavor of Japanese culture. He had great admiration for the spirit of Zen.[5]

---

[3]Ibid., 137.

[4]Michael Cooper, "Japan Described: The Reports of the Europeans," in *The Southern Barbarians*, 102.

[5]Ibid., 121.

If the Jesuit missioners in Japan early learned to admire and adopt many local cultural traits, they were no less purveyors of Western culture in turn.[6] The Japanese, then as today quick to adopt and adapt whatever they admire in the West, were so enthusiastic about Western music that Father Organtino wrote, "If we had organs, musical instruments, and singers, all of Miyako and Sakai would be converted without any doubt within a year."[7] This echoes a remark made a generation earlier in far-away Brazil by missioner Manuel da Nóbrega, to the effect that with enough musicians he could soon convert the whole continent to Christ.[8]

The Jesuits had already become professionally interested in astronomy. Valignano encouraged this in Japan. João Rodrigues was something of an astronomer as well as a linguist and included an account of oriental astronomy in his history of the Japanese mission. He also discussed astronomy with such important personalities as Tokugawa Ieyasu and Honda Masazumi. Carlo Spinola established an academy of sciences and together with his colleague Giulio Aleni made the first scientific observation of a lunar eclipse ever studied in Japan.

Meantime the Jesuit press continued to pour out books, both religious and secular. Perhaps the most influential original work published was a treatise on the merits of martyrdom, which according to Arimichi Ebisawa helped many Christians remain steadfast during the times of persecution. For Japan's opening to the West would last only until 1639, when *sakoku* (national isolation) became official policy. According to Hubert Cieslik, a leading Japanese church historian, at least 2,000 Christians died for their faith. Meantime, however, Valignano's policies had helped a great deal, at least for a time, for West to learn something about East and East about West.

Across the Sea of Japan, let us move back to China, then as now the world's most populous nation, with already some 150 million inhabitants. In China, another Italian, Matteo Ricci, was serving as Valignano's first emissary. For years before leaving for China, Ricci intensely studied Chinese language and customs. He so successfully mastered the language that the sinologist Joseph Sebes suggested that his grammatical errors in Italian "reveal a man more at home with Chinese than with his native tongue." He had also adopted a Chinese

---

[6]Ibid., 122.

[7]Ibid., 137. I must quote Organtino again, since present experience of Japanese musicians seems to bear out his judgment: "In all truth I confess that I learn from them every day, and I think that there is no other nation with such and so many talents and natural gifts as the Japanese."

[8]Clement J. McNaspy and Thomas D. Culley, "Music and the Early Jesuits (1540–1565)" in *Archivum Historicum Societatis Jesu* (Rome, 1971) 238.

name, Li Ma-tou, and learned to wear the robes of a Buddhist bonze to suggest that he was "a man of God." Later he switched to Mandarin dress, on discovering that the bonzes were not always in good repute, whereas the Mandarin status was higher, that of a scholar. In this role, together with a number of his colleagues, Ricci felt some natural affinity with the Chinese intelligentsia and educated officials. From the first he learned and used the Chinese kowtow (three kneelings and nine prostrations) accorded to officials, and first stressed scholarship and what he felt in common with his Chinese hosts. For example, from wide reading he became convinced that Confucianism, in its sphere of ethical action and social and political life, was a doctrine that was compatible in all essentials with Christianity. It seems significant that the first book he published in Chinese was an adaptation of Cicero's *De amicitia* (*On Friendship*).

At the same time, Ricci discovered in contemporary Confucianism, as in the forms of Buddhism he encountered, what he judged to be superstitious elements. Accordingly he worked to restore the earlier, what he called "pure" Confucianism, aware however that the "adulterated" later version had been official doctrine for six centuries. He was never naive in his fondness for inculturation.

Ricci was himself a skilled mathematician, astronomer, and cartographer. Sensitive to the Chinese respect for learning, he quickly composed a Chinese textbook on Euclid. Then he showed the Chinese how to construct sundials and make astronomical calculations. Further, he translated three of the astronomer Christopher Clavius's books on mathematics and wrote several of his own, plus a volume on hydraulics and another on Western memory techniques.

In *The Memory Palace of Matteo Ricci*, Jonathan Spence details how these extraordinary techniques enabled Ricci to read a page of 400 Chinese characters at a single time and then repeat them backwards or forwards from memory. His feat so impressed Chinese scholars that he wrote a book to explain how they could perform it, too. Basically the Ricci technique had enjoyed a long pedigree in Western literature, and he modestly credited the Greek poet Simonides with its discovery. It consists of creating combinations of images fixed in place which, through association of ideas or some specific mnemonic rule, would instantly yield a required piece of information.[9]

For all his gifts, it took Ricci some years to make his way to Beijing after arriving in China. Even so, he was frustrated in not being allowed to settle there. Two and a half years later he tried again, and this time managed to meet the emperor and compose eight songs for his court. Only then was he allowed permanent residence, which would terminate only with his death nine years later. Meantime, however, in other Chinese cities he had not been idle or ineffective.

---

[9]Jonathan D. Spence, *The Memory Palace of Matteo Ricci* (New York: Viking, 1984) 6-8.

With his lectures and writing with "tongue and brush," as the Chinese put it, he cultivated the local intellectual elites everywhere and spoke with them of science and philosophy, in the hope that these would lead to higher things. As Joseph Sebes put it:

> The key to Ricci's success lay in his learning and consummate tact. He refused to condemn ancestor worship, adopted a term *T'ien-chu* (Lord of Heaven) for God (unlike less tolerant later missioners who insisted on the Latin *Deus*), and he adapted the Roman liturgy to China.[10]

Ricci saw that the term "ancestor worship" was an unhappy translation of what meant veneration, and he had no trouble reconciling this concept with the Christian belief known as "the communion of saints."

Without compromising his own faith, Ricci stressed what pure Confucianism—as he saw it—held in common with Christianity. Meanwhile, he also tried to make himself and his fellow missioners generally useful as scholars, technicians, mapmakers, and the like. The Chinese were particularly fascinated by his maps, but at first dismayed to discover that China, the "Middle Kingdom," was not shown in the middle of the earth. Ricci then adroitly adjusted his world map, placing China honorably right in the center, without sacrificing cartographical accuracy, and thus satisfied everyone except some Europeans.

When Ricci died, there were in China some 50,000 Christians, many of them intellectuals. Though the journey from Lisbon to China was hazardous, the volunteers still came. Ricci's best-known associates and successors, Ferdinand Verbiest and Johann Adam Schall von Bell (often abbreviated to Adam Schall), both competent scientists and dedicated missioners, carried on his work, upholding the orthodoxy of "the Chinese Rites," as Ricci's method of cultural accommodation came to be called. They revised the Chinese calendar, bringing it into conformity with the earth's orbit and rotation, and were appointed official court astronomers. Somehow Verbiest also found time to publish twenty volumes on astronomy, and his observatory became so respected that even after two centuries it still stands high on the only part of the Beijing wall not torn down by the present government.

One curious episode in Chinese history may best illustrate the pivotal role in East-West relations during what Sebes called "China's Jesuit Century": it has to do with the Treaty of Nerchinsk (1689) settling the border between China and Russia, which had already expanded all the way to the Pacific.[11] This treaty is still in effect, though sometimes challenged by the former Soviet Union. The Treaty was negotiated by Fyodor Alekseyevich Golovin as Russia's high

---

[10]Sebes, "China's Jesuit Century," 175.

[11]Joseph Sebes, *The Jesuits and the Sino-Russian Treaty of Nerchinski (1689)* (Institutum Historicum S.I., 1961).

ambassador plenipotentiary, with two Jesuits representing Chinese Emperor K'ang-hsi (Hsüan-yeh): François Gerbillon and Tomás Pereira, both appointed by Ferdinand Verbiest, then superior of the mission. The Russian Golovin thanked the Jesuits for helping out, though when rumors got back to St. Petersburg that the sinister Jesuits had hoodwinked the Russians, Peter the Great expelled all Jesuits from his domains. Later, when better informed, he rewarded Golovin by making him a boyar and viceroy of all Siberia.[12]

The East-West influence, of course, went both ways. The movement of chinoiserie swept through Europe at the time of the Jesuit mission and in part because of interest in China stirred up by their constant communications. A more enduring influence proved to be that of Chinese books translated into European languages. The Chinese were, of course, preeminently people of books. In the seventeenth and eighteenth centuries Chinese books, notably those on ethics and political philosophy, would exert enormous influence on such Western thinkers as Voltaire and Rousseau, and even on the professional philosopher Leibnitz. Thus, as has been observed more than once, to Westerners, Ricci and his companions were the first Sinologists, while to the Chinese they were the first Occidentalists.

Yet not all contacts were to be tranquil, nor was this moment of East-West encounter to perdure long. What one calls today the "conservatives" in China were suspicious of these influential foreigners. One Chinese scientist went so far as to state that "he would rather have no good calendar than to have foreigners; it is exactly because of their excellent instruments that they are a potential enemy." Accordingly, before Emperor K'ang-hsi's Edict of Toleration (1692), persecution of Christian converts periodically swept through the provinces, though less so in the capital because of the emperor's swift intervention.

On the European side matters were perhaps worse. Professional imperialists accused the Jesuits of "selling out" Western superiority by accepting important offices in the government. Further, the arrival of new missioners (this time not Jesuits) stirred new problems. To the new arrivals, unfamiliar with Chinese culture, the Jesuit acculturation in liturgical matters seemed a betrayal. These newcomers attacked the veneration of ancestors, the use of Chinese dress and manners, even the use of "pagan" chop-sticks and other eating customs, and the like. They did not realize that Ricci had not been naive in such accommodation and that he did not hesitate to forbid Christians to practice certain customs that he found impossible to reconcile with their faith.

The internecine quarrel grew in intensity and eventually, in 1701, Rome sent a young French bishop, Charles Thomas Maillard de Tournon, to settle the matter. The young, inflexible, and discourteous de Tournon arrived three years

---

[12]Ibid., 131-37.

later and within weeks was undoing a century's work. The pope, for one thing, did not realize that a young man of thirty-four would be unacceptable as a diplomat to China, given the Chinese respect for age. Even worse, de Tournon had not come as an arbiter but as a promulgator of a papal decree roundly condemning the "Chinese Rites." Whereupon the emperor became infuriated and declared: "On reading this decree I conclude that the Westerners are small indeed and their religion no different from other small, bigoted sects of Buddhism or Taoism." The end had come. The feelings of the last Jesuit survivors were poignantly expressed by French Father Jean-Joseph-Marie Amiot, who left this epitaph: "Go away, traveler, congratulate the dead, condole the living, pray for all, marvel and be silent."

Two footnotes may be appended to this overview of what was really a complex episode. One is the familiar fact that in our time, especially since 1959 when Pope John XXIII announced an ecumenical council to promote Christian unity (Vatican II), the attitude in Rome has changed radically, now even endorsing what Ricci and his colleagues struggled for so earnestly, in the matter of adaptation and inculturation. Phrases from various documents of Vatican Council II almost read as if Ricci himself had written them. In 1982, when Pope John Paul II formally addressed Jesuit leaders assembled in Rome, one of the two points he especially signaled out for praise in the work of Jesuit history was the work of Ricci. The other point we shall touch on shortly.

The second footnote is a bit more recondite, but suggests that a person's influence may outlive immediate failure. A major article by cultural historian Richard Devine entitled "Hirata Atsutane and Christian Sources" appears in the spring 1981 issue of Japan's distinguished *Monumenta Nipponica*.[13] Coincidentally I was present at the article's genesis, three years before. My confrere Richard Devine fairly burst into my room at Sophia University and blurted out, "I just discovered that Matteo Ricci had a great influence on Hirata Atsutane!"

"And who is Hirata Atsutane?" I enquired with honest ignorance.

"Only the most influential Japanese thinker of the last century, the chap whose writings most effected the imperial court and those that led to the Meiji Restoration!" my friend explained.

He had, in fact, just discovered from documents that Hirata knew Ricci's work well and used it often, though never mentioning his name since Christian writings were at that time proscribed. After further research Devine satisfied both himself and Japanese scholars that the evidence was incontrovertible. Thus even

---

[13]Richard Devine, "Hirata Atsutane and Christian Sources," *Monumenta Nipponica* 35/1 (Spring 1981): 37-54.

in death and long after the partial failure of his mission, Ricci's work still enjoyed an unexpected, serendipitous influence in another important country.

One of the finest and most objective brief treatments in English on the China mission is the work of Columba Cary-Elwes, the distinguished English Benedictine historian. Let me cite a few key sentences from his *China and the Cross: A Survey of Missionary History.*

> Thus the first full-scale attempt of the West to make contact, to understand and be understood by the East, at this crucial point in the story failed. . . . Never perhaps had one civilization succeeded better in entering into the spirit of another and in being accepted by it, not by force of arms but by force of charity. . . . Perhaps the chief reason for the failure was the unpreparedness of many Catholic Westerners for approaching another civilized world, whose history was almost double that of their own in length. It so happened that the West at this period was entering upon its age of smugness, of superiority; it was the least propitious moment to attempt so great a task.[14]

II

An analogous attempt at adaptation and acculturation also took place in the world's second most populous nation. In July 1580, when Ricci was on his way to China, three of his colleagues were engaged in serious intercultural philosophical and theological discussions with another famous emperor, Abū-ul-Fath Jalāl-ud-Din Muhammad Akbar, or simply Akbar as he is generally known, head of what is today all northern India, Pakistan, and large parts of Afghanistan. Moreover, they had been invited by Akbar to be his guests in his newly constructed capital Fatehpur Sikri, not far from where his grandson Shāh Jahān would build the Taj Mahal. These three were Ricci's close friend Rodolfo Acquaviva, who had traveled with him from Lisbon to Portuguese Goa, and two companions, Antonio Monserrate, a Spaniard, and Francis Henriques, born a Muslim in Persia, but who converted to Christianity and became a Jesuit. Their letters back to Goa make dramatic reading, ranging from the sanguine to the disheartening, as it gradually became evident that the emperor of India would never become a Christian.[15]

In one letter Aquaviva expressed how close they came to death at the hands, not of the emperor, but of some of his more fanatical associates. Acquaviva

---

[14]Columba Cary-Elwes, *China and the Cross: A Survey of Missionary History* (South Bend IN: University of Notre Dame Press, 1957) 147-61.

[15]*Letters from the Mughal Court,* ed. and intro. John Correia-Afonso (Bombay: 1980).

returned to the district of Goa in February 1583 carrying a letter to his superior from the emperor himself:

> Regarding Father Rodolfo, since I like very much the book of the heavenly Jesus and desire to discover the truth of it, and with the aid of his skill to find out the meanings of those who have written in the past, therefore I have much love for the Father; and considering that he is wise and versed in the laws, I desire to have him every hour in conversation with me, and for this reason I refused him permission to leave. But as you asked it of me by several letters, I did so and give him permission.

Rudolfo got back to Goa only to learn of the martyrdom of Edmund Campion at Tyburn, England, and to lament his own unworthiness of a similar blessing. However, Rudolfo's hope for martyrdom was about to be fulfilled, for only five months later he was killed at Cuncolimin, on the peninsula of Salsete, by a mob enraged against the missioners.

Another Italian, Roberto de Nobili, a person of almost Riccian stature, began what one historian calls "one of the major breakthroughs in Western mission history."[16] Though only twenty-eight years old when he arrived in India, de Nobili quickly discovered that a new approach was needed, that of cultural adaptation to the great subcontinent. He therefore dressed according to the Indian equivalent of the Italian nobility to which he belonged, in order to be able to move freely among Brahmins and intermediate castes. He later dressed as a *sannyasi* (Indian "man of God") and ate only rice, fruit, and herbs. To master the Vedas he had to learn Sanskrit and in fact became the first European ever to do so, memorizing whole passages of the Vedas in order to understand India's deep religiousness. For years his methods proved useful, but when he tried to make Sanskrit the official liturgical language for Indian Christians instead of Latin, he ran into trouble. Most local theologians condemned his "going over to paganism," as the Portuguese archbishop of Goa put it. While he later met support from Rome, both from his superior general and from Pope Gregory XV, de Nobili's methods of acculturation did not last long, though they are finally accepted today by many Christian Indians.

Another important missioner to India was Thomas Stephens, who also knew Ricci during their stay in Goa. Stephens quickly mastered Konkani, the local native language. His Konkani grammar was the first of an Indian tongue to be published, except of course for Pānini's classic Sanskrit grammar (perhaps the oldest extant grammar in the world) written two thousand years before. But it

---

[16]William V. Bangert, *A History of the Society of Jesus* (St. Louis: Institute of Jesuit Sources, 1972). Bangert's treatment of the Roberto de Nobili episode is insightful and flawless.

was Stephens's *Christian Purana*, completed in 1616 in the Marathi language, that gave him immortality. This is a long poem, analogous to the Hindu Purānas, relating the story of both Old and New Testaments. For centuries Stephens's poem has been part of the cultural heritage of Indian Christians. By the time Stephens died, the entire population of Salsette, some 80,000, had been baptized, descendants of those who had slaughtered Rodolfo Aquaviva.

III

The final episode of Jesuit mission history I wish to consider is known as the "Paraguay Reductions." The term is, however, singularly infelicitous, since the so-called "Reductions" covered an area that included less than a fourth of Northeastern Argentina and most of the modern Brazilian State of Rio Grande do Sul. Further, the word "Reduction" is a clumsy transliteration of the Spanish *Reducción*, a technical term in Spanish colonial jargon meaning "mission" or an Indian settlement already Christianized or in process of evangelization. The Latin verb "reducere," from which the term is derived, means "to lead back" or "lead together." Thus some such term as "community" would actually be more appropriate.

The 1986 film "The Mission" as well as the play "The Strong Are Lonely," based on Fritz Hochwälder's "Das Heilige Experiment," performed around 1950 in Paris under the title "Sur la Terre comme au Ciel," both deal with a factual episode in "Reduction" history, the ousting of the Guaraní Indians from their Reductions on what is now the Brazil side of the Uruguay River. This tragic business transpired because of what is called The Treaty of Limits, signed in Madrid in 1750, purporting to settle incessant skirmishes between the two Iberian empires: Spain still claiming what had been allotted to it by the Treaty of Tordesillas in 1494, while Portugal, in the light of that Treaty's arbitrary line drawing, having realistic recourse to the fait accompli of conquest and occupation, pushing its way almost to the Andes. But how did all this affect the Reductions?

Quite simply because the Reductions were viewed by Spanish geopoliticians as a convenient buffer thwarting Portuguese imperialist ambitions. No one, of course, used such words in those simpler days, and in any case political vocabulary was then often obscured by real or fictitious overtones of piety. Some of the Spanish monarchs did indeed look upon the Conquest as a work of evangelization quite as much as a source of apparently endless supplies of gold and silver. Nor did they want the Portuguese to pilfer any of their precious metals.

In Asia missioners had encountered civilizations in some ways more sophisticated than their own, and it was easy to recognize their greatness and thus start missionary work with becoming modesty; in America the European found much to feed his arrogance. Understandably the proudest country in Europe, Spain had just emerged united after centuries of the *reconquista* finally expelling Arabs and Jews just as the *conquista* of America was about to get under way. Spain's self-image, according to Enrique Dussel, was that of a nation uniquely elected by God to be the instrument for the salvation of the world. Others, not least the English, relished a similar myth, but not for exactly the same reasons. Portugal's vision of its own position in the world is analogous to both Spain and England, and can be seen as its eloquent best in Luis de Camoens's incomparably proud epic *Os Lusiadas*.

Among the conquistadores, then, especially after the massive but fragile Aztec and Inca empires had been shattered, there could be little thought of adaptation or acculturation toward native cultures. This religious conversion or any other kind of contact was inevitably envisioned as vertical, from the top down. Such arrogance was inevitable. Indeed, for a time missioners were even troubled by the question whether the American Indians were fully human, thus capable of becoming Christians at all.

As well as I can understand the complex world of the *conquista*, much of the "Black Legend" is true enough. Yet it was not the envious French, British, or Dutch who first proclaimed it, often for sectarian or chauvinistic motives. Rather, it was the Spanish Dominican priest Antonio de Montesinos, who seeing the hideousness of his compatriot's behavior toward the Indians, vigorously excoriated them in an Advent sermon in December 1511, using words redolent of the liturgical text citing John the Baptist: "You are all living in mortal sin, and you will live and die in sin because of the cruelty and tyranny with which you abuse these innocent people!"

An even more famous Dominican, Bartolomé de las Casas, arrived in Hispaniola (Santo Domingo) from Seville in 1502 as a typical colonist. He soon recognized his own injustice. Returning to Seville in 1506, he was ordained a priest in Rome in 1507. (He would enter the Dominican order in 1522.) In 1514, in Cuba, he preached an even more flaming sermon against the *encomienda* system than had Montesinos, and shortly thereafter sailed to Spain to work for the Indians' human rights. Back again to America, and after repeated failures, he returned to Spain to arm himself with deeper juridical studies. Finally at the end of 1519 he was ready to defend the Indian cause at court against Juan de Quevedo, bishop of Panamá. Las Casas won his case, then returned to America, where again he failed and had to go back to Spain. It was there that he wrote his most important works, among them *De Unico Modo* (1534). Then Las Casas returned to America, becoming one of fourteen bishops whom Enrique Dussel calls "The Latin American Fathers of the Church." All were valiant men, some suffering martyrdom at the hands of their own compatriots for their defense of Indians' rights.

Now a word about what was going on in the Portuguese half of South America. In Brazil the Jesuits were pioneers, some of them as early as 1549, arriving with the first colonists and participating in the foundation of Salvador (Bahía) and São Paulo. Let me quote Dussel again:

> As they did in Mexico, the Jesuits in Brazil organized the Indians into villages or *reducciones*. The method used by the Jesuits was that of the tabula rasa ("clean slate" or "starting from scratch," for in Brazil no vestige of high civilization existed). Studying the Tupi language, Jesuit Juan de Azpilcuera Navarro produced a dictionary, while Anchieta developed the first grammar.

Dussel's use of the concept tabula rasa is, of course, familiar, even commonplace to anyone well read in the historical literature on Latin America, and is often contrasted to the Jesuits' techniques of adaptation and acculturation met in Ricci, de Nobili, and other pioneers in Asia. In fact, Dussel points explicitly to this contrast:

> The Spaniard, unable to understand the ultimate bases of the Indian culture and civilization, sought to obliterate every vestige of pre-Hispanic American civilization. Tragically, there was no adult interlocutor such as Matteo Ricci encountered in China or as Roberto de Nobili found in India; the indigenous American peoples lacked the philosophers and theologians who could have acted as bridges between the Hispanic and the American "ethicomythical nucleus." Moreover, the multiplicity of languages and cultures impeded the conquerors from absorbing the cultural wealth of the conquered tribes and peoples.[17]

I tend to agree generally with Dussel but venture to suggest he overstates the contrast. For I believe the Reductions did something that was more than merely the consequence of a tabula rasa approach, and I hope some of my reasons will become clear in the remainder of this essay. I have the same reservations regarding John Parker's fine epigram found in his *Windows into China*: "Valignano concluded that China, unlike the New World, was to be a field for scholars, not soldiers." The New World was to be more than just a field for soldiers, as John Parker knows well.[18]

Whether or not those pioneer founders of the Reductions, men like Antonio Ruiz de Montoya and Roque González de Santa Cruz, had read Bartolomé de las Casas's works, they surely were in agreement with him. Indeed Montoya's greatest book, the *Conquista Espiritual*, makes the same point again and again, as he was struggling to get permission for the Reduction Indians to bear arms in

---

[17]Enrique Dussel, *A History of the Church in Latin America: Colonialism to Liberation (1942–1979)*, trans. and rev. Alan Neely (Grand Rapids: Eerdmans, 1981).

[18]John Parker, *Windows into China* (Boston, 1978).

defense against the Portuguese and other invaders. And some of Roque González's published letters are at least as eloquent as las Casas's in defense of the
Indians, especially against his fellow Spanish Creoles.

In what precise way do I wish to suggest that their missionary techniques
were not reducible to tabula rasa? Granted, the South American Indians, even the
highly developed Andean civilizations, were not book people, unlike the Asian
civilizations we have looked at. Yet they were eminently people of the spoken
word. Further, their languages were every bit as sophisticated as any the
missioners had left behind in Europe. Every one of them who encountered the
language of the Guaraní wrote eulogistically about it. Ignace Chomé, esteemed
as a polyglot, had this to say:

> I confess that I was amazed to find in Guaraní such a combination of
> majesty and energy. I never could have imagined that here, in this barbarous
> region, such a language could be spoken, one which for nobility and
> harmony is in no way inferior to European languages I have learned.

Pedro Lozano, a Spaniard, concurred:

> Without doubt Guaraní is one of the richest and most elegant languages in
> the world. Men who know well both it and Greek find it little if any inferior
> to Greek and superior to other famous languages.

But Roque González carried adaptation farther than fluency in Guaraní. He
personally worked and sweated with the Indians as they built their new homes,
and made himself one of them. (Even so, he was not immune to the discomforts
of a missionary outside his native environment.) While the son of a conquistador—a disappointed conquistador, of course, as were all the Spanish who came
to Paraguay looking for gold and died disillusioned—Roque was as conscious of
the evil endemic in the system as Bartolomé de las Casas had been, and fought
it as vigorously. Among his many letters we have one directed to his elder
brother Francisco, then lieutenant governor of the area:

> I have received your letter and understand from it and from other letters the
> strong feelings and complaints you have regarding the Indians and especially
> against us. In part this was nothing new. The *encomendero* gentlemen (who
> in fact practice slavery despite Spanish law) and soldiers have long com-
> plained against us Jesuits. This does us great honor. I say this because the
> cause of the Indians is so just and because they have and always have had
> the right to be free from the harsh slavery and forced labor called "personal
> service." Indeed, the Indians are exempt from this by natural law, divine and
> human. The *encomenderos* live in such a state of blindness, that precisely
> for this reason no God-fearing priest will hear their confessions. For my own
> part, I tell you that I will not hear the confession of any one of them for
> anything in this world, since they have done evil and are not willing to
> admit it, much less are they willing to make restitution and amend their

lives. May God give the grace for His will to be fulfilled in everything, and may he preserve you, my dear brother.

Little wonder that Francisco, shortly after receiving this letter, gave Roque permission to establish new Reductions farther and farther away from Asunción. He was obviously eager to get this troublesome brother as far away as possible.

Not surprisingly Roque was to die a violent death. His murderers were not Spaniards or Creoles, however, but rather ironically Indians who did not live in the Reductions nor know Roque at all. We have a contemporary document that presents the case of the Indian chief Potirava, as remembered by another Indian who had heard him harangue his tribe:

> Aren't you afraid that these men who call themselves "fathers" are saying this to disguise their ambition and are really making slaves of those they call their "dear sons"? Do we need any more examples of what the Spaniards really are, when we see their promises held out to us as bait? All they want is their own wealth and our misery. Don't you feel the outrage toward your gods when a foreign, hateful law takes away what we received from our forefathers—a law that takes away our oracles, substituting the worship of a wooden beam they call the cross? Can we let a foreign lie overcome the truth of our fathers? This danger threatens all of us. But the blow will fall hardest on you if you don't stop these treacherous tyrants by killing them!

Change "Spaniards" to "Englishmen" or "Frenchmen" and one suspects that Potirava's same speech must have been heard occasionally in our own country. Despite their struggle for Indians' rights, the missioners often had to face suspicion that they were secret Spanish agents being used by the Spanish authorities.

Let us return to Ruiz de Montoya for a moment. What made his achievements in Guaraní linguistics so remarkable was the fact that he was born thousands of miles from Guaraní country in Lima, Peru. As a Jesuit novice there he volunteered for the remote Guaraní mission, and somehow during his studies mastered the difficult tongue. But he, like Roque, was primarily a man of action. For some years he worked in the first Reductions not far from what was one day to be the metropolis of São Paulo, then technically within the Spanish empire. As we have seen, constant raids from Portuguese half-breeds, the Bandeirantes, led to some 60,000 Christian Guaranís being enslaved. Ruiz de Montoya saw that the only safety for the survivors lay in flight. It took all his gifts as a speaker to persuade his fellow missioners and the remaining 14,000 Indians to embark on this humiliating course. Just in time, they managed to construct some 700 balsas (double canoes with a connecting platform) and started on what many historians have called the "Guaraní Exodus." Down the Paranapanema and Paraná they paddled, facing obstacles and threats from Spaniards all the way, and only after many narrow escapes they found themselves blocked by the seven cataracts of Itaipú. The cataracts were impassable, and Montoya and his Indians had to portage more than twenty-five leagues (some seventy-five miles) through tiger-infested jungles and sniping enemy Indians until they could regain the river and row to safety. Almost a thousand miles from home they resettled in what is now Misiones Province in Argentina.

But Montoya's work was far from done. Word soon came of more Bandeirante threats, and he was sent by his fellow Jesuits to persuade the Spanish monarch Philip IV to allow the Reductions the exceptional use of firearms in self-defense. He finally won his point, after years of waiting and bureaucratic hoops in Madrid, during which he used his time well. For it was then that he completed and published his grammar, dictionary, and catechism already mentioned, as well as the engaging account of the Reductions and their development in the much heralded masterpiece called *Conquista Espiritual*, in which he gives credit to almost all the missioners except himself.

The Paraguay Reductions have, of course, been vilified and eulogized with enormous fervor, often by writers who never set foot in them. Voltaire, for example, oscillated between the two extreme attitudes in his spoof in *Candide*, and the enthusiasm shown in his *Essai sur les moeurs* (chapter 154), where he rhapsodically dubs them a "triumph of humanity." Today's research tends to be on a more even keel, as dissertations and monographs continue to add to what is already a vast bibliography.

If I have stressed the linguistic aspect of inculturation there, it is because, with most linguists, I believe language is at the heart of culture, and that by promoting Guaraní and making it a written language as well, the missioners contributed to its permanence and helped make it a vehicle for a substantial literature that still goes on developing.

IV

The Paraguay Reductions and their missioners are sometimes understandably accused of paternalism. Given the difference between the neolithic life-style of the Guaranís and the more developed baggage they brought with them to America, this was probably inescapable. To them, quite likely, the only clear option lay between being paternalistic or tyrannical. Paraguay was not China. Yet I find it an exaggeration to suggest that they "kept" the Indians *in statu pupillari*, like innocent, docile children. In this I find Robert Bolt's script for the film "The Mission" generally close to Reduction reality.

To bolster this opinion, we have a number of letters written by the caciques (native Indian chiefs) who made up the Reductions' cabildos (councils), composed by the seven Reductions ordered evacuated by the Treaty of Limits in 1750.[19] The letters are preserved in the National Archives in Madrid, and are

---

[19]Francisco Mateos, "Cartas de Indios Cristianos del Paraguay," *Missionalia*

addressed to José Andonaegui, Spanish governor in whose jurisdiction the seven Reductions lay. They were composed in Guaraní and translated into Spanish, and I am assured by experts in both languages that while the texts are basically identical, the Guaraní is worded more vigorously. Here are several typical but key sentences translated from the Spanish:

> Lord Governor: We have received your letter but cannot believe that these are the words of our King. For they go against what King Philip V promised us: that if we are faithful vassals and defend his land, he will never surrender it to another king. The king, our king, cannot break his promise made to our forefathers and to us.
>
> We are all creatures of one and the same God. Can it be that He loves Spaniards more than us Indians? Why, then, would he want to deprive us of our lands and homes?
>
> Even wild animals love their dens and attack anything and anyone that threatens them. How much more do we Christians love the town God has given us and our great, beautiful church, all built out of stone by our own hands and sweat!
>
> In this land of ours have died our holy teachers, priests who wore themselves out for us and who suffered so much for God and His love. Surely if the present king understood all this he would not want us to leave our land but would be full of anger against those who do.
>
> We do not want war. But if war comes, trusting in Jesus Christ we say: Let's save our lives, our lands, all our property! If God wills that we die, then this is the land where we were born and baptized and where we grew up. Only here do we wish to die. And you, Lord Governor, will pay for this eternally in hell!

Hardly the sentiments of innocent, docile children.

One of Britain's leading contemporary anthropologists, John Hemming, in his recent volume *Red Gold* repeatedly praised the Jesuits' efforts in the Reductions:

> With intelligent and dedicated evangelists like Montoya, the Jesuits were soon able to create great missions. The Guaranís were relieved to find protectors among the white men. Groups of Guaraní volunteers were soon emerging from the forests to join the Reductions, or sending to ask the black-robed missionaries to bring them their magic. . . . [The Jesuits'] Paraguayan missions were the most successful attempt at conversion or acculturation of any South American Indians. Amid all the hypocritical claptrap about the benefits of Christianity, these missions demonstrated that in the right circumstances something could be done.

Hispanica (1949): 547-72.

Apart from the gratuitous phrase about "hypocritical claptrap," Hemming's tribute is appreciated.[20]

---

[20]John Hemming, *Red Gold: The Conquest of the Brazilian Indians, 1500–1760* (Cambridge: Harvard University Press, 1978) see esp. 258-74.

"No More War Parties": The Pacification and Transformation of Plains Indian Religion

Jesse W. Nash

Introduction

After his last war raid, the Crow warrior Two Leggings concluded his life story this way:

> Nothing happened after that. We just lived. there were no more war parties, no capturing of horses from the Piegans and the Sioux, no buffalo to hunt. There is nothing more to tell.[1]

The testimony here of the importance of warfare to one rather average Crow warrior is instructive. With the end of warfare, there is an end to the Plains Indian *way of life*, since all of that life, as revealed in Two Leggings's biography, is understood as preparation for warfare, being in war, or the direct result of war. We could even go further and suggest that the end of warfare was the end of traditional Plains Indian *religion*.

We are not accustomed to considering warfare a religious activity, and when we find such instances, as in some forms of contemporary terrorism, we are prone to dismiss these instances as aberrations or inauthentic moments in the history of that tradition. Such an understanding is naive, and in the case of the Plains Indians simply wrong. As in most tribal cultures, warfare was at the heart of the Plains Indian religious beliefs and practices and self-understanding.[2]

---

[1]Peter Nabokov, *Two Leggings: The Making of a Crow Warrior* (Lincoln: University of Nebraska Press, 1967) 197.

[2]Jesse W. Nash, "Elegant Weapons," *The New Orleans Art Review* 8/2 (September 1989): 11.

After the 1890 massacre at Wounded Knee, Indian warfare effectively came to an end. The resulting pacification of the Plains Indians also entailed a pacification or demilitarization of their religious traditions. There were essentially three options open to the Plains Indians after their conquest. Like Two Leggings, they could simply opt out of their system as if reality had suddenly come to a screeching halt. According to this position, the end of warfare spelled the end of the religious system. After pacification, there is really no need to be religious in the traditional Plains fashion.

A second alternative is complete Christianization, which the government wanted. This alternative was obviously resisted by the Plains Indians and was never completely realized. But this option made sense given the change in affairs after the victory by the whites. According to this option, military exploits, such as scalping and raiding, were taken out of the spheres of religion. According to Christianity, these activities were forbidden. The articulated goal of Christianity was personal, interior, and nonviolent transformation, not the counting of coup.

A third alternative is more complex and also more familiar. This option attempts to be transformative in nature. Consciously and unconsciously, a Christianized mysticism is proposed. This mysticism is simply the old warrior traditions denuded of military exploits and even antimilitaristic in their own way. I would suggest that this alternative represents the influence of Christianity on native traditions. The best example of this is that of the Oglala Sioux Black Elk (Hehaka Sapa, 1863–1950). In Black Elk's mysticism, the Plains Indian traditions are transformed into mystical, inward-looking religions of harmony, unity, and personal transformation. This alternative represents a partial pacification of the Plains heritage. It must be stressed that the demilitarization of Plains religious practices is only partial in Black Elk; he continues to desire revenge, which in many ways is at the heart of the Plains vision quest and is forbidden in the Christian tradition. There is also a semi-Christianization of the visions Black Elk receives, and an unlikely ideology of peace is developed. This position eventually tries to reconcile being an Indian with a changed and changing history, and it argues, quite effectively to judge from the number of its admirers, that the Plains Indians should be left alone, as if the Plains Indians themselves routinely recognized boundaries and tribal isolation.

We will eventually have to ask if such a partial transformation of the Plains traditions is successful and, if it fails, why.

Thus this paper will examine the major facets of the prepacification Plains Indian religious tradition and that tradition's most famous response to the crisis caused by the coming of the white man and his eventual triumph: Black Elk's mysticism. We will demonstrate the centrality of violence and war motifs in the tradition, specifically examining scalping, the sun dance, and the Okipa of the Mandan. Then we will demonstrate the centrality of a personal, psychological struggle in the transformation of that tradition by Black Elk. The latter, we will argue, does not represent a triumph of the Christian missionary effort but rather a triumph of the American military and its more secular self-understanding. Eventually, we will argue that Black Elk's vision fails because it is still too closely tied to the Plains Indian military traditions to be able effectively to mediate between the past and the present.

The Plains Indian Sacrificial Complex

Casual readers of *Black Elk Speaks*[3] often think they have stumbled on a congenial religiosity, and they typically admire Black Elk's spirituality. That text doesn't really introduce us to the "otherness" of Plains Indian culture. The problem, of course, is that traditional Plains Indian religious culture is very alien to us. Black Elk is not a good guide to the traditional culture; he has already been Christianized. To put Plains Indian religiosity into a properly alien context, we must first reconsider what we understand to be specifically religious activities.

In recent years there has been a resurgence of serious, scholarly interest in such related phenomena as human sacrifice, ritual and institutional cannibalism, trophy taking, the torture of captives, the nature of sacrifice in general, and even the religious nature of warfare.[4] The significance of this renewed interest cannot

---

[3]John Gneisenau Neihardt, *Black Elk Speaks, Being the Life Story of a Holy Man of the Oglala Sioux, as Told through John G. Neihardt (Flaming Rainbow)* (New York: William Morrow, 1932; various reprints including Pocket Books, 1959; University of Nebraska Press [Bison Book 119], 1979, 1988).

[4]See René Girard, *Violence and the Sacred*, trans. Patrick Gregory (Baltimore: Johns Hopkins University Press, 1977); Robert A. Paul, *The Tibetan Symbolic World* (Chicago: University of Chicago Press, 1982); Peggy Reeves Sanday, *Divine Hunger: Cannibalism as a Cultural System* (New York: Cambridge University Press, 1986); *The Ethnography of Cannibalism*, ed. Paula Brown and Donald Tuzin (Washington DC: Society for Psychological Anthropology, 1983); Marshall Sahlins, "Raw Women, Cooked Men, and Other 'Great Things' of the Fiji Islands," in *The Ethnography of Cannibalism*, 72-93; Sahlins, *Islands of History* (Chicago: University of Chicago Press, 1985); Valerio Valeri, *Kingship and Sacrifice: Ritual and Society in Ancient Hawaii*, trans. Paula Wissing (Chicago: University of Chicago Press, 1985); Walter Burkert, *Structure and History in Greek Mythology and Ritual* (Berkeley: University of California Press, 1979); Burkert, *Homo Necans: The Anthropology of Ancient Greek Sacrificial Ritual and Myth*, trans. Peter Bing (Berkeley: University of California Press, 1983); *Ritual Human Sacrifice in Mesoamerica, A Conference at Dumbarton Oaks, October 13th and 14th, 1979*, ed. Elizabeth H. Boone (Washington DC: Dumbarton Oaks, 1984); Howard L. Harrod, *Renewing the World: Plains Indian Religion and Morality* (Tucson: University of Arizona Press, 1987).

be overstated since it follows a period of general disinterest in and often avoidance of these topics on the part of professional students of religion and culture, especially those in the United States. That period was marked by ecological/materialistic explanations for[5] and outright denials of[6] the existence of such behavior. To some degree the attitudes of that period persist in many departments of religious studies and anthropology and in nearly every religious studies textbook I have seen.[7] Nevertheless, especially after the publication of the papers of the Dumbarton Oaks conference on human sacrifice in Mesoamerica,[8] the English translation of Walter Burkert's study of classical Greek sacrifice,[9] and

---

[5]See Michael Harner, "The Ecological Basis for Aztec Sacrifice," *American Ethnologist* 4 (1977): 117-35; Marvin Harris, *Cannibals and Kings* (New York: Random House, 1977).

[6]William Arens, *The Man-Eating Myth: Anthropology and Anthropophagy* (London: Oxford University Press, 1979).

[7]See Richard C. Bush et al., *The Religious World: Communities of Faith* (New York: Macmillan, 1982); Denise Lardner Carmody and John Carmody, *The Story of World Religions* (Mountain View CA: Mayfield, 1988). A good example of the problem in discussing certain essential aspects of Native North American religions is revealed in these two very different religious studies textbooks. The Bush textbook raises the specter of contradictory and conflicting images of the Amerindians created by television, novels, and films; this text prefers to ignore the reasons for this seeming set of contradictions and winds up merely repeating that Indians were in harmony with the universe and sometimes killed each other off; one gets the impression that Bush et al. would prefer the Indian to be a little more consistent and less colorful. Carmody and Carmody, on the other hand, get right to the heart of the matter—there is violence here—but then paint a misleading picture in their zeal to judge the Indians according to our standards. This text suffers from the same problems I am addressing in this paper. For example, the Sioux scalping and sun-dance practices are presented as totally different from and preferable to Aztec sacrificial practices which are then compared to genocide in the twentieth century. The Plains Indian practices of torture and total warfare (in the two volumes of his 1844 *North American Indians*, Catlin accuses the Sioux [Dakota primarily] of systematically wiping out the Mandan) are ignored in the text. This latter text wishes to teach our children a moral lesson, to be sure, but can only do so at the expense of real similarities and violence in the practices of the Plains Indians and their neighbors south of the border. Of course, it goes without saying that many religious studies textbooks simply do not mention the Native North American traditions.

[8]Boone, *Ritual Human Sacrifice*.

[9]Burkert, *Homo Necans*.

the rebirth of cross-cultural study of cannibalism,[10] we can no longer plead ignorance or even disinterest; these rather sensational activities seem to be at the core of what it has meant to be and possibly what it still means to be religious for many cultures and societies.[11]

Although these new works often address different cultural areas, focus on widely separated geographical regions, utilize different, sometimes conflicting methodologies, and examine different historical periods, we can draw some very general conclusions that might assist in the study and restudy of other cultural areas and historical periods.[12] First, these various activities are primarily religious

---

[10]Brown and Tuzin, *Ethnography of Cannibalism.*

[11]It should be obvious that my criticisms here are directed at a largely American audience of professionals and not European or non-American scholarship. Non-American scholarship—note Burkert's and Girard's influence—has in general had a completely different cast to it, in part because of its proximity to the various centers of critical thinking in Europe. See in particular Gerardo Reichel-Dolmatoff, *Amazonian Cosmos: The Sexual and Religious Symbolism of the Tukano Indians* (Chicago: University of Chicago Press, 1971); Marcel Detienne, *Les Jardins d'Adonis* (Paris: Editions Gallimard, 1972); Detienne, *Dionysos mis à mort* (Paris: Editions Gallimard, 1977); Detienne and J.-P. Vernant, *La cuisine du sacrifice en pays grec* (Paris: Editions Gallimard, 1979). The American scene, however, both in anthropology and religious studies is dominated by theologians, would-be theologians, and moralists. The American university exists to pass on civilized values. Frequently, American scholars cannot understand how a study of human sacrifice might be undertaken simply because the topic is interesting, much less that such practices might tell us a great deal about what it means to be human. Accordingly, Europeans and others have been more willing to study violence as a religious phenomenon. Americans, significantly, pretend that the violence is an aberration but a contagious one—to study violence is to "invite it into one's home and heart," so said one of my students upon reading Girard's classic on religious violence. Again, the difference might be put this way: in the U.S. even scholars of religion and other disciplines such as philosophy are concerned with how to be "authentically" religious. In this vein see John D. Caputo, *Radical Hermeneutics: Repetition, Deconstruction, and the Hermeneutic Project* (Bloomington: Indiana University Press, 1987) ch. 10. A largely European and social-scientific perspective is concerned with how people are religious, how they have been religious, and perhaps even why.

[12]See, however, Karen Gordon-Grube, "Anthropophagy in Post-Renaissance Europe: The Tradition of Medicinal Cannibalism," *American Anthropologist* 90 (1988): 405-409. Gordon-Grube reminds us that medicinal cannibalism in the West was practiced until recent times. Gordon-Grube's point is well taken and

by nature, as Davies[13] and others have consistently argued. Second, these activities are also sociopolitical realities and strategies.[14] Third, especially as several of the papers at the Dumbarton Oaks Conference[15] and the work of Burkert[16] indicate, these activities are intimately related to each other and may even form a behavioral and/or cultural complex of sorts, what I call "the tribal sacrificial complex."[17] On this point, then, it would seem that if one is to study tribal religious traditions one is going to have to study cannibalism, sacrifice, human sacrifice, and a whole host of other activities. If nothing else, and by way of example, the researcher may have to determine why a particular group sacrificed humans but did not eat them or why they have stopped either practice.

Finally, if all this is true, these practices are hardly peripheral to or aberrant in the cultures and historical periods in which they have been documented and noted.[18] Thus an understanding of such activities and practices will be central to

---

one we often forget. Even in the West until very recently the human body was understood as a repository of powers, magical, medicinal, and otherwise. Thus cannibalism was at worst a magical attempt and at best a religious act. See Jesse W. Nash, "European Witchcraft: The Hidden Tradition," *Human Mosaic* 21 (1987): 10-30.

[13]Nigel Davies, *Human Sacrifice in History and Today* (New York: William Morrow, 1981); Davies, "Human Sacrifice in the Old World and the New: Some Similarities and Differences," in Boone, *Ritual Human Sacrifice*, 211-26.

[14]See the very helpful discussion in Alberto R. W. Green, *The Role of Human Sacrifice in the Ancient Near East* (Missoula MT: Scholars Press, 1975) 17, 202.

[15]See the following individual papers of that volume, *Ritual Human Sacrifice*, ed. Boone: Betty Ann Brown, "Ochpaniztli in Historical Perspective," 195-210; Eduardo Matos Moctezuma, "The Temple Mayor of Tenochtitlan: Economics and Ideology," 133-64; Linda Schele, "Human Sacrifice Among the Classic Maya," 7-48; S. Jeffrey K. Wilkerson, "In Search of the Mountain of Foam: Human Sacrifice in Eastern Mesoamerica," 101-32.

[16]In addition to the Burkert works previously cited, see also "Urgeschichte der Technik im Spiegel antiker Religion," *Technikgeschichte* 34 (1967): 281-99; "Orpheus und die Vorsokratiker," *Antike und Abendland* 14 (1968): 93-114; "Jason, Hypsipyle, and New Fire at Lemnos," *Classical Quarterly* 20 (1970): 1-16; "Glaube und Verhalten: Zeichengehalt und Wirkungsmacht von Opferritualen," *Le sacrifice dans l'antiquité, Entretiens sur l'antiquité classique* 27 (1987): 91-125.

[17]See Karl Meuli, "Griechische Opferbräuche," in *Phyllobolia. Festschrift für Peter von der Muhll* (Basel: Benno Schwabe, 1946).

[18]The issue of discontinuity and continuity in the study of history and culture

any professional attempt to understand religiosity, culture, and, for that matter, humanity.

Naturally, certain problems persist, too many to possibly consider here. Let us, however, consider an observation made by George Catlin in the first half of the last century as an introduction to some of those problems—and it is immediately pertinent to our consideration of the Plains Indians. Catlin writes: "Human sacrifices have never been made by the Mandans, nor by any of the northwestern tribes (so far as I can learn), excepting the Pawnees of the Platte."[19] Now Catlin points out that the Mandan do sacrifice their own fingers, animals, weapons, meat, traded merchandise, effigies, perhaps even the scalps of their enemies, and so forth, but they do not practice "human sacrifice." An essential difference is being drawn; one can almost hear Catlin sigh with relief—"At least they don't sacrifice each other!" (But is he so sure after witnessing the Okipa?)

Hermeneutically, we might ask what Catlin's understanding of a human sacrifice is and/or might be; would he necessarily have known one if he had seen it; would he, or anyone for that matter, recognize all the possible variations? Would he have been in a position to know if the Mandan, in the past, had "never" sacrificed a human being? Moreover, is "human sacrifice" a Western category or a native one in this case? Did Catlin's Indian informants tell him that they did not sacrifice humans or did they tell him that the Pawnee had a different kind of sacrifice? Or was Catlin's information gained from other whites who were making distinctions the Indians themselves might not have made? Finally, what exactly is the religious difference between a human scalp taken in battle and a human victim sacrificed at the home village in a public ceremony that we Westerners would recognize as religious?[20] Very little. The crucial question then might be: What is the difference between sacrificing on the battlefield or sacrificing oneself in the sun dance, as in the tradition, or becoming one with the

---

is involved here. There is a certain sense in which we are prone to read aspects of history or cultures we are uncomfortable with as either "primitive" or "aberrant" and therefore not essential to understanding people, culture, or history. See Nash, "European Witchcraft," 29.

[19]George Catlin, *North American Indians*, 2 vols. (New York: Dover, 1973) 1:133.

[20]Note that even the way I have set up this question reveals a certain way of thinking I may not be able ultimately to defend and makes and presupposes modern secular distinctions between battle and religion, the warpath and religious ceremony. Also note that by focusing on scalp and victim, I am able to avoid discussing the actions themselves. One reason scalping is not understood as primarily a religious gesture is that the scalp is not associated with life while, as in Aztec and Maya ceremonies, the heart is.

Plains deity in meditation and trance, as in Black Elk's and other more contemporary Indian spirituality? A great deal.

These kinds of questions can be asked because there are inherent problems in our traditional classification of human sacrifice as distinct from other kinds of sacrifice and such related activities as autosacrifice or self-mutilation, trophy taking, torture, and killing in war. For example, to make a distinction between the sacrifice of humans and the torture of captives, as Knowles[21] consistently does, is to read certain practices from a rather recent, perhaps even befuddled, most assuredly ahistorical, rationalizing, and self-deceiving Western mindset.[22] In reality, Knowles commits the faux pas he wishes to avoid: accusing the Indians of simply being cruel and thereby actually fueling bigotry. Furthermore, to excuse the Plains Indians from the charge of sacrificing humans but to admit in turn that they tortured captives and then put them to death is to miss the essentially religious nature of the capturing of enemies and the subsequent torturing of those captives.

Consequently, pacification was so disastrous for the Plains Indians because the most fundamental elements of their religious universe were unhinged. The North American Plains Indians are not known in the scholarly literature for human sacrifice.[23] Such a position explains why we still have a problem understanding the Plains resistance and the near collapse of Plains culture after pacification. Killing in war was a form of worship. Without such killing, worship was basically inconceivable.

Driver's position[24] also suggests that to understand the religious tradition of the Plains and the crisis the whites precipitated, we need a more flexible system of classifying such obviously related religious activities and practices as scalping,

---

[21]Nathaniel Knowles, "The Torture of Captives by the Indians of Eastern North America," *Proceedings of the American Philosophical Society* 82 (1947): 151-225.

[22]Michel Foucault's works consistently remind us that we wish to see history as a continuous progressive flow, but that wish is also naive. To a great degree, Foucault's critique of history and historians can serve as a critique of anthropologists and other students of religion: history is an ideological reading of the past to protect the present from self-consciousness. See Michel Foucault, *Madness and Civilization*, trans. Richard Howard (New York: Pantheon, 1965); *The Order of Things*, trans. Alan Sheridan (New York: Pantheon, 1970); *The Birth of the Clinic*, trans. Alan Sheridan (New York: Pantheon, 1973); *Discipline and Punish*, trans. Alan Sheridan (New York: Pantheon, 1977).

[23]Harold E. Driver, *Indians of North America* (Chicago: University of Chicago Press, 1969) 325.

[24]Ibid.

warfare, and prayer, and we will need a system that will reflect the existence of connections and relationships among these practices. In particular, I want to argue that in a real sense Catlin is wrong: the Plains Indians *did* practice human sacrifice. To tease out this line of argumentation and explain my seemingly bizarre logic, I would like to suggest that among the North American Indians in general and the Plains Indians in particular we are dealing with a complex *set* of interrelated and therefore *interchangeable* activities and practices. Moreover, the distinctions we often make, for clarity's sake no doubt, actually obfuscate what is at the heart of many Indian practices and what unifies them in a complex of interrelated and interchangeable parts: the *sacrificiality*, if you will, of human beings and their world. This complex set of practices, from torture and human sacrifice in the East and Southeast to scalping on the Plains to headhunting in the Northwest, only make sense because the human is the sacrificial object of them all and are only performed because the killing of a human being is regarded as a religious exercise.

These activities and practices take place in and derive their possible meanings from the Indian religious universe.[25] By drawing from both structuralist and symbolic anthropological perspectives,[26] it is possible to gain a better understanding of that religious world and the role of sacrifice in that world.[27] To recast a

---

[25]Harrod, *Renewing the World.*

[26]In addition to the "structuralist" works of Burkert, Detienne, and Sahlins, one should consult the four volumes of *Mythologiques* by Claude Lévi-Strauss (*Introduction to a Science of Mythology*, trans. John Weightman and Doreen Weightman): (1) *The Raw and the Cooked*; (2) *From Honey to Ashes*; (3) *The Origin of Table Manners*; and (4) *The Naked Man* (New York: Harper & Row, [1] 1969; [2] 1973; [3] 1978; and [4] 1981; repr. Chicago: University of Chicago Press, [1] 1983; [2] 1983; [3] 1990; and [4] 1990). One should also consult Lévi-Strauss's more recent volume on South American mythology, *The Jealous Potter*, trans. Benedicte Chorier (Chicago: University of Chicago Press, 1988). A structuralist perspective is augmented in America by a symbolic anthropology perspective. In particular, the work of Turner is instructive: see Victor W. Turner, *The Forest of Symbols: Aspects of Ndembu Ritual* (Ithaca NY: Cornell University Press, 1967) and *The Ritual Process: Structure and Anti-Structure* (Chicago: Aldine Pub. Co., 1969).

[27]There are of course numerous criticisms that can be made of Lévi-Strauss and other structuralist/symbolic positions. Suffice it to say I do not understand the analysis I am proposing to be dealing with an invariable and necessary cognitive/biological structure. Human beings do not have to think this way. This is obvious. That religious people tend to think this way at certain times and places tells us more about religious thinking than mental structures as such.

phrase of Turner's,[28] that world is a "forest of symbols and symbolic actions." The elements of the forest, both symbols and symbolic actions, such as captives and scalps, buffalo and enemies, hunting a buffalo and hunting an enemy, butchering/hiding a buffalo and scalping an enemy, and so forth, are structurally equivalent and therefore interchangeable. In other words, the scalp and the victim are not mutually exclusive or even independent categories of classification. As symbols and themselves the results of symbolic actions, the scalp and the victim are structurally equivalent and derive their meanings and possible meanings from their very real and possible equivalences within the Plains Indian "symbolic forest." In this sense, to say that most Plains Indians scalped but did not sacrifice human beings is to have missed some very important connections. Both the victim and the scalp are sacrifices involving the taking of human life, the celebrating of the taking of that human life, the ritual justification of taking that life, and the further ritual dedication of that taken life to deities and/or ancestors.

Thus I will argue in this paper that there is a sacrificial/warfare complex among the Plains Indians in which scalping and other related practices are structurally and symbolically equivalent to what we have traditionally termed "human sacrifice." Additionally, I will attempt to demonstrate that the complex is rooted in the mythic life of the Plains Indians, and therefore those practices disclose an American Indian anthropology of sorts.

A further allusion must be nurtured and taken seriously. Warfare and the hunt are intimately tied together here in our earlier citation from Two Leggings's biography. The hunt for the great buffalo is on the same level as the battle with and for other humans. In the language of structuralism and symbolic anthropology, warfare and hunting as human activities are structurally equivalent. The consequences of such an equivalence are enormous and fascinating.

"Stealing horses" is also rated an essential, necessary activity, one that ranks equally with hunting and warring. To steal horses from the enemy was a significant feat and structurally equivalent to taking his scalp or hunting a buffalo. To steal a horse from someone was to have offended their masculinity or character. This could only happen if there was also some kind of equivalence at work between being human and being a horse, that is, between being a human and being an animal, as is already evident in the reference to the buffalo. "Stealing" is perhaps the wrong word in this context because of our association of stealing with private property and breaking the law. Stealing, in the Plains context, was a virtue precisely because stealing was a way of "scalping" or "hunting" or "killing" the enemy personally.

Stealing also occurred within the religious framework of the hunt and the war party. "Stealing horses" could be promised in visions and would be cele-

---

[28]Turner, *Forest of Symbols.*

brated as achievements of honor in warfare.[29] Stealing was sanctioned by religious forces, was carried out with the aid of those forces, appeased supernatural beings and ancestors, and contributed to the fulfillment of one's life. Stealing itself was another religiously sanctioned way to hunt and/or wage war, and the possible objects of that stealing, from horses to women to weapons, were always structurally equivalent to the possible objects of the hunt or the war raid. And a successful raid for horses would be concluded by appropriate sacrifices and an unsuccessful one would have to be supernaturally accounted for.

The hunt and the war raid were thus at the center of the religious life of the Plains Indians; they were religious acts that influenced the understanding of other acts, such as stealing or even marriage. We know that both hunting and warfare among the Plains Indians were preceded by religious rituals in which the hunter or warrior sought the assistance of various animal spirits in vision quests and dreams. Both the hunt and warfare were religiously regulated activities. This in itself should not surprise us.

Anthropologically, we have for a long time associated war and religiosity in general, and war and sacrifice in particular,[30] and hunting, religiosity, and sacrifice.[31] Burkert goes so far as to assert that hunting, warfare, and sacrifice were symbolically interchangeable in the ancient Western world.[32] The same might be said for the Plains Indian world as well, and we already have seen some good evidence of this from Two Leggings's biography. There is more.

When, where, and what does Two Leggings sacrifice? "Always, everywhere, and everything" might be the answer but most especially in conjunction with the

---

[29]Catlin, *North American Indians*, 1:145-54.

[30]See Robert H. Lowie, *The Crow Indians* (Lincoln: University of Nebraska Press, 1935) 215; Lowie, *An Introduction to Cultural Anthropology* (New York: Rinehart, 1940) 22; Lowie, *Primitive Religion* (New York: Liverwright, 1948) 15; Lowie, *Indians of the Plains* (Lincoln: University of Nebraska Press, 1954); A. M. Hocart, *Social Origins* (London: Watts, 1954) 141, 143; Henri Hubert and Marcel Mauss, "Esquisse d'Une Théorie Générale de la Magie," in *Sociologie et Anthropologie*, ed. Marcel Mauss (Paris: Presses Universitaires de France, 1950) 1-141; Hubert and Mauss, *Sacrifice, Its Nature and Function*, trans. W. D. Halls (Chicago: University of Chicago Press, 1964).

[31]See Turner, *Forest of Symbols*, 280-98; E. E. Evans-Pritchard, *Nuer Religion* (New York: Oxford University Press, 1956) 197-286. Meuli, in "Griechische Opferbräuche," 223-24, concerning the origins of Olympic sacrifices, concludes that much of ancient Greek religious and/or sports activities were derived from prior rituals associated with first the hunt and then warfare.

[32]Burkert, *Homo Necans*, 46-48; see also Burkert, *Structure and History*, 119-21.

hunt and the battle or the war raid. Two Leggings sacrifices before the battle at his vision quest(s), at the sun dance, on the battlefield, after the battle, and before and after the hunt.[33] He sacrifices away from the village and in the village, and even on the battlefield, in one telling instance, he holds aloft a scalp to the sun as a sacrifice.[34] And he also sacrifices skin from his fingers,[35] a blanket,[36] and himself in the sun dance.[37] He even tells the deity to "eat my flesh."[38] We might say that the world for Two Leggings was a place of sacrifice, and everything, himself included, could be sacrificed precisely because everything could be hunted or killed in battle.

As has been indicated, the symbolic elements and activities of Two Leggings's religious universe are such that they are structurally equivalent. We can then see how hunting and warfare are not simply prepared for by sacrifices, as in the vision quest or the sun dance, but they themselves become sacrificial activities. A flexible typology of sacrifice would recognize warfare and hunting as sacrificial activities. The killing of the game is structurally equivalent to the killing of the enemy and both are structurally equivalent to offering a sacrifice to the deity or deities. Moreover, as Burkert points out, "The hunter equals the victim."[39] Two Leggings is somewhat conscious of this when he says that a warrior is lucky to die fighting.[40] Eventually and fundamentally, every sacrifice is always a human sacrifice and also a self-sacrifice.

If we can follow Burkert's suggestions on these points, we would expect not only hunting and warfare to resemble sacrificial ceremonies but we would also expect sacrificial ceremonies to resemble hunting and warfare. In fact, we should be able to say that a sun dance, for example, is like a hunt or going to war; we would also be saying that we cannot understand one activity without the others since they are structurally equivalent and mimetic.[41] These three activities so

---

[33]Nabokov, *Two Leggings*, 45, 53-54, 64, 81, 105, 172.
[34]Ibid., 164.
[35]Ibid., 53-54, 62.
[36]Ibid., 146.
[37]Ibid., 45.
[38]Ibid., 63.
[39]Burkert, *Structure and History*, 120.
[40]Nabokov, *Two Leggings*, 26.
[41]Mimesis here is never exact, as deconstructionist and postmodernist theories have taught us. The religious system merely gives the impression of being mimetically perfect, but upon closer inspection the mimesis is always called into question. Note the ambiguity surrounding the Christian liturgical saying "Do this in memory of me."

inform and form each other that they seemingly imitate, complement, and complete each other.

The structure of all three activities is almost if not identical, and all three activities share a common universe of symbols and symbolic actions. Since symbols and actions are notoriously multivalent,[42] the meanings can easily switch or change. A hunter in one activity is already the hunted in another area; more complexly but more realistically, because the hunter is always the hunted on some occasion, the meaning of the hunter is always tinged by that of the hunted; that possible and real occasion of being the hunted always, already informs what it means to be the hunter and vice versa. The nature of the symbolic forest is such that the structure of ritual and mythic activity disseminates itself throughout the society.

The Sun Dance

Let us examine the structure of one particular, rather tame version of the sun dance, that of the Shoshoni.[43] After an initial period of ritual preparation and purification, young men are sent out, like hunters, a war party, or scouts, to find a certain cottonwood tree to serve as a center pole for the sun dance lodge. The tree stands for the original tree of myth, the tree that is the source of life. The warriors "count coup" upon the tree as if the tree were in fact an enemy. Once the tree is felled and carried, like captives, stolen horses, or scalps, to the sun dance field, it is raised amid the clapping of hands and war whoops. The war motif is even more evident earlier in the ceremony. The returning company of young men are met by an opposing army and a mock battle takes place. The sun dance is preparation for war and before one can even participate in that ritual, a battle must take place. One might think that war itself is the most fitting image of the American Indian understanding of the universe; if so, what is normally understood as Amerindian notions of "harmony" might have to be revised, including Black Elk's.

Imagine at this point the Plains Indian sacred pipe and its decoration of a snake consuming a frog, a fitting image for both the hunt and the war raid. Fittingly enough, explicit hunting motifs also enter into the picture with the raising of the sacred pole. Attached to the center pole is a stuffed buffalo head, and one of the connecting lodge poles will support an eagle and eagle's nest. The dancing that follows increases in tempo and earnestness as the days pass, and as the days pass war whoops are heard over the drumming and singing. The abstention from water is a form of ritual renunciation, which is historically and cross-

---

[42]See Turner, *Forest of Symbols*, ch. 1.

[43]See Ake Hultkrantz, *Native Religions of North America* (New York: Harper and Row, 1967) 68-76.

culturally associated with hunting, warfare, and sacrifice.[44] As one might expect, a sip of water at the end of the dance signals that the ritual is at an end. Among the festivities that evening, however, war dances are evident. This pattern itself seems to hold as well for the ancient Western world.[45] The sun dance rejuvenates the world but a part of that rejuvenation process is war. In fact, war might be the name of that process.

It should also be noted that the sun dance is a dance for "blood revenge" *and* a rite of initiation.[46] The sun dance is thus associated with the battlefield in its genesis, that is, the death of kin and fellow tribesmen. The sun dance must be completed on the battlefield, where revenge is won. The victory dance and/or mourning rituals celebrate the exchange of one death for another. Significantly, trophies and/or scalps are brought back as proof that revenge has been exacted. War is thus the object and raison d'être of the sun dance and the life of the Plains Indian.[47]

Thus the emergence of a young man and his life as an adult are associated with the battlefield, hunting, and killing. During the actual "struggle with the sun" in the ritual, the initiate strains against the sun, tearing flesh from his body. His flesh and blood are at one and the same time sacrificial offerings to the sun and trophies.[48] The sun dance, like any rite of initiation, is a killing of the initiate.[49] The killing of the initiate is a structural and symbolic equivalent of the desired and intended killing of the enemy, with all the necessary overtones of death and resurrection, sacrifice and war, food and abstinence, obligation and gift.[50]

That the sun dance is also a quest for blood revenge makes its connection with warfare even more apparent. This aspect is sometimes used to argue that the sun dance is not a religious ritual at all; such an argument suffers from a modern secular perspective. Westermarck has forcefully argued that quests for blood revenge are primarily forms of human sacrifice.[51] Revenge, being a duty to the

---

[44]Burkert, *Homo Necans*, 48-72.

[45]Ibid.

[46]Lowie, *Indians of the Plains*, 178.

[47]William K. Powers, *Oglala Religion* (Lincoln: University of Nebraska Press, 1975) 96-100.

[48]See Harrod, *Renewing the World*.

[49]See Mircea Eliade, *Rites and Symbols of Initiation*, trans. Willard R. Trask (New York: Harper, 1958); Turner, *The Ritual Process*.

[50]Sir James George Frazer, *The Golden Bough*, abridged ed. (New York: Macmillan, 1922) 12-105; Hubert and Mauss, *Esquisse*; Marcel Mauss, "Essai sur le Don," in *Sociologie et Anthropologie* (Paris: Presses Universitaires de France, 1950) 145-279; Eliade, *Rites and Symbols*, 3, 81-102.

[51]Edward Westermarck, *The Origin and Development of Moral Ideas*, 2 vols.

dead, is pursued for religious purposes. More exactly and in line with Wester-marck's often neglected insight, in traditional, especially tribal societies, to kill the enemy is already to sacrifice him or her. Both Valeri[52] and Sahlins[53] point out that, in Pacific island cultures, enemies that fall in battle are dedicated to the gods and are considered sacrificial victims. Two Leggings's behavior, as we have seen, is quite similar. The Plains Indians do not have to wait until they reach home to practice a human sacrifice—they do so on the battlefield. To take someone's scalp is much the same thing as taking a heart and offering it to the sun especially since the scalp is offered to the sun as well, as in Two Leggings's case. Moreover, the scalp *is* the victim, and to get a victim, the warrior has to be willing and able to exchange himself symbolically and ritually for the victim.

The logic of the sun dance is as impeccable as it is inescapable. To gain the object of the sun dance, a vision of success in war, the initiate must become that object, the flesh and blood of the enemy or his horse, and offer it to the sun. What he foresees doing to the enemy he does symbolically to himself. In the sun dance, the Plains warrior identifies himself with the sun, the animal spirits, his ancestors, his people, and his enemy. In particular, the structural and symbolic equivalence of the warrior and his intended victim are writ large in the sun dance. Before he can sacrifice the enemy, the Plains warrior must sacrifice him-self. And pledging to sacrifice the enemy is precisely what the sun dance is all about. This is *not* comparable to a modern decision to invade enemy territory. It is a ritual that understands the enemy to be religious food, a *Speiseopfer*, a sacri-fice. The sun dance reiterates that, but also the fact that the warrior/initiate is himself that food. The tug of war with the sun only heightens the symbolism in the rite, and the symbolism is that of exchange. The initiate exchanges himself for power and will later exchange a scalp for himself. To exchange oneself is to sacrifice oneself; to scalp another is to sacrifice him in exchange for oneself; and, of course, to sacrifice the other is to sacrifice oneself. Again, structurally and symbolically, every sacrifice is always a human sacrifice and also an autosacri-fice.

As we have seen, in the sun dance the intense association of the victim and the hunter, leading to what I have referred to as structural equivalence, is readily manifest. To underscore this point, we need not merely focus on the initi-ates/participants themselves. The identification of the victim and the hunter, the sacrificed and the sacrificer, is apparent in the reactions of those who watch the young men in their sun dance and often imitate the very scene they are viewing. Two Leggings describes his ordeal with the sun:

(London: Macmillan, 1917) 1:481-82.

[52]Valeri, *Kingship and Sacrifice*, 337.

[53]Sahlins, *Islands*, 81.

I envied the other dancers when I heard them calling out a horse, a scalp, or some other vision they had seen. I prayed for something soon so my suffering would be over. As I jerked on the thongs and tried to dance faster the left skewer tore loose and blood ran down my body. Now the right side became very painful. As I danced close to the pole where the rope had wound itself I thought something appeared beside the doll (the Crow equivalent of the buffalo's head or eagle's nest of the Shoshoni). A vision seemed about to come. I prayed harder and jerked with all my strength. I must have been reeling when I realized that someone beside me was crying. It was a young woman, a cousin, who had been watching my suffering. She stabbed herself in the forehead until her face was covered with blood.[54]

Two Leggings's battle with the sun and his sacrifice of himself invites his young cousin to mutilate and therefore sacrifice herself. Sacrifice implies and invites self-sacrifice. But also sacrifice invites a human sacrifice. Interestingly enough, the young woman cuts herself where Two Leggings will cut his enemies—she symbolically scalps herself in imitation or anticipation of Two Leggings's desired performance on the battlefield. By doing so, she performs as the enemy. On the other hand, because her actions are symbolically multivalent, she can be understood as imitating Two Leggings, performing an autosacrifice that assists Two Leggings's autosacrifice. We do not really have to choose between the two possible interpretations. Within the Plains Indian symbolic forest, the young woman symbolizes both the enemy and Two Leggings in her actions.[55]

The sun dance then can be understood as a preparation for war and as such we already find an identification of the human being and sacrificial food (the *Speiseopfer*) the initiate/participant and the desired victim, the sacrificer and the sacrificed, hunting and war, and killing and sacrifice. Thus we have intentionally blurred those carefully drawn lines we normally find in discussions of North American Indians. In doing so, we have at least laid the foundations for understanding why Plains Indian religious practices were so energetically regulated and repressed by the federal government. The sun dance was declared illegal. Plains Indian religion makes of all people possible combatants, warriors, and the subjects of blood-revenge feuds. A nontribal government, such as the American federal government, cannot abide such a religious and individualistic ideology in its bosom.

Now it is time to look at the Mandan Okipa as a variant of the Plains sun dance and see why Catlin and others were so frightened by that ritual.

---

[54]Nabokov, *Two Leggings*, 49.

[55]This would be the typical interpretation of her actions. I am of course suggesting that her actions are more complicated and symbolically multivalent.

The Okipa

> Oh! *horrible visu—et mirabile dictu*! Thank God, it is over, that I have seen it, and am able to tell it to the world.[56]

And so Catlin begins his ambivalent description of the Mandan Okipa. He recognizes that it is a religious ceremony but that it can also be compared to, perhaps even "surpassing, if possible, the cruelty of the rack or the inquisition."[57] The Okipa celebrates, among other things, the subsiding of the primeval flood waters, the coming of the buffalo, and the initiation of young men. Of the latter, Catlin notes:

> This part of the ceremony, as I have just witnessed it, is truly shocking to behold, and will almost stagger the belief of the world when they read of it. The scene is too terrible and too revolting to be seen or to be told, were it not an *essential part of a whole*.[58]

That initiation ceremony was performed to provide warriors and chiefs. Warfare as a theme is already apparent at the beginning of the ritual: "at sunrise, we were suddenly startled by the shrieking and screaming of the women, and barking and howling of dogs, as if an enemy were actually storming their village."[59] The noise registers the sighting of "First Man" on the horizon:

> The whole community joined in the general expression of great alarm, as if they were in danger of instant destruction; bows were strung and thrummed to test their elasticity—their horses were caught upon the prairie and run into the villages—warriors were blackening their faces, and dogs were muzzled, and every preparation made, as if for instant combat.[60]

The opening of the annual religious ceremony is analogous to an attack from an enemy, and as we have seen in the sun dance, the religious ceremony imitates the battlefield and vice versa.

First Man enters the village and goes straight to the medicine lodge and opens it. There piled together are human and buffalo skulls, showing that the two are alike.[61] First Man takes death and transforms it. That this death theme is re-

---

[56]Catlin, *North American Indians*, 1:155.
[57]Ibid, 156.
[58]Ibid, 157, emphasis added.
[59]Ibid, 158.

[60]Ibid, 159.
[61]Ibid.

lated to sacrifice is made apparent by Catlin: each tent sacrifices a tool to the waters in memory of the primeval flood.[62] While describing the initiation ceremonies that follow First Man's visit/attack, Catlin drops the sacrificial language at first and uses the language of "torture" and "self-torture." And yet it is obvious that the young men are being sacrificed and that their ordeal is in preparation for the eventual sacrifice of the enemy on the battlefield. Catlin is uncomfortable with using religious language here but is forced to; he has recourse to the language of "torture" which diminishes the religiosity of the "curious" scenes but that he relates such religiosity to torture probably reflects at least an unconscious recognition of the religious nature of the origin of torture in the West.[63] The initiates are prepared for the "Cutting Scene" with a scalping knife and their bodies are appropriately butchered.[64] After being hoisted up and whirled, the initiate appeals to the Great Spirit to protect him from his trials and tormentors—the tormentors are his own people.[65] The initiates are turned until they are "entirely dead" and look like "corpses."[66] From Catlin's description, the initiate is treated as if he were an enemy being tortured by the village but also like a butchered animal. The series of equivalences pointed out earlier still seem to be operative. Remember, First Man, the ancestor of the Mandan, pays the village a visit but the village prepares as if it is being attacked. And then to transform its young boys into men and warriors, the village "attacks" and "butchers" them in much the same way it does buffalo and its enemies. First Man is to be feared because he brings death, but, paradoxically, life comes from death.

The sacrificial language and imagery become clearer as Catlin describes more of the ceremony.[67] Young men "sacrifice" their left little finger on a buffalo skull; more exactly, their finger is also sacrificed for them—they do the offering and another chops it off. The sacrificial schema we noticed in the sun dance also applies. The sacrifice is a human sacrifice and an autosacrifice. The observers, dignitaries and chiefs, also mutilate themselves.[68] And we can augment our chain

---

[62]Ibid, 160.

[63]See Talal Asad, "Notes on Body Pain and Truth in Medieval Christian Ritual," *Economy and Society* 12 (1983): 287-327; Asad, "Medieval Heresy: An Anthropological View," *Social History* 11 (1986): 345-62.

[64]Catlin, *North American Indians*, 1:170.

[65]Ibid, 171.

[66]Ibid.

[67]Ibid, 172.

[68]I have only begun to study the Mayan glyph material, but already I am struck by the similarities. In this iconographic material, hunted animals, especially the deer, captives, and then the hunters/sacrificers themselves seem to serve the same structural roles. That is, what is done to an animal is structurally what

of structural equivalences: the sacrifice of the individual is the sacrifice of the community. From the perspective of the war party, these series of self- and communal sacrifices mirror the desired killing and sacrifice of the enemy.

The identification of the young men and buffalo is heightened at the end of the ceremony when the young men are weighted down with skulls and dragged about the camp. The initiate is ritual food, and his symbolic death allows for the regeneration of the world of the buffalo; similarly the death of the enemy is a part of the regeneration of the world. Only religious language can express the paradox without blushing: to kill is to gain life; to sacrifice life is to preserve life; to die sacrificially is to participate in the preservation of life.

In the Okipa, the initiate himself is cut by the scalping knife and chopped by a hatchet as if he were an enemy or a buffalo. He is literally butchered like an animal and treated as if he were an enemy. He is a victim, but also a sacrificial victim. His symbolic death mirrors the death of the hunt and the war party. But given the nature of the Plains Indian religious universe, everyone and everything is a potential victim. In this sense, there is no killing that is not a sacrificial killing, which helps explain the notorious Indian valuation of dying in battle and not in the village: to be killed is to be sacrificed. The wearing of scalp locks among some of the Plains Indians reflects this sentiment very well: it is a duty to be a potential sacrificial/warfare victim.[69] To be a victim of sacrifice or warfare is to be food. And thus we have entered the terrain of an American Indian anthropology.

American Indian Anthropology: An Initial Sketch

If nothing else, I think we have to think of the scalp as a kind of sacrificial victim. They are both offerings that fulfill more than one religious need. The scalp is sought after in the same fashion as a victim for a "more typical" sacrificial ceremony and fulfills the same purpose. A person has to be killed to obtain the scalp in much the same way a person has to be killed for a heart to be extracted in Mesoamerican ceremonies. The death of the individual in both situations is sacrificial. The individual in both situations is a religious victim; that is, his or her death serves some religious benefit for the slayer.

is done to a sacrificial victim, which the sacrificer ultimately does to himself or herself.

[69]Catlin, *North American Indians*, 2:23-24; Francis LaFlesche, *War Ceremony and Peace Ceremony of the Osage Indians*, Bulletin of the American Ethnology Bureau 101 (1939); Elizabeth Hooker, *An Ethnography of the Huron Indians, 1615–1649*, Bulletin of the American Ethnology Bureau 190 (1969).

It is also becoming more and more obvious that an intimate relationship is claimed to exist between the killer and the killed. Following Girard,[70] it is equally obvious that the victim is a "double" for the slayer and his community. This identification is important, and one that scholars as diverse as Girard, Burkert, Sahlins, and Valeri all recognize. There is a fundamental structural equivalency of victim and slayer. In this sense, every sacrifice is always a human sacrifice and always a self-sacrifice. The nature of religious sacrifice demands such an equivalency. Let us flesh out a "why" for the Plains Indian.

A brief look at the mythology of the Plains and other Indians of the Americas will yield a preoccupation with food, as the work of Lévi-Strauss has made abundantly clear. Harrod[71] goes a little further and points out that in a Plains context the Indian life situation is understood as benefiting from a primeval exchange of sorts. At one time, the animals ruled and were masters of the earth. For the humans to occupy their present situation, they had to supplant the animal-persons. This supplanting occurs within the context of the animals, especially the buffalo, becoming food; in the Northwest it is the salmon and bear; even when we are talking about the corn mother in the southeast and agricultural communities, we are talking about a primeval plant-person becoming human food. More specifically, the animal-persons had to be sacrificed so there could be human life as we know it. Life as we know it depends upon a prior death or sacrifice. Before the primeval sacrifice the animals were not food, and there is even the myth that at one time the buffalo hunted human beings. Food and death go together then; the myth forces a "strange" logic upon the Indian, a logic that is not so different from that of very traditional Christian religious and liturgical language.

Let us tease the logic out further. The death of an animal-person is the origin of life. There is a primeval exchange and in every exchange there is a debt incurred and owed; and this primeval exchange is no different. The spirit of the dead animals must be placated. More exactly, as the logic seems to go, the animal spirits and people are really dependent on each other; human beings exist dependent on the sacrifice of animal- and/or plant-persons. It is also clear in this mythology that these animal-persons are also the origins of human life—humans are derived from these creatures themselves or are created by them. In this sense, humans eat only because something is willing to and/or can be cajoled (in the Eskimo case) into dying. Death is the origin of human culture, and eating is a mark of that culture according to this mythic logic.

Harrod rightly points to a fundamental ambivalence on the part of the American Indian toward his killing, but it is not because they have qualms with

---

[70]In his *Violence and the Sacred.*
[71]Harrod, *Renewing the World.*

killing. Life itself is ambivalent, being derived from the death of often superior animal- and or plant-persons. A Sioux legend captures the irony perfectly. There is an old woman who weaves and cooks. When she stops weaving to stir the cooking pot, her only companion, a dog, unravels her quilt/blanket. If she were to finish her weaving the world would end; the dog insures the world's survival by destroying the weaving. Such a logic is really only possible because the American Indians understood their cosmos to be built upon a primeval death or series of primeval deaths, a series of exchanges they themselves had to reenact in battle and other religious rituals.

In the sun dance, this reliance on death and irony is at play. The dancer offers his flesh to the sun and battles with the sun. The dancer sacrifices himself and sacrifices his scalps and other trophies to the sun and his ancestors and to the various animal spirits that help him. Death and killing are the keys to the universe. The mythology of the Indians accounts for the origin of human existence in a primeval exchange. The rituals of the Indians are designed to produce men who can kill and placate those who have died. Scalping, like the sacrificial practices of Mesoamerica, fulfills a cosmological function—the universe depends upon killing and dying. The war raid repeats the hunting party. Food assumes cosmological importance. And the sun dance indicates that the dancer himself is food as are his female relatives dancing nearby. The world, in such a logic, becomes ritual food and is quite capable of being sacrificed or killed. Because human beings are identified with their world, they are always sacrificing themselves in their killing.

The ambivalence Harrod points to lies here: because of his logic, the Plains Indian kills himself by killing others. Two Leggings is already aware of this; we think of suicidal impulses at this point. The enemy exists to be killed but because of the various structural equivalences that exist in the system, the enemy is never simply the enemy. The ambivalence is most perfectly realized when the Crows and others of Two Leggings's encounters sing to and call each other "Girl" or "Woman." The romance of killing on the Plains may well have been just that, a romance.

From such an anthropology, the war party or the raid is practically mandatory. To show one's love for the deities and spirits, to show one's harmonious relationship with the earth, and so forth, one had to kill both game and humans. The whites wiped out the buffalo and deritualized the killing of game or hunting. More importantly, the whites demilitarized the religion in general, making it illegal for an individual to kill another human being. Now note the radical difference in cultures. It was not illegal to kill another human being in Plains Indian cultures; it was religiously mandatory. Traditional Plains Indian religiosity died with the last of the war parties.

Another Vision?

It should be repeated that visions were quite often sought by young Plains warriors and would-be warriors. Catlin and others describe in some detail the vision process, and Two Leggings confesses that the vision is primarily to assist one on the war path. It would not be an exaggeration to suggest that prior to Black Elk every major vision was related to war and warriors and the success of war parties.

At first glance, Black Elk speaks a different language of visions:

> And as they walked the third ascent, all the animals and fowls that were the people ran here and there, for each seemed to have his own little vision that he followed and his own rules; and all over the universe I could hear the winds at war like wild beasts fighting.[72]

In the text, immediately below this passage, is a curious footnote:

> At this point Black Elk remarked: "I think we are near that place now, and I am afraid something very bad is going to happen all over the world." He [Black Elk] cannot read and knows nothing of world affairs.[73]

Neihardt and others think Black Elk is actually foretelling the future, like a prophet, and speaking of current events. But not really. Black Elk foresees the destruction of his people, and *that* is a tragedy, not necessarily the destruction of all people or an increased incidence of hostilities. The death of the Plains Indians is significant, not the death of the white soldiers he has learned to hate.

Black Elk is of two minds regarding the matter. He has been influenced by the whites at the reservation. He abhors the death of women and children. About Wounded Knee he complains:

> There was a big blizzard, and it grew very cold. The snow drifted deep in the crooked gulch, and it was one long grave of butchered women and children and babies, who had never done any harm and were only trying to run away.[74]

Such sentiments resonate with chords in us, but they do not sound like a Plains Indian warrior. As Knowles[75] and others have made perfectly clear, women and children were killed in the war raid and in sacrificial and torture ceremonies. War

---

[72]Neihardt, *Black Elk*, 31.
[73]Ibid.
[74]Ibid, 223.
[75]Knowles, *Torture of Captives*, 1-2.

as practiced on the Plains knew no age or gender limits. Black Elk sounds like a white man here.

It is also curious that many readers of Black Elk ignore his confession of his own involvement in and his typically Plains Indian reaction to killing in battle. His friend Iron Hawk recounts what happens after one battle:

> The women swarmed up the hill and began stripping the soldiers. They were yelling and laughing and singing now. I saw something funny. Two fat old women were stripping a soldier, who was wounded and playing dead. When they had him naked, they began to cut something off that he had, and he jumped up and began fighting with the two fat women. He was swinging one of them around, while the other was trying to stab him with her knife. After awhile, another woman rushed up and shoved her knife into him and he died really dead. It was funny to see the naked Wasichu [white man] fighting with the fat women.[76]

Black Elk describes his own involvement in the battle of the Little Big Horn this way—and pay attention to who does the killing in his recounting:

> Before we got there, the Wasichus were all down, and most of them were dead, but some of them were still alive and kicking. Many other little boys had come up by this time, and we rode around shooting arrows into the Wasichus.[77]

Black Elk's visions are essentially military and prophetic in nature, but even when they are prophetic, they are so in the sense that they foretell the military future of his people. His last visions recount the loss of the land to the whites. They are not visions of peace and harmony. They are visions of conquest and subjugation mingled with a nostalgia for a peaceful Plains that never existed. They are the stuff of mysticism, a mysticism that sees the end of everything holy and natural to the Plains Indian:

> And I, to whom so great a vision was given in my youth—you see me now a pitiful old man who has done nothing, for the nation's hoop is broken and scattered. There is no center any longer, and the sacred tree is dead.[78]

It is the end because the war is over and cannot be fought again. It is the end because the visions come only to a warrior, and after pacification, Black Elk is no longer a warrior. The Plains Indians are no longer warriors, and because of that there can be no more real religion. It is all over.

---

[76]Neihardt, *Black Elk*, 103-104.
[77]Ibid, 105.
[78]Ibid, 230.

Conclusion

In retrospect, the fate of the Plains Indian religion may help us understand the notorious vitality and popularity of many militant religious movements today, such as fundamentalist Islam and certain varieties of Hinduism and Christianity. Every major contemporary religious tradition has a history of violence, and that violence is, perhaps unfortunately, related to its longevity and vitality. It is as if a religious tradition needs enemies. It is as if every major religious tradition, including Buddhism in Southeast Asia, defines itself militaristically. Not even Christianity is exempt from this militaristic complex; missionaries followed the military into the Plains area and even cooperated with the military. More pointedly, Christianity has historically used the military to assure conversions or at least to eliminate opposition.

This comfortable relationship between religion and violence should come as no surprise. These traditions, like the Plains Indian sacrificial complex, all have their origins in that old Paleolithic sacrificial complex, whereby the sacrificed/hunted animal goes to heaven and returns as young animals, a complex which by its very symbolism associates death with rebirth, death with life, killing with sacrificing, killing with pleasing the deities. All religions are sacrificial in their origin, then, and thus it is easy to understand the violence that actually occurs in many religious traditions today and the violence that always threatens to boil over in any of these religious traditions. We have to face the truth of the matter: to be religious is to be violent. Violence is perhaps the most primitive form of worship or religious activity. Similarly, nonviolence does not become a religious tradition, not as long as any religious tradition, like the Islam of Salman Rushdie's *The Satanic Verses*, can say: "To live, first you must die," which is of course another way of saying "to kill is to sacrifice."

The Beginning
of the Southern Bible Belt

John Boles

The region of the United States known as "the South" has had a number of identifying characteristics—many of which have not been favorable. Despite a generation of unprecedented change that has erased many of the more unpleasant
images, that of the "Bible Belt" persists. For many Americans the states below
the Mason-Dixon line no longer seem economically backward, and the strikingly
modern skylines of Atlanta and Houston are light years removed from the rural
squalor popularized in the sleazy novels of Erskine Caldwell fifty years ago.
Racial problems are no longer an exclusively Southern concern, and the proliferation of franchised motels and fast-food emporiums lining the standardized inter-
state highway system makes one part of the nation look very much like any
other.

But the popular stereotypes of Southern religion—Bible-thumping, sweating
revivalists shouting and wildly gesturing beneath shabby little tents, black
ministers awash under waves of passionate oratory, simpleminded scriptural
literalists fighting Darwin still, sophisticated media ministers with their polished
television extravaganzas, snake handlers and holy rollers praising the Lord with
tears streaming down their cheeks—all these and more represent Southern
religion to many outsiders. It should not be necessary to point out here that these
are stereotypes, often greatly exaggerated, which leave no room for the many
millions of Southerners who attend mainline churches and worship with dignity,
order, and quiet emotion.

Yet while these exotic images must be cautioned against, it must also be said
that religion in the South is *different*. Practically every poll of American attitudes
shows that the level of religiosity is highest in the South, whether the measure
is of those who say they believe in God, accept the Bible as literally true, or
attend church regularly. This is not solely a rural phenomenon, for urban,
educated Southerners are also much more traditionally religious than their
counterparts elsewhere in the nation. Conservative, evangelical Protestantism
dominates the Southern religious scene today, and the newer kind of theological
fundamentalism (premillennial dispensationalism and biblical literalism) that first

took root in the Northeast and on the West Coast between 1880 and 1920 now also thrives in the land of Dixie. But it was not always thus.

The South as the nation's Bible Belt of evangelical Protestantism is an early nineteenth-century development, and the phrase itself—along with its negative, condescending connotation—derives from the iconoclastic H. L. Mencken during the Scopes-trial controversy of the 1920s. It was the Great Revival of 1800, the South's "First Great Awakening," that set the South on the path to evangelical dominance and thus changed the entire historical landscape of the region. The camp-meeting revivals on the Southern frontier at the beginning of the early nineteenth century were a cultural watershed for the South; their origins, development, and consequences are the focus of this essay.

If there had been an H. L. Mencken in the seventeenth century, he would have labeled New England the Bible Belt. The storied Pilgrims were of little significance, but the thousands of tough-minded, theologically informed Puritans who founded the Massachusetts Bay Colony had an immeasurable influence on the molding of the American character. Further to the south, the Quakers in Pennsylvania and the small Catholic presence in Maryland lent a special flavor to those two colonies. Yet from Virginia southward organized religion was far weaker; after all, relatively few immigrants to the Southern colonies came for religious reasons. The pattern of settlement in the South was much more sparse, with miles of almost impenetrable forests separating one agricultural outpost from another. The scattered population and the horrendous roads made nearly futile all attempts at joint community action, with public schools and regular Sunday worship merely two of the most prominent social casualties. By the first quarter of the eighteenth century the South was already the region of many-acred plantations growing tobacco and rice with slave work forces, though the bulk of the population were poor whites, former indentured servants now competing for land and slaves. Religious activities were extremely limited in the South, and those who had a sense of mission aimed for personal aggrandizement, not the expansion of Christendom.

New England, on the other hand, had in 1725 a rich religious heritage, with learned ministers, a tradition of education and scholarly sermons, stable, well-established churches, and a populace sharing a belief system whereby the expectations of God and the responsibilities of man were clearly defined. Puritans had come to the New World with a vivid sense of mission, to establish in "New" England a Holy Bible Commonwealth where the civil laws conformed to the Bible—in itself, they believed, a good thing—but more importantly, to found in New England such a model community that their example would lead to religious and social reform in England and eventually to the completion of the yet unfinished Reformation begun by Luther and Calvin. After a century of spectacular success in New England, however, the Puritans (Congregationalists) discovered that their own accomplishments had led them away from their earlier reliance on Providence. It was becoming easier to see their own hand in what they had achieved, and, in Daniel Boorstin's marvelous phrase, pride slowly replaced Providence as the Puritan surveyed his Boston—no longer a "city upon a hill" but rather a bustling seaport. The Puritan had become a Yankee, shrewd, practical, thrifty, and always looking out for the main chance.

And yet, and yet, the religious spark was still there. New Englanders saw what was happening, only partly understood it, and knew it was not what they had intended, but were they to be lazy and extravagant so as not to prosper? Somehow, in doing what was right, they were reaping what was wrong; but they could not help themselves. A sense of grief and frustration, even guilt, crept in, exacerbated by social tensions engendered by the growth and prosperity. The result, by the mid-1730s, was an outbreak of religious revivals wherein the guilt was assuaged, religious practice intensified, and a new sense of religious mission discovered. For a decade a series of culturally transforming revivals swept through New England and portions of what are now called the Middle Atlantic states, and these revivals, collectively known as the First Great Awakening, were the most significant cultural event in the colonies prior to 1776.

Although textbooks and general religious histories portray the First Great Awakening as a colonies-wide occurrence that helped create a common colonial identity, even nationalism, that in turn prefigured the coming of the American Revolution, it is my contention that the South was left relatively untouched by the momentous religious events of the 1730s and 1740s. Jonathan Edwards had no Southern equivalent, and the young British evangelist George Whitefield, who had such sensational success in New England and the greater Philadelphia region, found mainly dispute and disappointment in the South. The religious foundation in the Southern colonies was so weak in the mid-eighteenth century that the greatest spiritual awakening in the nation's history to that point left the South comparatively untouched. Why was the future Bible Belt so "unreligious" in the 1740s, and when did the religious terrain undergo the seismic shift that eventually produced the Great Revival?

A religious revival does not occur in a vacuum. Several prerequisites must be met before an awakening can happen, and unlike the Northern colonies, the South was not "ready" for a significant, intense, region-wide revival until the very end of the eighteenth century. There had been, of course, small scattered outbreaks of religious fervor in the South—which have often been erroneously interpreted as the Southern phase of the mid-eighteenth century Great Awakening—but these limited revivals are more properly seen as preliminaries to the Great Revival, preliminaries that helped the South meet the prerequisites for a genuine, region-wide awakening. Before there can be a general awakening, there must be a network of churches and ministers in a region, there must exist a prevailing belief system—shared ideas about God, man, and redemption—and there must be a sense of religious crisis, a feeling that there exists a powerful need to invigorate the spiritual life of a community. A series of small revivals centered in the colony of Virginia between 1740 and 1776, whereby the Presbyterian, Baptist, and then Methodist churches were established with a coterie of revival-minded ministers, began the process that would eventually transform the religious history of the South. It is to that story of mini-Awakenings we now turn.

Before the seventeenth century ended, the Church of England was the legally established church in the colony of Virginia, but geography and personnel problems severely hindered its effectiveness. Virginia's small population was sprinkled across an immense sweep of land, with parishes so huge that weekly attendance at worship would have worked an insurmountable hardship for all but the most devout; for others, a vital church life was practically impossible. To compound this very real dilemma, the Anglican clergy in colonial Virginia were as a group not the sort who engendered great affection for the church. Tales of their immorality, drunkenness, and arrogance have surely been exaggerated, but there is a hint of truth in the charges. Few American-born men entered the ministry because one had to journey to England to be ordained, and British ministers often regarded accepting a call to an American parish as only one stop short of abandoning the civilized world. Consequently the Virginia ministry contained some rejects and misfits, and the church suffered. Most clergy were well-intentioned, of course, but even for them their sparsely settled parish made a sense of religious community almost unobtainable.

In Maryland and Virginia, as nowhere else in the colonies, the clergy were entirely supported by a colony-wide church tax, with no assistance from the Society for the Propagation of the Gospel. This led to perennial debate, with the annoying matter of clerical salaries creating a negative image of the Anglican ministers that limited their effectiveness. Moreover, the vestries that controlled the local churches (in the absence of an American bishop) were composed of the gentry, who gave the Anglican endeavor a tone of aristocratic control. The common folk found the church difficult to travel to, the minister occasionally less than inspiring, his salary a constant irritation, and the church administration removed from their participation.

Consequently, the plain people did not identify with the official church of their colony. The situation seemed to invite other types of ministers and church organization that would make an energetic effort to reach out to the masses, offer them a sense of belonging, and give them an opportunity to govern their churches. First the Presbyterians, then the Baptists, and finally the Methodists invaded Virginia (and the South) and waged a spiritual war for the hearts and minds of the common folk. The Anglican Church, even with the arm of the law behind it, was no match for this three-prong evangelical invasion.

About 1740 several families in Hanover County, just north of present-day Richmond, began meeting together in a farmhouse for informal religious services, with several laymen leading them in makeshift worship services. Somehow an old volume of sermons by Martin Luther turned up, and for months readings from this book sufficed for preaching. In the early 1740s an opportunistic Presbyterian minister from across the Blue Ridge in the Valley of Virginia heard of this infant and impromptu revival in Hanover County. Reasoning that if 200-year-old printed sermons were awakening the people, his spoken sermons should reap a harvest of believers, the Reverend William Robinson entered Hanover and swept the worshipers away from Luther and into the Presbyterian Church. (A sprinkling of Presbyterian ministers had accompanied the Scotch-Irish settlers who had migrated down the Valley of Virginia from Maryland and Pennsylvania a generation earlier, but until this moment they had stayed in the backcountry and had not tried to reach out to the main population centers of the colony.) A pulsating Presbyterian revival was soon underway in central Virginia. Dozens of new churches were established and other Presbyterian ministers—including the great Samuel Davies, later appointed president of Princeton—entered the field. By 1755 or so, the revival had ebbed and subsequent church growth was much slower, but the foundations of Presbyterianism had been firmly erected in Virginia.

While the roots of Presbyterianism were being planted in Virginia, the Great Awakening was roaring across New England. Among the multitude of results was an increasing number of fervent converts who believed the Congregational church had lapsed into error and irrelevancy; they called for like-minded worshipers to separate from their mother church. For a while these born-again believers called themselves Separate Congregationalists, but as their theology developed they slowly came to realize that they had essentially become Baptists. Soon the extremely evangelical converts began calling themselves "Separate Baptists." Two Connecticut Separate Baptists, Shubal Stearns and Daniel Marshall, became convinced God intended them to spread the gospel to the South, so with their families and several others they came in 1754 to what is now West Virginia. Meeting no success there, these two Connecticut Yankees took their evangelical style of Baptist faith to North Carolina, founding a church in 1755 at Sandy Creek, just south of the Virginia boundary. Stearns was an especially gifted evangelist, and the two of them found quick success on their missionary forays into the surrounding countryside. By 1760 Separate Baptists churches were springing up in southern Virginia like mushrooms after a soaking rain, and by the mid-1760s much of the southern half of Virginia east of the Blue Ridge had become a hotbed of Baptist activity.

If the Anglican establishment in Virginia had at first looked askance at the Presbyterian presence—for despite their tradition of a learned ministry and orderly church services, the Presbyterian growth challenged the unitary religious community that was the official goal of the Church of England in Virginia—then imagine how the invasion of superevangelistic Separate Baptists with their highly emotional style of preaching and worship shocked the staid church establishment. With their uneducated itinerant ministers who preached anywhere at any time, and who advocated a warm personal faith nurtured by a close-knit community of faith—the local congregation—where foot washing, baptism by immersion, and laying on of hands suggested a "felt" religion a world apart from the "cool" abstractionism of Anglicanism, the Baptists represented a stark challenge to the ruling establishment. Of course they were persecuted, and persecuted harshly, by the legal and religious authorities, but Baptist ministerial perseverance under pressure only strengthened the resolve of the laity and gained new adherents for the sect. When the Separate Baptist revival waned in the early 1770s, it was only after a strong network of Baptist churches had been founded in Virginia and North Carolina. (Earlier, the North Carolina governor had tried to disband some of the Baptist churches, suspecting them of fomenting civil unrest, but he only caused the Separate Baptists who left the colony to spread their faith throughout further regions of the South.) In each colony several thousand persons who had had only a nominal relationship with the established church now had a strong religious commitment, and literally dozens of farmer-preachers who served without pay or formal education had arisen to broadcast the seeds of their faith upon the fertile soil of the common people. A folk religion had emerged within the shadows of the aristocratic establishment of Virginia.

The Methodist or Wesleyan movement in the mid-eighteenth century was the evangelical arm of the Church of England, and the first Methodist missionary to America arrived in New York in 1766. More important for our story was the advent in 1773 of the first missionary to Virginia, Robert Williams. Arriving in the southeastern corner of the state, Williams luckily found a cooperative Anglican priest, Devereux Jarratt, who smoothed the way for the British evangelist. Since Methodist ministers were not allowed to administer the sacraments, they depended upon willing Anglicans. Jarratt was more than willing, and in fact for a while became himself a Methodist in everything but name. With his help, Williams found quick success; Jarratt travelled with him to neighboring parishes, even into North Carolina, and within a year the Methodist movement was firmly rooted in the Old Dominion.

The Methodist scheme of organization was ideally suited for a sparely settled colony. One of the problems of the Anglican establishment was the size of the parish; worshipers often found it extremely inconvenient to travel on Sunday to the distant church, and there were not enough ministers to staff a greatly increased number of churches. The Methodists pioneered the idea of the itinerant preacher, usually an unmarried man not tied to one location. The itinerant travelled on horseback around a huge circuit that could stretch over several counties. Instead of a centrally located church building, the itinerant preached on regularly scheduled days at a variety of locations—private homes, barns, public buildings—spread across his circuit. The handful of worshipers at any one location might have their minister there for only one or two days a month, but in his absence a local committee (called a class or band) conducted informal worship and oversaw the spiritual life of the nascent community. By taking the gospel to the people instead of waiting for them to travel to a faraway church, the Methodist itinerants made religion seem more personal and more relevant, and allowed a single minister to reach effectively a far higher percentage of the people in a rural area. With this ecclesiastical system and a growing number of fervent preachers drawn largely from the common folk, Methodism spread quickly. A Methodist revival surged across Virginia, Maryland, and North Carolina before the region was embroiled in the American Revolution.

Because the founder of Methodism, John Wesley, was an outspoken Tory, Methodists in America came under severe criticism after 1776. The war itself nipped the Methodist revival, and many prominent Methodist ministers found it prudent to lay low for several years; some even went into exile. But their work had been done: Methodist churches dotted the countryside, a number of ministers were available to preach once peacetime arrived, and hundreds of pious Methodist laypersons awaited a resumption of active church life.

Had the American Revolution not occurred in 1776, Virginia and neighboring Southern states might have experienced a Great Awakening-type religious revival then, for two of the prerequisites for such an event were in place: a series of churches of the major evangelical denominations had been founded along with a contingent of evangelical ministers, and the very existence of the churches and ministers was evidence that at least a segment of the population had accepted an evangelical worldview. Yet the third prerequisite, a shared sense of religious crisis—a situation that, the faithful believed, could be rectified only by a special act of Providence—had not been fulfilled. True, the earlier Presbyterian and Baptist revivals had cooled off, and the Methodist movement was crimped by the outbreak of hostilities, but most evangelicals expected the Revolution, once completed, to usher in an era of political liberty *and* religious expansion. The delay, even decline, was presumed to be temporary.

That optimistic expectation seemed confirmed when, in the mid-1780s, a revival began in central Virginia. What made this development especially heartening was that, for the first time, all three denominations experienced revivals simultaneously and in the same region. On a small scale, the 1785–1788 Virginia revival seemed like a Great Awakening both in intensity and in universality. But the grandiose expectations were soon dashed when the local revival faded. In fact, throughout Virginia and the South the decade after the mid-1780s was disastrous for the state of religion. Several reasons have been advanced to explain why religious growth faltered after the initial indications of expansion. The late 1780s, which saw the Constitution written, fiercely debated, then ratified, with a new government soon in place, was an era when political concerns replaced religious ones for many people. The Southern economy had been severely disrupted in the final years of the Revolution, and economic affairs—rebuilding barns, fences, and irrigation systems; working out new markets for staple products; adjusting to the new demands for land and slaves after the invention of the cotton gin in 1793—became an understandable preoccupation for many persons. The trans-Appalachian frontier was now open, and thousands—many of whom were Revolutionary War veterans possessing land bounties from the government—were making the trek westward. This massive migration actually left some seaboard regions depopulated, and on the frontier the onrush of settlers outpaced the ability of institutions such as churches to keep up even as churches to the east were nearly emptied. For these and, no doubt, other reasons, the decade that had opened in 1785 with such religious promise had within just a few years turned into a decade of despair.

This despair only deepened as the years passed, and fears of deism and infidelity (stoked by news and rumors of the revolution raging in France) were soon added to more prosaic worries about religious indifference and decline. As one reads the letters and diaries of ministers and laypersons in the early 1790s, it becomes apparent that a perceived "religious declension," a sense of crisis, gripped many believers. This turn of events brought to many clergy a sharp loss of morale that only exacerbated the problem. Deadened ministers hastened the departure from the church of nominal Christians already distracted by economic or social developments. Church membership actually dropped in many regions of the South, and nowhere was religious growth staying abreast of general population growth.

Religion plays many roles in any society, and one of its major functions is to provide an explanation system for the joys and tragedies of life. There is a deep human desire to find a larger purpose for the myriad dramas of daily life, and this religion provides. Not just the ultimate mystery of death but the everyday concerns of living cry out for a context of meaning. For an age when religious interpretations of all human events were far more dominant than today, we should not be surprised to discover that ministers and laypersons desperately sought a religious explanation for the perceived spiritual crisis of the 1790s. The widespread sense of despair sent ministers searching for God's presumed purpose, for it was axiomatic that God knew of their dilemma and in some manner was the author of their plight. Their means for deliverance was to be found within this beginning assumption.

Precisely because ministers were worried about the state of religion, they confided their fears to their diaries and corresponded with likeminded clergy, seeking consolation perhaps in the knowledge that others were as worried and ineffective in their ministries as they were. In this correspondence, dejected ministers often revealed their thoughts as to the causes of the present decline in religious interest. A consensus slowly began to emerge, and one reads similar interpretations from the pens of preachers of all denominations in all regions of the South. Beginning with the axiomatic assumption that an all-knowing God was aware of the "declension," the question was: For what purpose was the religious aridity sent?

Clergy pondering this problem quickly concluded that God was chastising the churches (and their members) for some error or sin, intentional or unintentional. Almost as soon as the problem was posed, ministers had a list of supposed faults: a rampant preoccupation with crops, slaves, and land; arrogant trust in human endeavor to shape the future, as revealed in resort to war and statecraft; negligence in the spiritual life as the dreary details of hardscrabble existence on the Southern frontier crowded contemplation and devotion out of the conscience. In writing constitutions and moving west, in buying slaves and speculating in crops, Americans had slighted the role of God in the affairs of the world. To indicate the shortsightedness of such indifference, and to reveal His displeasure with such a turn of events—or so the clergy argued—God had sent a harsh message: spiritual death and despair were the fruits of not giving Him his due. By the mid-1790s various clergy across the region were pointing to economic speculation and political wrangling as the major causes of the malaise in the churches.

Once people recognized their errors, acknowledged God's proper role in life, and communicated their sense of repentance to him, they could, the ministers wrote, confidently expect God to lift his displeasure and send a renewal of religious vitality. How were contrite parishioners to reveal that they had learned the lesson God had intended? Organized days of fasting were an ages-old method of ceremonializing a community's penitence, and prayer was the traditional way of imploring God's blessings. All across the South in the last years of the 1790s churches were participating in fast days and prayer societies specifically to acknowledge their sins and to pray for a revival. Over and over again ministers in public sermons and in private writings expressed their confidence that God was a loving and forgiving God who would hear and respond to their heartfelt requests. No one could predict where and when God would signal approval, but "showers of blessing" could be expected eventually. What had started out as an attempt to understand their dilemma ended up as a hopeful expectation of what they typically called "deliverance." From the Virginia Piedmont to the Georgia pinelands to the Cumberland region of Kentucky and Tennessee, there came to be by the end of the eighteenth century a strong undercurrent of anticipation of a religious resurgence.

In retrospect, it is clear that the much-discussed "declension" of religion was exaggerated, and we can understand now that even as concerned clergy worried about religion's future in the South, the prerequisites for a major revival were in place. The mini-revivals of the 1740s through the 1770s had produced the initial establishment of evangelical churches in the region, and although the Revolution intervened, by the mid-1780s the three primary denominations had experienced a simultaneous revival. Though cut short for a variety of reasons, this intermediate revival enabled the Baptists, Methodists, and Presbyterians to gain members, establish new churches, and—especially important—produce a phalanx of able young ministers who would gradually spread their respective messages across the South.

The three popular denominations employed different techniques to enforce religious discipline among their faithful, but the Methodists with their "classes" and "bands" (perhaps "cells" would have been a more descriptive term) and the Baptists with their monthly "business" sessions, where the business was the moral supervision of their members, were particularly successful in teaching their beliefs to the people. An evangelical culture was established, with specific ceremonies like "love feasts," the "right hand of fellowship," footwashing, and stylized forms of preaching and singing to cement members of local congregations into small but intense communities of the faithful. A religious folk culture with a corresponding institutional network were two of the prerequisites for the kind of foundation-shaking revival that would transform the society. Ironically, contemporaries were more aware of the factors that were temporarily (it now seems) depressing religious expression than they were of the underlying forces that were to make possible the so-called Great Revival of the South.

What seems to have been critically important was the sense of religious crisis that contemporaries felt so threatened the future of religion. Clearly there were, as we have seen, underlying social factors that contributed to the perception of crisis, but perhaps none was more important than the massive human migration westward in the decade and a half after the American Revolution. Churches in the seaboard regions often lost a good percentage of their members, and the younger, more energetic members as well, which helped produce an almost tangible sense of decline. Moreover, the thousands of newcomers on the Kentucky and Tennessee frontiers found that they had moved beyond the perimeter of the established churches—it simply took a decade or so for the institutional network of the denominations to catch up with the onrush of settlers in the West.

Newcomers to the region westward of the Appalachians, bereft of the kind of institutional support they had known, if only nominally, on the eastern seaboard, and lonely for family and friends left behind, revealed what can only be described as a profound hunger for the comforting church community they remembered or romanticized back at the old home place. The absence of churches in the West, then, resulted in an intense desire to recover what had been lost—the support of the religious community—and the real decline of membership in the East produced a related desire to regain somehow a sense of religious optimism. Both concerns reinforced the perception of a larger cultural dilemma and strengthened the theological argument that only a Providential deliverance could overcome the spiritual loss. For complex social, demographic, and theological reasons, the entire South at the end of the 1790s was ripe for a resounding religious revival.

It is one thing, of course, to talk of abstract causes, societal tensions, and perceived crises, and another to explain how, at one time and place, a broad social movement is set underway. Ultimately, history must come down to particular people acting in a specific place at a precise moment. Until we can pinpoint these individual actors, any historical interpretation is discomfortingly vague and impersonal. Luckily, the pivotal individual in this story can be identified and his catalytic role described. The Reverend James McGready, a man of imposing size, piercing eyes, and penetrating voice, was the person who provided the vital nexus between the background causes and the actual historical movement.

Born in 1758 in North Carolina and educated in Western Pennsylvania in the homes ("log colleges") of two Presbyterian ministers who had been revival promoters since the famed Great Awakening of the 1740s, James McGready was, by the time of his ordination in 1788, predisposed to support evangelistic preaching. Up to that moment, however, his commitment to evangelism was theological, not based on personal experience. As he traveled from Pennsylvania back to his birthplace in North Carolina, where he planned to begin his ministry, he happened to travel through central Virginia just as the Old Dominion was set ablaze by the—as it turned out—shortlived revival of 1785–1788. Everywhere the impressionable young minister saw the fruit of evangelical preaching, but nowhere more tellingly than at Hampden-Sydney College, at the moment in the midst of a student-led revival skillfully stoked by the college president, the Reverend James Blair Smith. Had McGready needed further evidence of the efficacy of revival preaching, the striking success of President Smith offered the clinching proof. With the confident determination of youth, McGready set out for North Carolina ready to single-handedly win the Piedmont for the Lord. But the planters of the Piedmont were more eager to be prosperous than pious, and McGready, despite some hints of success, ultimately was frustrated.

McGready's hard-hitting sermons and pointed critiques of giving one's highest allegiance to land and slaves won some converts, and his earnestness even helped several young Carolina sons decide to devote themselves to the ministry, but McGready soon found himself sharply at odds with the planter establishment. When not-so-subtle suggestions failed to dampen his zeal, McGready's secular foes ransacked his church and left a threatening message written in blood on his pulpit. This note pricked McGready's attention; having already received several requests from former parishioners to follow them to Kentucky, the beleaguered minister decided he had best seek another portion of the Lord's vineyard to cultivate. In the winter of 1795–1796 he moved to Logan County, Kentucky, just above the Tennessee line, a near-frontier region of the Blue Grass State so rough and ready that Methodist minister Peter Cartwright, in his famous autobiography, called the county a "rogue's harbor." There, on the western fringe of the South at the end of the eighteenth century, McGready took charge of three small churches.

By his own sad experience McGready knew the sense of dashed potential and religious crisis that gripped much of the quasi-religious South in the mid-1790s. Yet he, too, shared the wider belief that somehow a benevolent Providence would rescue the South once the chastised people acknowledged their guilt to God and prayed for deliverance. No sooner had he arrived in Logan County than he organized the faithful remnant in the Red River, Gasper River, and Muddy River Presbyterian churches into prayer societies, both to admit their sins jointly and to implore God to send a spiritual renewal. At first there was little evidence of change, but with McGready's constant assurance that God would hear their heartfelt prayers and answer their requests, an air of expectancy began to be perceptible. This slight, almost intangible change of tone emboldened McGready to exhort his congregations more fervently. His hope proved contagious, and by 1799 there was a general anticipation of a wondrous revival soon to burst forth, but no one knew where or when.

One June weekend in 1800, when the more faithful members from all three of McGready's tiny churches were meeting together at the Red River church for a combined sacramental service (a monthly meeting for celebrating communion), two visiting ministers (brothers) en route from North Carolina to Ohio—one a Presbyterian, the other a Methodist—asked McGready for permission to participate in the services. Ordinarily, McGready would not have cooperated with the Methodist, but since he knew the Presbyterian—had in fact converted him back in the Tar Heel State—McGready allowed both to preach and assist in the administration of the sacraments.

Nothing unusual happened Friday evening or Saturday; on Saturday night, however, with the worshipers no doubt tired to the point of exhaustion and their emotions stretched taut, the Methodist itinerant suddenly jumped up and began to preach. Then, just as suddenly, completely overcome with emotion, he began to shout and cry, exclaiming that he felt God's presence in their midst with special vividness. The normally sedate Presbyterian congregation was stunned by this display of emotion and not sure either of its cause or their proper response. All at once at the rear of the church a woman began shouting and collapsed in tears. Like an electrical shock, excitement swept through the congregation, and people right and left, in unconscious imitation, began to sob almost uncontrollably. McGready himself, never having experienced such a scene, stood back in amazement, but he quickly concluded that here, before his very eyes, was the sign—long prayed for, fervently hoped for—of a providential deliverance of the region from the grasps of irreligion and apostasy.

Interpreting this event as a minor miracle, McGready quickly determined to make the most of the opportunity presented. No sooner had the worshipers departed than he began laying preparations for an even bigger sacramental occasion the following month, July 1800, at his Gasper River church. Notice was sent far and wide, with everyone invited to come prepared to *camp out* so services could continue until another miraculous outburst occurred. It is difficult to overestimate the effect these preparations and the rumors of the previous meeting had on the rural people scattered across the lonely frontier. Desiring to recapture the sense of congregational community they warmly associated with the past (or back east across the mountains), and led by years of sermons to expect some day a glorious renewal of religious fervor, an almost pathetic sense of expectation existed among many of the people. This only increased the more they heard about and imagined the novel events at Red River. In an age when God's hand was seen behind most otherwise inexplicable events, the unusual occurrence in June was easily interpreted at the first premonition of God's miraculous plan to send "refreshing revivals of religion" or "showers of blessing" to the spiritually parched South.

Historians today employ different interpretive schemes to explain the series of events leading up to the outbreak of revivalism in Kentucky and thereafter across much of the South. They speak of societal tensions resulting from rapid migration and the transformation of the Southern economy; they point to the disproportionate number of youths under twenty-one in those regions where revivalism flamed and note that revival converts are always disproportionately drawn from the young; they describe the religious culture that led people to expect a God-sent revival and then believe that *was* what was occurring when novel religious events were observed; furthermore, they suggest that religious culture provided models for behavior in such situations—sobbing, falling unconscious, and so on—that in turn were themselves interpreted as proof of a major revival; they use terms like crowd psychology, hysteria, and revitalization movements to lend an aura of social-science respectability to their descriptions of what apparently occurred. But while we, from our perspective, properly use such concepts—along with the language of functionalism and cultural anthropology—to explain what happened, it is important to recover the viewpoint of the participants, holding, as it were, the two modes of interpretation in abeyance.

If one tries to place oneself in Logan County in early July 1800, one can almost feel the excitement building and the curiosity running rampant as people anticipated the religious services advertised for the Gasper River Meeting House during the last weekend of the month. As the date drew near, hundreds of laypersons of all persuasions and perhaps two dozen ministers of several denominations made preparations to attend. With provisions loaded in their wagons along with makeshift tents, the crowd began to build on the fateful Friday. By evening, several thousand had gathered, an absolutely unprecedented crowd for this semi-frontier region. With the people camped out among the trees, a constant roar of sound rose as the babble of idle conversation mingled with preaching and hymn singing and the occasional noise of draft animals and dogs; the whole landscape was eerily lit by the flames of torches and bonfires, and smoke mixed with human and animal odors suffused the whole mix as strange shadows danced against the background of trees.

All the senses were engaged by the spectacle. To the lonely backcountry folk primed to expect a miracle, this truly seemed a God-sent event. Caught up by the carnival-like excitement and overcome with emotion, many worshipers fainted, sobbed, and became hysterical—behavior that seemed further to legitimate the popular belief that this was a miraculous event. Huge numbers of people, having come to the religious services expecting and wanting to experience a miracle, interpreted the unprecedented size of the crowd, the interdenominational nature of the preaching, and the fervor of those who "fell" converted as proof of what they sought.

Like a self-fulfilling prophecy, the Gasper River meeting, the first of many so-called camp meetings that were to become a staple of Southern religious life, galvanized churchpeople in the region into vigorous activity, and as the sensational news of events in Logan County spread, emboldened ministers elsewhere announced that the long-anticipated revival had at last commenced and scheduled massive outdoor religious services themselves. The outdoor revivals, first called "camp meetings" in 1802, accommodated crowds far larger than any of the church buildings could have held, and suggested in addition the new religious forces supposedly at work. The pace of religious activity quickly accelerated, with rumors of success feeding more feverish efforts to hold meetings and preach. The very ministers who only a few years before had commiserated with one another about the dearth of real religious sentiment were now buoyant. Camp meetings spread across the entire South, ministers and devout laypersons—exhilarated by the prospects—preached with renewed ardor and effectiveness, and the Great Revival was in full swing. Given its geographical extent, its interdenominational appeal, the intensity of the religious fervor, the numbers of persons added to the church rolls (membership doubled and tripled in some areas), this was the South's First Great Awakening.

The revival spread almost as if by contagion. The events of the last decade had so conditioned the entire region for a crisis-ending religious explosion that time and again a mere description, either heard directly from an eyewitness or read in a letter, pamphlet, or missionary magazine, prompted imitative revivals elsewhere. The largest camp meeting of the period was held in central Kentucky in August 1801 at Cane Ridge. Contemporary estimates of attendance ranged as high as 25,000 and though this was surely an inflated figure, it suggests the gargantuan size of the event. Dozens of ministers preached from hastily erected preaching stands, and literally hundreds of listeners claimed to have been converted. Here, too, were seen many examples of the sometimes bizarre physical manifestations of religious ecstasy that quickly became associated with the revivals. Worshipers fell unconscious to the ground, shook spasmodically and uncontrollably, and laughed or cried or exhorted hysterically, all of which "revival exercises" were taken to be legitimating proof of the authenticity of the revival. Cane Ridge was the quintessential camp meeting of the Great Revival, and dozens of participants left written and oral testimony of the spectacle. As far away as New England, news of "the Kentucky Revival" splashed across the pages of the religious press, and, particularly in the South, Cane Ridge became the symbol and inspiration of the Great Revival.

By 1803 the entire South was caught up in a paroxysm of revivalism, and though the most intense phase of the movement was over in a year or two and the whole movement in quick decline by 1805, the die had been cast. The three major evangelical denominations—Baptist, Methodist, and Presbyterian—had been so invigorated by the revival, whether measured in raw converts, churches established, or ministers called, that their cultural dominance in the South was never again doubted. After 1805 the South was on the way to becoming the Evangelical Protestant Bible Belt of the nation.

What were the cultural consequences of the Great Revival; what difference did it make for the South? A series of answers must be provided. History itself does not teach lessons; rather, people, looking back at experience, draw "lessons" from history. These so-called lessons are not always correct, particularly when they are applied at different times to different situations. Be that as it may, the three popular denominations, in their desire to maximize conversions and minimize denominational conflict in the midst of the Great Revival, recognized that theological precision and sophistication were unnecessary, perhaps even counterproductive. The issue at hand was to move a broad spectrum of people toward conversion, an emotional, "felt," conversion that could be fixed in time and place.

Downplaying theology and emphasizing emotion not only lessened the possibility of denominational arguments, but it apparently increased the probability of an experiential conversion. Because it worked in the most practical sense, the evangelicals' predisposition to undervalue theology seemed validated by revival successes. Religion was more a matter of the heart than the head. The relative poverty of the region and the sparseness of settlement, not to mention the regional inattention to higher education in general and seminaries in particular, were to reinforce this revival "lesson." The dominant Southern religions were for a century and a half to pride themselves on a simple biblicism that hardly extended beyond scriptural literalism, a reliance on the narrative power of the Bible, and the emotionally wrenching story of the crucifixion and the need to "give one's life to the Lord." The end-all and be-all of Southern evangelicalism was the conversion experience.

In large part because one's conversion was considered by all the evangelical denominations to be entirely a matter between an individual sinner and God, with no place for mediating institutions, Southern evangelicalism was strikingly privatized and individualistic in emphasis. Obviously, groups of converted individuals united together in congregations, and these local communities of the faithful played a powerful role in the cultural life of the people. But the sense of community seldom extended beyond the local congregation, with a felt responsibility for the larger society noticeably weaker in the South than in the Northeast and Midwest where the lengthened shadow of Puritanism left a strong societal dimension to popular religion. Perhaps the attenuated commitment to the larger society was an evangelical reaction against their only personal knowledge of societal religion, the established Anglican Church of late colonial days that had vigorously persecuted the fledgling evangelical denominations.

Moreover, the presence of slavery, which all other Southern institutions had to acknowledge, forced Southern churches to develop an exquisite ability to distinguish between things of this world and the other. In their first few decades the evangelicals—especially the Baptists and Methodists—had been outspokenly antislavery, but they very quickly discovered that if they wanted to have a viable ministry in the South, and be allowed to preach to slaves at all, they would have to throttle their emancipationist principles. There were a number of ways Southern white evangelicals consciously and unconsciously rationalized their compromise with slavery, but one way was to label slavery a matter of civil society and hence place the institution of slavery beyond their religious responsibility. Of course, they could and did minister to individual slaves and bring thousands of them into the churches; in doing so, however, they were careful to attack sin but not slavery.

The necessity of dividing life into civil or legal spheres and moral spheres reinforced the tendency among evangelicals to define religion almost entirely in terms of simply converting individual sinners. Until the most recent decades of the present century, the mainstream Southern evangelical churches have been noticeably different from churches outside the South in their hesitancy to address societal evils. They would extend Christian charity to the unfortunate and support temperance to remove temptation from potential backsliders, but not develop a critique of the societal institutions that produced poverty or alcoholism, much less portray a vision of a perfected society. Southern evangelicalism focused on individual conversion, not social reform.

Confident and energetic after their spurt of growth during the Great Revival, the three major evangelical churches emerged in the early nineteenth century in a good position to dominate the South, and dominate they did. Even today in many regions of Dixie these three churches claim upwards of ninety percent of the church members, and except in isolated pockets—Catholics in South Texas, South Louisiana, and near Miami, and Jews in certain areas of Florida—no other denomination or faith comes close to challenging the evangelical phalanx, not even the holiness and pentecostal sects that proliferated in the decades on both sides of 1900. The evangelicals grew from a despised minority to a respected majority in about a half century. The Great Revival helped make this possible, for the three soon-dominant denominations now had vitality, a network of churches, a corps of committed ministers, a revival theology, and a conversion technique—the camp meeting—to ensure continued growth. The camp meetings proved to be especially effective in the rural South, and although the Presbyterians and Baptists temporarily abstained from them because they were deemed too emotional, the camp meeting itself was soon calmed down, domesticated, and organized by rules—camp-meeting manuals were even published.

In thousands of locations through the South, the camp meeting grounds were as established and recognized as a park would be today, and the camp meetings were held on regular schedules, a clear indication that they were then seen as a purposeful human technique, not a miraculous visitation of the Holy Spirit. In settled urban areas the camp meeting evolved into the protracted meeting, a series of prayer sessions and worship services held throughout the town in homes, churches, and auditoriums, with appropriate organization and advertising. Church membership grew in spurts, with the long-term trend always upward, and the demographic spectrum of evangelical converts widened far beyond the mainly lower classes of colonial days to include the planter and urban elite. By the 1830s the upper classes were as apt to be Presbyterian or Baptist as Episcopalian in all areas of the South except a narrow swath along the eastern seaboard. Much of the vaunted localism and exaggerated individualism, paradoxically along with the cultural and social conformity that are often listed as characteristic of the South, probably owe more to the dominant religion than any other factor.

While it has been said before that the South was more solid religiously than politically in 1861, few have realized how biracial the Southern religious culture was. From the earliest days when the members of the infant evangelical churches, seen by the establishment as radical dissenters, condemned slavery, they had welcomed slave converts as members. This was especially true of the Baptists and Methodists, and in many churches of those denominations black members outnumbered whites after 1800. (This success in converting slaves was one of the ways Southern churches justified their soft-pedaling of emancipationism, for as a result of compromising with slavery the churches were granted access to the slave quarters, and with evangelical good results. Eventually white evangelicals came to defend slavery as the institution God had devised to bring the gospel to the slaves.) Time and again one will find slave members listed on the initial charters of incorporation, their names often indicated by an "X" with the name inserted afterwards by the church clerk. In antebellum church records through the Civil War this black presence in the so-called white churches was remarkable, with black members being present in significant numbers in all areas of the South.

These slave members usually sat in the same sanctuaries (though in a balcony or at the rear), heard the same sermons (though often at the end of the regular sermon special acknowledgement of their presence was shown by a paternalistic "slaves-obey-your-master" type homily that was typically introduced by the phrase: "and now a few words for our black brothers and sisters"), took communion with the whites, and were buried in the same cemetery. Slave members, like whites, were addressed as brother and sister, and their "letters" of admission and dismissal necessary for joining new congregations were identical to those of whites. Blacks even participated in the church disciplinary proceedings, testifying at times against whites and having their testimony weighted at least almost equally with the white if there was a conflict. What is notable about this is that, in civil society, nowhere in the South could a slave even testify against a white in court. In the church court there are many instances of white testimony against slaves being overruled because of counter testimony by the accused slave or other slaves, and there are even instances of whites being punished on the basis of black testimony.

While no one would argue that the slaves, sitting literally and figuratively at the back of the churches, were treated as equals in the "white" churches, one may argue that there they found a greater degree of equality than anywhere else in Southern society. In this relative equality of discipline and address, and diverse other ways within the church, slaves found through their participation in the evangelical denominations many opportunities to enhance their sense of self-worth and autonomy. Confident that in the eyes of God there was no bond or free, they found in religion the spiritual wherewithal to survive slavery without becoming psychologically enslaved. Moreover, slaves from various plantations and farms could openly come together at worship, and sitting together in their segregated seating may very well have helped bond them as a people.

After the Civil War the black members withdrew from the so-called white denominations and founded their own separate institutions, but the theology, ecclesiology, and tone of the churches remained similar. It was no accident that when white Southern Baptist Jimmy Carter wanted to communicate with blacks, North and South, he typically went to their churches. In ways perhaps neither completely understood, they shared a religious tradition.

Although white women in the antebellum South were by no stretch of the imagination as oppressed as slaves were, they were, like slaves, also a comparatively powerless minority. They could not vote in the political arena, had few property rights, and were subject under the law to the whim of their husbands. Also, like slaves, their role has often been slighted by historians. Yet women found in the churches an agency for purposeful social action, a means to create a woman's sphere broader than the home and to have significant impact on their local community, and an arena for developing their leadership skills. Throughout the nation women came to play such major roles in the churches that ministers began to be judged in part at least by their ability to work comfortably with them. This, of course, contributed to what has been called the feminization of the church in America, a term that suggests not only the role of women in the church but also the fact that the church's concerns began to be shaped by their presence and desires.

Southern rural women found in their church a sense of local community (and an incipient idea of sisterhood) that helped to break down the isolation of plantation and farm life. Through their work in a variety of church committees and societies women provided Sunday Schools (raising the funds for the schools, often renting the halls, and doing the teaching), helped build and maintain the church structures, bought church bells and organs, helped raise operating funds, visited the sick and those delinquent in tithes or pew rents, ministered to "backslidden" members. In short, women were often the backbone of the churches even though by legal precedent men made up the governing vestries and boards of deacons and elders. Women's prayer societies, women's auxiliaries, sewing societies, and the like were prominent parts of church life. To overlook women's role in the churches and religion's influence on women's life, in 1850 as in 1950, is seriously to misunderstand the universality of the evangelical worldview in the South. Because of the all-important nurturing function in the past of women in our society, and the consequent impact of childrearing, perhaps the indirect ministry of "petticoat preachers" has had more to do with shaping the evangelical mind of the South than any other single factor.

Evangelical religion has been central to the culture of the South, for it has been a nearly universal bond that within individual churches linked together white and black, male and female, rich and poor in a common language of resignation to this world and hope for another. In its Southern expression mainstream evangelical religion in the antebellum period generally recognized and legitimated a stratified society even as people in the church conceived of themselves as constituting the family of God. White Southerners at least usually accepted or acquiesced to differences of status in this world in the belief that ultimately everyone would bow together at God's knee. Differences of class, gender, and race—real enough, God knows—could be minimized within the small-scale congregational communities of mutual obligation where interpersonal relationships often transcended concrete divisions in status. The lines between gender and race were never denied, and outside the church were rigorously insisted upon, but within the local fellowship of believers people shared enough of a common faith to develop a biracial religious culture.

The boundaries of class division among whites in the Old South were more nearly obliterated by the folk religion, helped along by the practically universal white attitude toward slavery. Emancipation provided the impetus for blacks and whites to separate religiously, and their religious cultures have since grown somewhat apart. Economic and political divisions have erupted among whites from time to time since Reconstruction, and the mainstream denominations have occasionally contained discordant divisions within themselves over pressing issues, but still a shared religious grammar has shaped the vocabulary even of political protest. There can be no understanding of Southern history without an understanding in part at least of the role of religion in the matrix of peoples' lives.

Every Southerner knows the strength today of religion in his region and appreciates the role it plays in shaping mores and attitudes, and visitors often are surprised to discover how openly religious the South is, with football games and rodeos opened with prayer and the airwaves saturated on Sundays with sermons and hymns. It is easy to assume that the South has always been a hothouse of religion, and the "secular North" a seedbed of free thinking. But in colonial days those stereotypes were reversed, and it was the Great Revival of 1800–1805 that marked the transition from one South—the one Thomas Jefferson once remarked would some day be dominated by rational Unitarians—to another, Mencken's Bible Belt and our present-day stronghold of conservative evangelical Protestantism with its growing fundamentalist bloc. From a Yankee Puritan theocracy in the seventeenth century with an unchurched South to a possible Baptist theocracy in twentieth-century Dixie with a secular New England—that, perhaps, is the greatest irony of all Southern history.

Selected Bibliography

Most of this essay is derived from my own earlier work, *The Great Revival, 1787–1805: Origins of the Southern Evangelical Mind* (Lexington: University Press of Kentucky, 1972), still the most detailed treatment of the coming of the revival. This account should be supplemented with Dickson D. Bruce, Jr., *And They All Sang Hallelujah: Plain-Folk Camp-Meeting Religion, 1800–1845* (Knoxville: University of Tennessee Press, 1974). My *Religion in Antebellum Kentucky* (Lexington: University Press of Kentucky, 1976), using Kentucky as a test case, discusses religion throughout the antebellum period and covers slave religion as well. Donald G. Matthews in *Religion in the Old South* (Chicago: University of Chicago Press, 1977) covers much the same material in more depth, and more abstractly, and broadens his account to include a perceptive treatment of women. Anne C. Loveland provides a detailed history of white male clerical attitudes in *Southern Evangelicals and the Social Order, 1800–1860* (Baton Rouge: Louisiana State University Press, 1980).

A most provocative though not entirely persuasive account of evangelicalism in colonial Virginia is Rhys Issac, *The Transformation of Virginia, 1740–1790* (Chapel Hill: University of North Carolina Press, 1982). For the role of religion in colonial America see Patricia U. Bonomi, *Under the Cope of Heaven: Religion, Society, and Politics in Colonial America* (New York: Oxford University Press, 1986). The most extensive treatment of slave religion is Albert Raboteau, *Slave Religion: The 'Invisible Institution' in the Antebellum South* (New York: Oxford University Press, 1978), though Raboteau greatly underestimates the significance of the biracial religious community. For a corrective see Kenneth K. Bailey, "Protestantism and Afro-Americans in the Old South: Another Look," *Journal of Southern History* 41 (November 1975): 451-72, and *Masters & Slaves in the House of the Lord: Race and Religion in the American South, 1740–1870,* ed. John B. Boles (Lexington: University Press of Kentucky, 1988).

The most recent brief synthesis of antebellum Southern Protestantism is John B. Boles, "Evangelical Protestantism in the Old South: From Religious Dissent to Cultural Dominance," in *Religion in the South,* ed. Charles Reagan Wilson (Jackson: University of Mississippi Press, 1985), 13-34, but consult the entire book.

There are several essential works for the period after the Civil War. The single most important book on southern religion is Samuel S. Hill, Jr., *Southern Churches in Crisis* (New York: Holt, Rinehart, Winston, 1966), which, though it emphasizes the post-Civil War era, also provocatively analyzes the antebellum period. One should also consult Charles Reagan Wilson, *Baptized in Blood: The Religion of the Lost Cause, 1865–1920* (Athens: University of Georgia Press, 1980); Kenneth K. Bailey, *Southern White Protestantism in the Twentieth Century* (New York: Harper & Row, 1964); Samuel S. Hill, Jr., *The South and the North in American Religion* (Athens: University of Georgia Press, 1980); and the monumental *Encyclopedia of Religion in the South,* ed. Samuel S. Hill, Jr. (Macon GA: Mercer University Press, 1984).

Two especially useful collections of essays are *Varieties of Southern Evangelicalism,* ed. David E. Harrell, Jr. (Macon GA: Mercer University press, 1981) and *Varieties of Southern Religious Experience,* ed. Samuel S. Hill, Jr. (Baton Rouge: Louisiana State University Press, 1988).

For a relatively complete historiographical essay on the subject of southern religion, broadly conceived, see John B. Boles, "The Discovery of Southern Religious History," in *Interpreting Southern History: Historiographical Essays in Honor of S. W. Higginbotham,* ed. John B. Boles and Evelyn T. Nolen (Baton Rouge: Louisiana State University Press, 1987) 510-48. *Bibliography of Religion in the South,* ed. Charles H. Lippy (Macon GA: Mercer University Press, 1985).

The Transformation
of Fundamentalism
between the World Wars

William Martin

Introduction

The last twenty years have seen a notable increase in the attention given to
evangelical and fundamentalist religion. At the beginning of the 1970s, the Jesus
Movement captured attention, time, and space in the popular media. With the
coming to prominence of Jimmy Carter, another surge of interest occurred.
Newsmagazines and television specials focused on "Born Again Christianity,"
and "The Evangelical Empire." Then, since 1980, the "Electronic Church" and
the "Moral Majority" have held a dominant position in religious news. As one
known to have had personal contact with actual, living evangelicals, I was often
approached, especially around the time of the 1976 elections, by people who
were genuinely anxious about the possibility that a born-again Christian might
be elected to public office. The conversations often went something like this.

"It sounds spooky. Is it anything like being a Moonie?"

"No, it's more like being a Baptist."

"Is it really true there are forty to fifty million evangelicals in America?"

"That is what we are told. I know a good many personally."

"How did a religion like that get out of the rural south and infect the rest of
the country?"

"Fundamentalism *is* widespread in the South, but its strongholds throughout
the nineteenth century and, to a considerable extent, even during the twentieth
century have been urban and northern. In fact, Philadelphia and Chicago have
probably been as important as Nashville and Dallas."

"I thought fundamentalism died a long time ago, at the Scopes trial."

"Well, it was real sick there for several years, but it didn't die. You know
how it is. They put the spectacular news on the front page, and the less notewor-
thy gets buried on the back pages. It's a good story. If you've got about forty-
five minutes, maybe I can explain it to you."

Fundamentalism/Evangelicalism

First of all, let me explain what is generally meant by the terms, "fundamentalism" and "evangelicalism." Both terms can be and have been applied to the same set of religious beliefs and practices. In the nineteenth century, these beliefs and practices were commonly known as "evangelical." From 1900 to 1940, "fundamentalism" was the term preferred both within and without the movement. Since 1940, some adherents to these beliefs and practices have preferred to call themselves "evangelicals," while others have clung tenaciously to the "fundamentalist" label, which they wear as a badge of honor. The differences between fundamentalists and evangelicals are not so much cognitive and doctrinal as they are matters of outlook, temperament, and style. Billy Graham is the epitome of an evangelical; Jerry Falwell and the recent presidents of the Southern Baptist Convention are fundamentalists. But that gets ahead of the story. I will come back to that distinction at the end of the essay.

The hallmark of evangelical/fundamentalist belief is acceptance of the Bible as inspired, inerrant, infallible, the supreme rule of Christian faith and practice. It is regarded as literally true, though most evangelicals will make allowance for obviously figurative language and other literary devices. Following from this belief in the accuracy and authority of scripture are various other beliefs. Grace and salvation are available through, and only through, Christ. Jesus is the literal son of God, born of a virgin. He lived a sinless life, performed miracles, substituted himself in crucifixion as an atonement for our sins, rose from the dead in his physical body, ascended into heaven, and will come again at the end of the age. In the most common version, the second coming is followed by the millennium, a thousand-year period of peace and prosperity preceding final assignment to heaven or hell. Some have made lists of five or seven or fourteen fundamentals, but the fact is that denial of the truth and relevance of any rather straightforward biblical story or claim is enough to have one's credentials as an authentic evangelical called into serious question.

This is not, of course, a new form of Christian belief. The same basic assumptions have lain at the heart of Protestant Christianity since the days of Martin Luther and John Calvin, and most are shared by Catholic and Orthodox Christianity though these construe the authority of scripture in a somewhat different light. To be sure, there were significant elements of American religious and cultural life that did not share these assumptions, but it was not until the latter decades of the nineteenth century that their ascendancy met massive challenge.

The challenges were several. Extensive immigration brought an influx of Jews, Roman Catholics, and Orthodox Christians who weakened Protestant control of the nation. Urbanism and an attendant increase in secularism also alarmed evangelical Protestant leaders. An increasing interest in social service, in what came to be called the Social Gospel, undercut evangelicalism's tradition-al emphasis on personal salvation.

Two challenges, however, stood out above others as posing singular threats to the then-dominant form of American Christianity. The first was the advance-ment of science and increasing confidence in the inductive scientific method of attaining truth, as distinguished from deducing truth from a recognized repository, such as the Bible. The key symbol of this threat from science was the Darwinian theory of evolution, which constituted a direct challenge to the biblical account of creation and even to theism itself. The second critical challenge was the development of modern biblical criticism, which approached the Bible as it would any other collection of human documents, applying the same critical principles to it. This approach had arisen and developed primarily in German theological schools, particularly in Tübingen during the mid-1880s, and was subsequently adopted into many American seminaries. And it struck at the heart of the evangelical view of scripture.

Many churches and some entire denominations accommodated to these chal-lenges rather smoothly, conceiving of God as using evolutionary processes to accomplish God's ends, and of the Bible, human though it be in origin, as bearing witness to the revelation of God in Christ. Quite often, this accommoda-tion included an enthusiastic endorsement of the social gospel. As it has charac-teristically done when its worldview has been threatened so severely, evangelical Christianity experienced a notable revival, a revival that spanned several decades, with Dwight L. Moody at one end, in the 1870s, and Billy Sunday, the "Calliope of Zion," at the other end, with his heydey coming during and immediately after World War I.

At the beginning of the era of our concern, the movement possessed a well-thought-out and consistent view of the inspiration of the scriptures, thanks pri-marily to the work in the 1880s of Professors Charles Hodge, A. A. Hodge, and Benjamin Warfield, all of Princeton Theological Seminary. A widely distributed set of twelve pamphlets entitled *The Fundamentals*[1] financed by Californians Lyman Stewart and Milton Stewart, founders of Union Oil Company, not only

---

[1]*The Fundamentals: A Testimony to the Truth*, 12 vols., ed. Amzi Clarence Dixon (1-4), Louis Meyer (5-10), and Reuben Archer Torrey (11-12). Originally published 1910–1915 in Chicago by Testimony Publishing Co. as 12 booklets under the auspices of Moody Memorial Church and Moody Bible Institute as initi-ated and underwritten by the Stewart brothers; reorganized by Torrey, combined into 4 vols., and reissued in 1917 in Los Angeles by the King's Business, later the Bible Institute of Los Angeles. Repr.: 4 vols. (Grand Rapids MI: Baker, 1970); repr.: 4 vols., ed. with intro. by George M. Marsden, Fundamentalism in American Religion series (New York and London: Garland Pub., 1988).

set forth basic doctrines in the words of some of the most respected men in the movement, but proved crucial in getting the name "fundamentalist"[2] established as the most common appellation for the conservative Protestant wing of the church. This was further strengthened by the founding of the World's Christian Fundamentals Association following the 1919 World Conference on Christian Fundamentals at Philadelphia, attended by as many as 6,500 delegates and led by such notables as Billy Sunday, John Roach Straton of New York City (the "pope of Fundamentalism"), Paul Rader of Chicago, and William Bell Riley of Minneapolis.

The War and the Bolshevik Revolution of 1917 provided fundamentalism with what was to become one of its major elements: religious nationalism. Sunday, Riley, and other fundamentalist leaders declared that Satan himself was directing the German war effort, and hinted strongly that it was part of the same process that had begun with the development of biblical criticism in German universities. According to Sunday, the Kaiser called his statesmen to the Potsdam Palace in 1895 and "outlined his plan for world domination, and he was told that the German people would never stand by and endorse it, as it was not in line with the teaching of Martin Luther. The Kaiser cried, 'Then we will change the religion of Germany,' and higher criticism began."[3] Other preachers linked Ger-

---

[2]The term "fundamental*ist*" itself is found following the summer of 1920 when it, evidently, was coined by Baptist *Watchman-Examiner* editor Curtis Lee Laws with reference to the conservative faction in the Northern Baptist Convention. Laws probably specifically had in mind his fellow ultraconservative William Bell Riley and Riley's World's Christian Fundamentals Association (WCFA), those who were ready to do battle for the "Fundamentals." But the "Fundamentals" Laws had in mind were probably those itemized in the nine-point confession of faith adopted by the World Conference on Christian Fundamentals (WCCF) in late May 1919 rather than in the 1910–1915 *Fundamentals*. The birth of organized fundamentalism may well be identified with the WCCF and its continuum, the WCFA. In fact, in 1973, militant fundamentalist George Dollar suggested *The Fundamentals* are *not* the fundamentals of the fundamentalists but "the Fundamentals of Orthodoxy": "Fundamentalist fellowships never used [*The Fundamentals*] as a complete statement of their faith." Dollar of course sharply distinguishes between "orthodox" and "fundamentalist": what orthodox Christians stand for is correct; it is just not enough. See Dollar, *A History of Fundamentalism in America* (Greenville SC: Bob Jones University Press, 1973) esp. 173-83 (ch. 10, "Orthodox Allies"); quotes above from 175.

[3]William G. McLoughlin, Jr., *Billy Sunday Was His Real Name* (Chicago: University of Chicago Press, 1955) 281.

man barbarism and German theology. Modernism, they asserted, had turned Germany into a godless nation, and would do the same thing to America.

The combination of prewar nativism, war-heightened patriotism, the rise of communism and the rash of strikes, bombings, and advocacy of radical causes immediately following the war helped produce the Red Scare, and fundamentalists were among the most scared. In 1919, Billy Sunday offered his audiences this solution to dealing with radicals: "If I had my way with these ornery wild-eyed socialists and IWW's [Industrial Workers of the World], I would stand them up before a firing squad." As for Reds, he said he would "fill the jails so full . . . their feet would stick out the windows."[4] Sunday was given to hyperbole, of course, but the churches, particularly the conservative Protestant churches, touted religion as a major bulwark against radicalism and had a definite tendency to identify Christianity and one-hundred-percent Americanism.

Another service performed for fundamentalists by the turmoil of the decade was to call into serious question the assumption of the Social Gospelers that the world was improving so rapidly that the Kingdom of God was just around the corner. In fact, the fundamentalist contention that things would get steadily worse until Jesus came to usher in the millennium no longer seemed so farfetched.

Finally, fundamentalists had participated heavily in bringing about Prohibition, which became a legal fact on January 16, 1920. Sunday, who had ranted against booze for years, even held a mock funeral for "John Barleycorn." So, in 1920, Fundamentalism appeared on the surface to be in pretty good shape. It had its intellectual act together, it was riding on a crest of patriotism, and it had shared in what was apparently a stunning moral victory. And yet, within ten years, this formidable movement would be devastated by defeat and dissension.

The Fundamentalist Controversy

Though I may be guilty of some academic parochialism, I think it is fair to say that the most significant development in American religion during the 1920s was what has come to be called the Fundamentalist Controversy. That controversy had two distinct components, corresponding to the two major challenges to orthodox faith noted earlier: evolutionism and biblical criticism. The fight against evolutionary teaching was waged primarily in the South. The major battles over biblical criticism occurred in and around Philadelphia. Some of the same people were involved in both aspects of the controversy and key events occurred contemporaneously, but it makes sense analytically to discuss them in turn, rather than to move through the decade in strict chronological fashion.

---

[4]Sidney Ahlstrom, *A Religious History of the American People* (New Haven: Yale University Press, 1972) 900.

The Fight against Evolution. The first and perhaps most familiar of the battles was over the right of public schools and colleges to teach scientific theories thought to be incompatible with scripture. The focus, of course, was on Darwinian evolution. If Darwin's view of the evolution of species was correct, then the Bible's account of creation as having occurred in six twenty-four-hour days could not be true. Since the Bible is true, evolutionary thought is therefore false and must not be taught as if it were true.

Some liberal Christians thought it might be possible to reconcile the biblical account with current scientific theory. Perhaps the "days" were not twenty-four-hour periods, but great ages, long enough to allow evolution to occur much as Darwin had described it. And perhaps the creation story in Genesis was not meant to be taken literally, but was simply an assertion that "back of the universe is God," and in his infinite wisdom, God may have used evolutionary processes to bring creation into being.

Fundamentalists would have none of this. Their most notable champion, former secretary of state and three-time candidate for the presidency William Jennings Bryan, declared flatly that "All the ills from which America suffers can be traced back to the teaching of evolution. It would be better to destroy every other book ever written, and save just the first three verses of Genesis."[5] Bryan not only contended that evolution was a pernicious doctrine, but felt that Christians had a perfect right to suppress it if they were able. In true populist fashion, he argued that when religion and science came into conflict, the issue should be decided by the will of the common people, not by "those who measure men by diplomas and college degrees."[6] "Why," he asked, "should the Bible, which the centuries have been unable to shake, be discarded for scientific works that have to be corrected and revised every few years?"[7] Richard Hofstadter quotes Walter Lippman as having observed that "the religious doctrine that all men will at last stand equal before the throne of God was somehow transmuted in Bryan's mind into the idea that all men were equally good biologists before the ballot box."[8]

In keeping with this approach, antievolutionists throughout the South and Southwest made concerted efforts to prohibit the teaching of evolution in the public schools.[9] Some of these ran aground rather early. Virginia, West Virginia,

---

[5]Maynard Shipley, *The War on Modern Science* (New York: Knopf, 1927) 254-55, as quoted by Richard Hofstadter in *Anti-Intellectualism in American Life* (New York: Vintage, 1962) 125.

[6]Quoted by Hofstadter, *Anti-Intellectualism*, 128.

[7]Quoted in Norman E. Furniss, *The Fundamentalist Controversy, 1918–1931* (Hampden CT: Archon books, 1963) 122.

[8]Hofstadter, *Anti-Intellectualism*, 128.

[9]The following sketch of these efforts is based primarily on Furniss, *The*

South Carolina, Georgia, and Alabama, for example, refused to pass restrictive acts, despite strong affirmations of orthodoxy.

In other states, academic freedom and science escaped more narrowly. In Kentucky, for example, a teacher was brought to trial in 1922 for teaching that the earth was round, and was dismissed from his job when the plaintiff, using the scriptures, convinced the judge that the earth was flat. Sensing the presence of kindred spirits, Bryan lent his influence to the cause in Kentucky and a bill that would have restricted the teaching of evolution was defeated in the legislature by only one vote.

In Missouri, a newspaper reporter with a mischievous spirit got friends in the legislature to introduce an antievolution bill, with no intent more serious than to enliven the political news. At first, the representatives refused to take the bill seriously. One moved to table it until the year 2000, to allow time for mature consideration. Another suggested fines for all those suspected of teaching evolution. And another proposed that any who were convicted of teaching evolution be housed in the St. Louis Zoo for not less than thirty days or more than forty nights. When the bill came to a vote, however, it lost by only twenty votes (82–62), and vigorous late action by a worried American Association of University Professors may have kept it from being even closer.[10]

In some states, restrictive measures *were* enacted. Oklahoma prohibited evolutionary texts from 1923 to 1925. Bryan helped prepare a resolution that was passed by the Florida legislature in 1923, though in 1925 efforts to turn the resolution into law failed. "Ma" Ferguson, then governor of Texas, adopted a policy of selecting textbooks that did not mention evolution or of snipping objectionable passages from books that did mention it, and of threatening teachers with dismissal and prosecution if they used unapproved texts. By 1927, however, teachers were free of legal constraints on their scientific instruction. Similarly, the governor of North Carolina rejected two texts in 1924, observing that he did not want his daughter "or anybody's daughter to have to study a book that prints pictures of a monkey and a man on the same page."[11] Still, an attempt in 1927 to pass restrictive legislation failed.

During the same period, Mississippi passed a law against the teaching of evolution, and both Arkansas and Louisiana placed some restrictions on science teachers. But the most notable success of the antievolution forces occurred in Tennessee, where George Washington Butler, farmer, part-time school teacher, and clerk of the Round Lick Association of Primitive Baptists, got himself elected to the legislature on a platform whose only plank was a pledge to outlaw

---

Fundamentalist Controversy, 78-100; and Ahlstrom, *A Religious History*, 909-10.
[10]Furniss, *The Fundamentalist Controversy*, 95-96.
[11]Ibid., 85.

heretical instruction. True to his word, Butler drafted a bill that was accepted by the Tennessee House by a vote of 71–5 and by the Senate by a 24–6 majority. On March 6, 1925, Governor Austin Peay signed into law a bill making it illegal "for any teacher in any of the universities (or public schools) of the state to teach any theory that denies the story of the divine creation of man as taught in the Bible and to teach instead that man has descended from a lower order of animals."[12]

For various reasons—probably the most important being that the lopsided vote in the Tennessee legislature was a reasonable reflection of popular sentiment—the passage of the bill did not stir great public reaction. But, as historian Norman Furniss tells it, one afternoon a few months later in 1925, several young men were sitting around in Robinson's Drug Store in Dayton, Tennessee, sipping lemon phosphates and talking about the new law. One of them, George Rappelyea, pointed out to his friend John T. Scopes that his biology classes at the local high school were in violation of Butler's law, since Scopes was using George Hunter's *Civic Biology*, an evolutionist book, as a text. They speculated that the law was probably unconstitutional, noted that the ACLU had agreed to support any teacher who would challenge it, and decided Rappelyea would challenge Scopes in order to provide a test case. Scopes agreed, Rappelyea challenged, and Scopes was subsequently indicted by a grand jury and shoved into the middle of one of the more remarkable arenas of intellectual and spiritual conflict in American history.[13] (It is interesting to note that the case was not initiated by fundamentalists.)

Dayton became the center of attention in the national press and attempted to make the most of it. Accommodations for 30,000 were announced as available, stores sold little cotton apes and lapel pins that said, "Your old man's a monkey." Circus performers entertained crowds with chimpanzees, and visitors included such notable attractions as Wilbur Glenn Voliva of the Christian Catholic (Apostolic) Church at Zion (Illinois), leading exponent of the flat-earth school of geography, and Lewis Levi Johnson Marshall, "Absolute Ruler of the Entire World, without Military, Naval, or other Physical Force."[14]

Scopes's lawyers included Maynard Shipley, the most noted fundamentalist fighter of the time, and, of course, Clarence Darrow. The fundamentalist prosecution, with William Jennings Bryan in the lists, felt up to the challenge. The lines of the conflict were clearly drawn: All the prosecution had to do was show that Scopes had broken the law, which was not really under dispute. The defense would argue that the law was unconstitutional because it violated the

---

[12]Ibid., 4.
[13]Ibid., 90.
[14]Ibid., 7.

mandate of the Tennessee constitution to "cherish literature and science" and, further, that it ran counter to the U.S. Constitution's guarantees of religious and intellectual freedom.

It was obvious from the outset where the court stood on the matter. Judge John T. Raulston opened the trial with a prayer calculated to persuade the defense it was in error and, until Darrow's objections obtained its removal, sat underneath a banner that said, "Read Your Bible Daily."[15] The jury, drawn from the community, was similarly inclined. The trial itself was rather dull until Darrow, who had not been allowed to summon expert witnesses, put Bryan on the stand and began to grill him in such a manner as to make him appear shallow and foolish to those who adored him. That evening, Bryan set about to draft a response he hoped would vindicate him, but the district attorney instructed him not to continue, lest their case be further weakened. Scopes was convicted and ordered to pay a fine of one hundred dollars. As a "consolation prize," he was awarded a scholarship to pursue graduate studies at the University of Chicago and had a successful career as a geologist. On the day following his humiliation at Darrow's hands, Bryan left Dayton. A few days later, he died after a heavy meal at a friend's home.[16]

Though it had ostensibly won the case, the fundamentalist movement was severely wounded in the Scopes trial, both in the loss of its most dynamic and respected leader and in the ridicule to which it was subjected by the national and international press. Within less than five years, despite strong feelings by millions of Americans that evolutionary teaching is diabolical and false, all legislation forbidding its being taught in the public schools and colleges would be repealed and no further serious efforts to legislate the content of scientific instruction would be mounted for half a century. The fundamentalists may not have descended from monkeys, but they had been made to look like them.

The Fight against Biblical Criticism. The second, and probably more important, struggle of the fundamentalist controversy was that occasioned by the steady increase in acceptance of German biblical criticism into Protestant churches and seminaries. It was possible, though not easy, to make accommodation between science and scripture. Since the Bible was written for prescientific people, perhaps God had used language they would understand to describe the same processes now being described by scientists. But biblical criticism rather thoroughly undercut the notion that scripture was inspired in any special, supernatural way. Its authors were seen to be men, creating sacred literature by the same processes used to create secular literature. That made claims of

---

[15]Ibid., 79.
[16]Ibid., 90-91.

inerrancy and infallibility and authority impossible to maintain. Since these claims constituted, as we have seen, the bedrock principle of fundamentalist faith, it was absolutely essential that they not be surrendered.

The fight over fidelity to the scriptures was also important because it highlighted the tendency of fundamentalists to fight among themselves with fully as much enthusiasm as they fought against more clearly marked enemies. Some churches escaped great turmoil. The Congregationalists and Methodists were barely troubled, mainly because "modernism" (as it was called) was so widely accepted in their circles. Similarly, Lutherans and Southern Baptists escaped serious upheaval because their ranks contained so few who had extended the right hand of fellowship to the new ways of thinking. The Holiness and Pentecostal churches, which were experiencing notable growth but which were not really part of the fundamentalist movement despite many similarities in basic assumptions, were untouched by the whole controversy.

The key struggles came within the Presbyterian Church USA, and the Northern Baptists. And the areas involved were not backwater burgs in the South, but New York, Princeton, and Philadelphia. Recall that the World's Christian Fundamentals Association had been formed in Philadelphia in 1919. A Statement of Belief adopted at the meeting made it clear that only those who were totally loyal to a literal understanding of the Bible could be born-again Christians. Bolstered by this show of strength, heady with the successes it had enjoyed in the decade of the teens and convinced it was time to press for purity of faith, the fundamentalists set about to root out error wherever they found it and to separate themselves from its perpetrators.

Conflict within the Presbyterian church was inescapable. Its polity enabled rather tight control over its ministers. Its two seminaries, Union (New York) and Princeton, were excellent, so that serious consideration of biblical criticism was a scholarly responsibility. Its tradition of treating doctrinal matters with utmost seriousness insured that the hard questions could not simply be finessed. In 1910, and later during the war (1916), the Presbyterian General Assembly had affirmed a fundamentalist platform ("The Five-Point Deliverance") and was insisting that ministers subscribe to it, a policy that was driving out some liberals, particularly among the younger men who had attended seminary recently. Throughout the denomination, fundamentalists were demanding public tests of orthodoxy for ministers and seminary professors. They were calling for the resignation of dissenting church journal editors, and attempting to purge liberals from denominational office. And they succeeded in getting the denomination to withdraw from the ecumenical Interchurch World Movement.

The first major Presbyterian fundamentalist campaign of the twenties revolved around a Baptist, Harry Emerson Fosdick. He had studied at Union, then become a professor there in 1908. Because of his growing reputation and skill as a preacher, he was invited to become the regular "guest preacher" at the

First Presbyterian Church in New York. In that prestigious pulpit, he expressed his own liberal theological views, which did not include belief in the inerrancy of scripture, the virgin birth, the second coming, and other fundamentalist tenets. Then, in 1922, he preached a sermon and wrote an article entitled, "Shall the Fundamentalists Win?" in which he made a frontal attack on the beliefs and, even more, the tactics of ultraconservatives, whom he saw as trying to restrict religious liberty and freedom of thought.

The sermon was widely circulated, in part with the financial backing of prominent layman, Ivy Lee, and fundamentalists gave notice that, yes, they would win if they were able.[17] William Bell Riley, a noted fundamentalist revivalist, gave his reply in a sermon called "Fundamentalism v. the New Faith, or Riley v. Fosdick." John Roach Straton, the New York Baptist preacher who was known as "The Man Who Fights Broadway," preached a sermon called "Shall the Funny Monkeyists Win?" in which he characterized Fosdick as "a Baptist bootlegger, a Presbyterian outlaw . . . the Jesse James of the theological world."[18] And throughout the denomination, conservatives called for Fosdick's removal from First Presbyterian's pulpit. Rather than reply to the substance of the criticisms, Presbyterian liberals pressed for Fosdick's resignation on the grounds that he was a Baptist, a maneuver that led Fostick to accuse them of running a closed shop. Fosdick did leave First Presbyterian in 1925, but not without consolation. From 1925 to 1930, he preached at Park Avenue Baptist, John D. Rockefeller's church, and in 1931, he moved into the magnificent non-denominational Riverside Church, which Rockefeller funded, and was, well into the 1940s, perhaps the most influential preacher in America.

As the Fosdick affair had shown, Union Seminary was hopelessly lost to the liberals. That made the battle to save Princeton all the more crucial. If Princeton fell, then fundamentalism—true Christianity itself—would be lost. Princeton had remained conservative since the days of the Hodges and Warfield, who had fashioned the fundamentalist position on inerrancy. Its faculty in the 1920s contained such distinguished conservative scholars as Oswald T. Allis, Robert Dick Wilson, and the preeminent scholar of the entire fundamentalist movement, J. Gresham Machen.

Machen was a graduate of Princeton College and Seminary and had studied at Marburg and Göttingen. He was intelligent and an authentic scholar. He was also an uncompromising fundamentalist, as his 1923 book *Christianity and*

---

[17]Ibid., 132; Ahlstrom, *A Religious History*, 911.

[18]Riley Sermon, cited in George W. Dollar, *A History of Fundamentalism* (Greenville SC: Bob Jones University Press, 1973) 118; Straton, "Shall the Funny Monkeyists Win?" in *The Faith-Fundamentalist* (New York: Calvary Baptist Church, December 1925) quoted in Dollar, 137-38.

Liberalism made plain. Machen believed no liberals should serve on seminary faculties or boards of directors. No liberal seminarians should be ordained to the Presbyterian ministry. Liberal ministers who had already been ordained should be censured. He pressed his case again and again with great vigor, but again and again he lost as the General Assembly, the final arbiter in the Presbyterian church, refused to root out the liberals. With the appointment of a new president (J. Ross Stevenson) at the seminary it became clear that Princeton itself was moving in a more moderate direction. With that, Machen abandoned the fight and decided to "come out from among them." In 1929, he and several colleagues pulled out of Princeton with a handful of students and moved to Philadelphia to establish Westminster Theological Seminary. One of the students was the president of the junior class, an aggressive, articulate man named Carl McIntire (b. 1906). This would not be McIntire's last act of separation from a body he found excessively impure.

The Westminster faculty and student body launched a program of bold criticism of the parent church, even charging its missionaries in China with being procommunist. In 1933, Machen and his associates formed the Independent Board for Presbyterian Foreign Missions, with the aim of supporting only those missionaries who were doctrinally sound. This, plus continued intemperate attacks on the larger body, led to the expulsion of Machen and McIntire from the church in 1935 and the formation in 1936 of the Presbyterian Church in America, later (1938) renamed the Orthodox Presbyterian Church.

Within a year, McIntire and his followers had found Machen and Westminster insufficiently pure and in 1937 split off to form the Bible Presbyterian Church and Faith Theological Seminary. Machen had died on the first day of 1937, leaving his wing without strong leadership and McIntire without strong opposition. These struggles left scars in the Presbyterian body, but it was clear who had won. The fundamentalists, intent on driving out the liberals and seizing control of the denomination, had themselves been driven out and more moderate forms of Christianity had prevailed.

Similar events occurred within the Northern Baptist Churches. Many of the leading liberal theologians were Baptists and its seminaries, including Newton, Colgate, Rochester, Crozer, and especially the University of Chicago Divinity School, were respected centers of learning. At the same time, however, many of the leading fundamentalists such as Straton, Riley, and Amzi Dixon (who had co-edited *The Fundamentals*), were also Baptists, determined, like their Presbyterian counterparts, to keep their denomination pure. Conservative forces were able in 1920 to lead their denomination out of the ecumenical Interchurch World Movement of North America. More important, however, was the formation of parade-nominational fundamentalist alliances that gave full attention to creeping liberalism.

Straton and Dixon led in the forming of the National Federation of Fundamentalists (1920) and Riley guided the Baptist Bible Union (1923). Through their drives to set up and demand adherence to rigid doctrinal statements and to eliminate heretics from the mission fields and seminaries, these fundamentalist groups created widespread disruption in Baptist churches and turned their conventions into occasions of considerable acrimony. They won some victories, but most of them were qualified and watered down so that by 1930 it was clear that Northern Baptists, like the Presbyterians, had opted for a more flexible form of Christianity than suited the fundamentalists.

At the end of the decade of the 1920s, then, fundamentalism appeared to have been defeated and relegated to a minor position. It had not only lost virtually every confrontation it had created but had been exposed to ridicule by its tendency to intellectual rigidity and obscurantism, by the intemperate nature of its actions, and by its propensity for attracting and lending support to anti-Semitic, anti-Catholic, and other nativist and right-wing political elements, and its uncritical equation of Christianity with one-hundred-percent Americanism. The Depression had diverted attention from theological wrangling and it was becoming apparent that the great victory of Prohibition would soon be overturned. It appeared that increased acceptance of science and modern biblical criticism would continue inexorably until the last fundamentalist had withered and died with a sour whimper.

This expectation was so strong that some noted historians—including Richard Hofstadter, William McLoughlin, and Norman Furniss—as much as declared that it had happened, despite considerable evidence to the contrary. That oversight, probably attributable at least in part to a desire of intellectuals to see such an anti-intellectual movement disappear, helped make the revival of the 1970s more of a surprise than it need have been. Fundamentalism did pass through a wilderness, but it did not enter the grave. In fact, fundamentalist Christianity not only failed to disappear during the 1930s, but it underwent a transformation that left it in a reasonably strong position by the end of the decade. It is to that transformation that I want to turn now.

The Transformation of Fundamentalism

The transformation of fundamentalism, which began in the 1920s, involved shifting and realigning and reorganization of the base of fundamentalism. Since the fight for control of denominations and seminaries had been lost, the fundamentalists set about to create a whole new set of institutions and structures, in which the true, pure, and unadulterated Christian message could be preserved and preached. In some cases, the steps taken were new; in others, they were elaborations of existing precedents. Let me mention some of the most important.

In keeping with a tendency to lionize its most vocal and sometimes most outrageous leaders, fundamentalists often formed themselves into independent congregations centered on—in fact, if not in name—a notable hero of the faith. John Roach Straton in New York City, Paul Rader in Chicago, J. Frank Norris in Fort Worth, Robert "Fighting Bob" Shuler in Los Angeles (not to be confused with today's Robert Schuller), William Bell Riley in Minneapolis, Carl McIntire in Collingswood, New Jersey, and many other lesser lights in other cities gathered the faithful into enclaves of aggressive purity. These served as important bases for flourishing revivalistic preaching both by their pastors and itinerant preachers who rode the circuit. It also gave opportunity for men like Gerald Winrod and Gerald L. K. Smith to tout racist, anti-Semitic views without check.

Often with the leadership of such key men as these, individuals and congregations formed fundamentalist alliances which they hoped would multiply their strength and effectiveness. I have already mentioned the World's Christian Fundamentals Association, the National Federation of Fundamentalists, and the Baptist Bible Union. These were the most notable, but there were dozens of others. Some catered to churches within a particular denominational group, like the American Baptist Association (with 3,300 churches), the General Association of Regular Baptists, the World Baptist Fellowship, and the Fundamental Presbyterians. Others, such as the Independent Fundamentalist Churches of America and the Associated Gospel Churches, catered to congregations that had thrown off the yoke of denominationalism. Still others consisted primarily of individuals from various denominations, many of whom felt a call to one particular segment of the battle for truth.

Representatives of this group included the Bible Crusaders of America, the Interdenominational Fundamentalist Association, the School-Bag Gospel League, the Bryan Bible League, the Defenders of Science vs. Speculation of California (Shuler and Riley), Victorious Life Testimony, and Gerald Winrod's Defenders of the Christian Faith, whose Flying Fundamentalists toured the Midwest attacking modernism, evolution, and, later, Jews, Catholics, Franklin Roosevelt's "Jewish New Deal," the "Negro Menace," and Communism. Large numbers of individual Christians also attended Bible conferences at places like Winona Lake, Indiana, and Stony Brook, Long Island, where the giants of fundamentalist faith assured them that they were not the only ones who had not bowed the knee to Baal, that thousands of others were still faithful to the Word as God had personally written it.

Another extremely crucial development, far more lasting in its impact than the various alliances, was the substantial increase in the number of Bible colleges and Bible institutes. The desire to have institutions to train ministers and Christian laymen, of course, had been at the roots of a number of prestigious American educational institutions, including Brown, Harvard, Yale, and Princeton. But the encouragement of the liberal arts in these schools had inexorably weakened their commitment to truth more narrowly conceived. What was needed was a new set of schools whose teaching was impeccably orthodox and whose entire curriculum would be devoted to inculcating the "faith once received" and training students to spread and cultivate it effectively.

The model was the Moody Bible Institute (MBI), founded in Chicago in 1886, with R. A. Torrey as the first superintendent. By 1929, MBI had trained more than 69,000 students to be ministers, church musicians, educational directors, Sunday school teachers, personal workers, and missionaries. It also operated a vigorous publishing house, sponsored numerous conferences, and by 1930 owned a radio station dedicated to Christian broadcasting. The Bible Institute of Los Angeles, known by the acronym Biola and now Biola University, had been founded by Lyman Stewart and Robert A. Hadden in 1908 and enjoyed similar status on the West Coast. Other such institutes and Bible colleges had sprung up in the early decades of the century, but fundamentalist losses in the twenties spurred further growth and their number increased from forty-nine in 1930 to 144 in 1950.[19]

Finally, fundamentalists made extraordinarily wide use of publications and the new medium, radio. Fundamentalism seems to bring out the editor and pamphleteer in its leaders, who conveyed their message in publications with names like the *Christian Beacon*, the *Essentialist*, the *Crusader's Champion*, the *King's Business*, *Conflict*, *Defender*, and *Dynamite*. Some fundamentalist publications were inflammatory and irresponsible. More were unimaginative, repetitive, and dull. But they were publications, and they were being read. And they formed a habit of reading among fundamentalists, with one result that every year the real bestsellers in American publishing are not those that appear in the *New York Times* lists but books that are sold by and to evangelical Christians.

Perhaps even more significant, fundamentalists quickly seized the opportunity offered them by radio. With their emphasis on proclamation and the prospect of a vast and ever-growing audience, they immediately saw radio as a tool of great potential. They were not alone, of course, in seeing its potential application to religious purposes. The first voice broadcast on radio, in 1906, had been a Christian celebration that included the singing of "O Holy Night" and a reading from Luke's Gospel. And on January 2, 1921, a month after KDKA in Pittsburgh became the first licensed broadcasting station in America, the Calvary Episcopal Church in that city began broadcasting its Sunday evening service. In 1922, Paul Rader began airing services at his Chicago Gospel Tabernacle over his own station, WJBT ("Where Jesus Blesses Thousands"), and soon saw his crowds swell mightily as people came to see in person the man they had heard on radio. (Later, he preached the revival at which Richard Nixon gave his life to Jesus.)

By 1925, one in ten of the more than six hundred radio stations in America were owned and operated by churches and other religious organizations. A tightening of licensing regulations led to a selling off of about half of these by

---

[19]Ahlstrom, *A Religious History*, 913.

1933, but the potential had been seen. Aimee Semple McPherson spoke for others when she said, in 1923, that:

> It has now become possible to stand in the pulpit, and speaking in a normal voice, reach hundreds of thousands of listeners. . . . We fully expect to reach with the preached word the prairie wife with her little family; the mountaineer amid the rugged crag and timbers of his alpine abode; the desert dweller amidst the sand dunes, cactus, and sage brush; the Indian chief . . . ; the blue jacket who sails in Uncle Sam's warships; the cripple in the wheelchair; the businessman as he sits at his luncheon.[20]

The two antenna towers of her station KFSG ("Kall Foursquare Gospel") were, she said,

> alive, tingling, pulsing spires of steel, mute witnesses that at Angelus Temple every moment of the day and night, a silent and invisible messenger awaits the command to carry, on the winged feet of the winds, the story of hope, the words of joy, of comfort, of salvation.[21]

Sister Aimee asked people to kneel by their radio while she prayed with them and to place their hands on the receiver for a sense of contact and presence. And when she wished to broadcast a baptismal service, she placed a microphone near the edge of the baptistery, so that not only her voice, but the splash of the water and the exhilaration of the newly baptized could be heard.[22] Though her own skills for promotion and drama helped no little, her use of radio made Aimee one of the best-known religious personalities of her time, and the first nationally known Pentecostal evangelist.

Other fundamentalist evangelists were not so imaginative as Ms. McPherson, but still proved successful at using the medium as an extension of their pulpit. In 1927, New York City's foremost fundamentalist John Roach Straton began broadcasting from Calvary Baptist Church, a radio ministry that continues today as the country's oldest. R. R. Brown, who began preaching over WOW in Omaha in 1923, came to be known as the "Billy Sunday of the Air," at least in part because he did not trust microphones and shouted and gestured at the half-million listeners who heard him each week as if they were with him in the studio.

---

[20]Aimee Semple McPherson, *Four Square* (December 1923), quoted by Harold Ellens, *Models of Religious Broadcasting* (Grand Rapids: Eerdmans, 1974) 24.

[21]Ibid. McPherson's radio station, the third established in Los Angeles, was (and still is) KFSG, "Kall Foursquare Gospel," referring to the "church" she established, the International Church of the Foursquare Gospel.

[22]Ibid., 72.

In 1928, Donald Grey Barnhouse, a graduate of the Bible Institute of Los Angeles and evangelical pastor of the Tenth Presbyterian Church in Philadelphia, became the first religious broadcaster to buy network time when he began broadcasting the church's evening services over one hundred CBS stations. In Los Angeles, "Fighting Bob" Shuler reached millions with broadcasts that usually included sensationalist moralizing and racy exposés of corruption and wickedness among Los Angelenos, Christian and otherwise.

M. R. DeHaan began the Radio Bible Class in 1938, a program that, with his son as speaker, is still heard over hundreds of stations and is the parent to the widely televised "Day of Discovery" broadcast (since 1968). Theodore Epp began the "Back to the Bible" broadcast in 1939, a program for which he is still a principal speaker. In 1935, J. Harold Smith began the "Radio Bible Hour," a program that has given him the distinction of having preached more different sermons on the radio than any other individual, living or dead. And, though virtually all fundamentalists would rule him out of their number as a heretic, Herbert W. Armstrong also began the broadcasts of the "Radio Church of God" (later called "The World Tomorrow") in 1934, a ministry that expanded until, at its peak in the 1970s, it was utilizing fifty million watts of broadcasting power each week as son Garner Ted Armstrong proclaimed the "plain truth about the world tomorrow" for a half-hour daily over 380 radio and seventy-five television stations throughout the world. Herbert's son and "World Tomorrow" star Garner Ted walked out on his father in 1983, but Herbert managed alone until his death on January 16, 1986, at age ninety-three, at which time "The World Tomorrow" was rated fourth among all religious programs.

Moody Bible Institute's WMBI has broadcast continuously since 1925, two years before the establishment of the Federal Radio Commission. WMBI not only launched an ambitious mixture of Christian programming, including music and drama as well as preaching, but developed many productions that it made available to other Christian stations. John Zoller (from 1922), Walter Maier ("The Lutheran Hour," also 1922–), Peter Edersveld, and numerous other capable preachers also made wide and effective use of radio, but none, perhaps, was more successful than another Biola graduate, Charles E. Fuller.

Fuller began his broadcasting career in 1923, and by 1924 was teaching bible lessons over the Biola Station in Los Angeles. In February 1930 he began broadcasting services from his independent Calvary Church, and included a phone-in segment, one of the first audience-participation talk shows in radio. Though Fuller was its founder, Calvary Church did not approve his efforts and he left the church in 1933 to enter a full-time radio ministry, supported solely by contributions from listeners. Despite the fact that it was at the low point of the Depression, contributions ran ahead of expenses and Fuller began to add stations. By 1937, the program was called the "Old Fashioned Revival Hour" and was being heard coast-to-coast on thirty Mutual network stations. Six weeks after obtaining this coverage, Fuller expanded to eighty-eight stations and by 1939 was broadcasting on all 152 stations in the Mutual system, reaching an estimated ten million listeners. By 1943, the "Old Fashioned Revival Hour" and a second Fuller program, "The Pilgrim's Hour," were being heard over 1,000 stations at a cost of $1.5 million for airtime alone, and Fuller's Gospel Broadcasting Association was buying fifty percent more time than the secular company in second place. His success soon led him to found Fuller Theological Seminary (in 1947), which is today perhaps the most respected of all evangelical schools. Fuller retired in 1967 and died in 1968; in 1969 his successor on the "Old Fashioned Revival Hour," David Hubbard, changed the program's name to "A Joyful Sound."

Following the Scopes "monkey trial" of 1925, some historians, liberal clergymen, and learned professors in major seminaries may have believed, certainly hoped, that Fundamentalism was dead. Millions of Americans knew better. Not only had the radio ministers kept evangelical doctrines before the people, but they had, by their astonishing success, made it clear that unnumbered legions still built on the firm foundation, still walked on the ancient pathways, and would teach their children to do the same.

Carl McIntire recognized that fundamentalism was stronger than it had been in more than a decade and moved in 1940 to form a national fundamentalist organization that would be "militantly progospel and antimodernist." Despite its desire for numbers, it would also be separatist, barring any churches or denominations that had truck with modernists or that belonged to the liberal Federal Council of Churches, the forerunner of the National Council of Churches. In 1941, the American Council of Christian Churches (ACCC) came into being, with McIntire as its first president. It was from the beginning a protesting council. It badgered the radio networks to give it a share of airtime equal to that given the Federal Council of Churches. It obtained a quota of chaplaincy slots from the armed services. And, through McIntire's paper *The Christian Beacon* and his syndicated radio program "The Twentieth Century Reformation Hour," the ACCC mounted unending attacks on the Federal Council and, indeed, on any group or individual less pure than itself.

Fortunately, some fundamentalists, exposed by schools and conferences and radio to men of more irenic spirit, were able to see that the quarrelsomeness of men like McIntire seemed inevitably to result in an endless sequence of splittings into units that grew smaller and smaller, in spirit as well as in number. Less than a month after McIntire's ACCC was formed, a group of more moderate conservatives met at the Moody Bible Institute with the aim of establishing an association that could represent all evangelical believers in all denominations, including those affiliated with the Federal Council of Churches. The group, which included such men as Harold John Ockenga, Carl F. H. Henry, and J. Elwin Wright, invited representatives of the ACCC to present their ideas, in the hope of achieving unity with them. Their theological differences were minor.

Their differences in spirit were irreconcilable. The National Association of Evangelicals (NAE) was organized April 7, 1942, at the National Conference for United Action among Evangelicals in St. Louis. The NAE, the organizers said, was determined to break with apostasy but wanted no "dog-in-the-manger, reactionary, negative, or destructive type of organization," and was determined to shun all forms of "bigotry, intolerance, misrepresentation, hate, jealousy, false judgment, and hypocrisy."[23] The NAE was, in several words, determined not to be like Carl McIntire and the American Council of Christian Churches.

This brings us to the end of the period between the world wars. Forty years later, in the 1980s, the dual alignment of conservatives still persists, though the more moderate group prefers to be known by the less pejorative term "evangelical" and now includes large segments of the pentecostal/charismatic movement, who are usually excluded from fundamentalist circles. Doctrinally, "fundamentalist-conservatives" and "evangelical-conservatives" still share a great deal. In temperament and behavior, they are quite distinct.

Fundamentalists are still represented by men such as Carl McIntire—though today McIntire is in the Where-are-they-now? category—and the current ostensible champions of orthodoxy within the Southern Baptist Convention, Paige Patterson, Paul Pressler, and others. They continue to manifest a separatist attitude and fissiparous spirit, willing to divide Christians into sheep and goats at the drop of a double-edged sword, splitting off from others over differences often perceived by others to be minor. Evangelicals, of whom Billy Graham is the best-known exemplar, tend to overlook minor theological differences and to express a more charitable spirit of brotherhood toward those who accept the basic tenets of evangelical faith.

In political matters, fundamentalists typically espouse a strident kind of patriotism, with an emphasis on anticommunism and strong national defense, an uncritical attitude toward laissez-faire capitalism, and a disdain for social-welfare policies. Most evangelicals also line up on the more conservative side of the political spectrum, but have shown an increasing ability to be critical of weaknesses and shortcomings in the standing order. Where education is concerned, fundamentalists show a preference for tight control over content and method by teachers and administrators known for sound doctrine and unlikely to infect the young with disruptive qualities of critical analysis so often, and properly, associated with education. The burgeoning "Christian School" movement of recent years has received much of its impetus from the ranks of fundamentalists troubled by the threat of secular education. Evangelicals have typically demon-

---

[23]As quoted, e.g., by Martin E. Marty, in *Pilgrims in Their Own Land: 500 Years of Religion in America* (Boston: Little, Brown, 1984) 411.

strated sufficient openness toward the liberal arts and legitimate scholarship in various fields, including the study of the Bible, to avoid being identified with unremitting anti-intellectualism.

Another notable difference between fundamentalists and evangelicals, one often noted by themselves, is that of style and temperament. Fundamentalists tend to see evangelicals as soft and unsound on matters of doctrine, and compromising in their relationship to the world. Evangelicals, for their part, are apt to regard fundamentalists as unloving and harsh, even belligerent, in manner and spirit, more concerned with assuring themselves they are right than with manifesting the spirit of Christ.

For most of the last four decades, evangelicals seemed clearly to be winning out over the fundamentalists. During the 1980s, however, fundamentalists have scored enormous gains and once again have forced their more moderate brethren into a defensive posture, as exemplified by their gaining control of the presidency of the Southern Baptist Convention for several years and pressing attacks, in language remarkably reminiscent of that used in the 1920s, in such denominational citadels as Baylor University and Southern Seminary. There is a marked tendency of fundamentalists to move into the evangelical camp as they achieve success. A shift in the opposite direction is far less common. Whatever the outcome of the current struggle, both fundamentalists and evangelicals are enjoying robust health at a time when more liberal forms of Christianity appear decidedly less vital.

It is useful and worthwhile to pursue the reasons why evangelicalism/fundamentalism is flourishing in the last quarter of the twentieth century. That is not the purpose of this essay. But if and when one does consider that question, I recommend remembering at least two things. First, a vital and healthy evangelical religion is not a new element in American life, but an authentic, major tradition that has never come close to disappearing, and that by far the greatest number of its adherents come to it by normal processes of socialization, that is, by growing up in it. And secondly, at least a significant part of the current vitality of evangelicalism/fundamentalism is directly traceable to developments that were an integral part of its transformation between the World Wars.

Biblical Justification of Apartheid in Afrikaner Civil Religion

Robert Hamerton-Kelly

> This identity, I would insist, is founded ultimately on a wound, a feeling of having been victimized.　　　　　　　　　—Vincent Crapanzano

Afrikaner group identity was forged between the hammer of British imperialism and the anvil of black resistance. It contains two powerful motivating forces: the sense of being a victim of injustice and arrogance—in this case at the hands of the British—and the exhilaration of being the victor over unfavorable odds—in this instance over the superior numbers of the blacks in battle.

When placed within the interpretive context of the Christian religion, both these impulses receive the added impetus of imaginative identification with the great Christian archetypes of the Crucifixion, in the first instance, and the Resurrection in the second. Victimization and victory are the two fundamental moments of the apostolic preaching and the two fundamental moments of Afrikaner group experience. When placed within the context of the whole Bible this experience takes on the superadded energy of the belief that God acts in the history of nations to vindicate the chosen people against their oppressors.

Before we consider the specific passages on which the Afrikaner churches have, until recently, based the biblical justification of Apartheid, we shall consider the more general themes of victimization, victory, and chosenness.

Two events provide the poles of the Afrikaner national myth: the 1816 rebellion in Cape Colony at Slagtersnek (or Slachter's Nek), which is the victimization pole, and the three-hour "Battle of Blood River" (on the Ncome River in Zululand) on December 16, 1838, which is the victory pole. Suspended between the two is the sacred canopy of chosenness. That these memories comprise a myth is shown by the fact that they were first interpreted nationalistically only in the period after the British annexation of the Transvaal (South African Republic) in January 1877 and especially after the Boer victory over the British in the Boer rebellion (variously the "Anglo-Boer War," "War of Independence," or "Freedom War," 1880–1881). Prior to that time, these events went relatively unremarked.

Slagtersnek and "Blood River" were recalled and transfigured under the influence of the pious rhetoric of Paul Kruger in the Transvaal, as he sought to whip up opposition to the annexation, and of the nascent cultural consciousness in the Cape, heralded by the founding of the True South Africans (1875) and the Afrikanerbond (1879), and the launching of the "First Language Movement" by the Stellenbosch clergyman-educator Stephanus Johannes du Toit's (1847–1911) *De Christelijke School in hare verhouding tot Kerk en Staat* (*The Relationship of the Christian School to Church and State*, 1876) and *Die Geskiedenis van ons Land in die Taal van ons Volk* (*The History of Our Country in the Language of Our People*, 1877), the first full-length books in Afrikaans language.

Prior to the Transvaal annexation in 1877, "Afrikaner" was used to designate only those who had trekked (migrated) out of Cape Colony during 1834–1838 and colonized the two Boer republics of the Orange Free State and the Transvaal. During the time of the annexation and the first Anglo-Boer (Freedom) war, the sympathy shown by the Cape and Free State Afrikaners for the plight of the Transvaal drew all Dutch-speaking burghers together and the name "Afrikaner" was extended to the Dutch-speaking inhabitants of the Cape and Natal. A trans-regional consciousness based on a common religion, language, culture, and on a common history of persecution by the British and victory over the blacks, began to come to being.[1] This common consciousness, dating from 1877–1881, is the spiritual fact that we must attend to as we seek to understand the role the Bible played in Afrikaner civil religion, which issued eventually in the policy of Apartheid.

The Slagtersnek rebellion is a convenient symbol of the "victim" pole of the mythology, and a good illustration of the way history is turned into myth in order to promote the political interests of the mythmakers. The salient fact of the case is that in 1816 the British authorities hanged five Boers at a place in the Eastern Cape called Vanaardtspos, in the district of Uitenhage, for having led an armed rebellion. The authorities were at fault, the rebels argued, because they had sent out a force of blacks to arrest a recalcitrant white man. This racist rationale went unquestioned by either the British or the Boer version of the event, showing thereby that the bedrock on which the mythology is founded is racial discrimination, and raising the question whether the religious justification is for the most part rationalization. The historical details show that the episode was typically ambiguous, but the mythical retelling turned it into an unambiguous instance of British tyranny, exemplified by the fact that the ropes broke in four of the five cases, but the execution went on nevertheless and each of the four survivors was hanged seriatim from the one sound rope. The very name Slagtersnek, which was

[1]Floris van Jaarsveld, *The Afrikaner's Interpretation of South African History* (Capetown: Simondium Publications, 1964) 41.

chosen to designate the incident was incendiary, meaning as it does "the ravine of the butchers." It was chosen by the later mythmakers for its emotional punch.

Slagtersnek became a symbol only after S. J. du Toit made it one in his *Geskiednis* (1877), where he devoted six of 235 pages to the rebellion. Other writers took up the theme, and transformed a sordid incident into a heroic episode in the struggle for national identity.[2] This was grist to the anti-British mill of the Transvaalers during the first war, and became even more useful during and after the second war of 1899–1902 (commonly called either the "Boer War" or the "South African War").

Although it originated during the first war (1880–1881), the burgeoning and consolidation of Afrikaner national consciousness followed the second Boer (Freedom) war of 1899–1902.[3] Confident that God would bless their arms as he had in 1881, the Boer republics declared war on Britain in 1899. This time they suffered defeat, although Kruger, displaying Calvinist resilience, said upon receiving the news of the surrender that God was merely testing his people and that they would eventually triumph. Who can say that he was wrong, given the history of the last eighty years?

The victorious British instituted a policy of Anglicization of the Boers after this second Boer War, which provoked, as might be expected, the Second Afrikaans Language Movement. A truly distinguished Afrikaans lyric poetry came to word at this time through the genius of men like clergyman-poet Jakob Daniel du Toit (pseudonym Totius), Jan F. E. Celliers (whom Moodie calls the "poet laureate of the Afrikaans civil faith"),[4] Eugène Marais, and many others. Marais's "Winternag" ("Winter Night") was the first of the new poetry to be published (in *Land en Volk* in 1905), but for our purposes the work of Totius is most interesting.

Totius was the son of S. J. du Toit, leader of the First Language Movement. He was a minister of the Gereformeerde church, educated at the Free University of Amsterdam (where he wrote his doctoral thesis on Methodism), and became professor of theology at the Dopper theological school at Potchefstroom in 1911. His poetry gave lasting expression to the Calvinist element in the Afrikaner myth, which Calvinism went back in this form to that other equally famous Dopper, Paul Kruger. "Like an Old Testament prophet, Totius interprets his People's

---

[2]See Leonard Thompson, *The Political Mythology of Apartheid* (New Haven: Yale University Press, 1985) 126-43.

[3]Irving Hexham, *The Irony of Apartheid: The Struggle for National Independence of Afrikaner Calvinism Against British Imperialism* (New York: Edwin Mellen Press, 1981) 6.

[4]T. Dunbar Moodie, *The Rise of Afrikanerdom: Power, Apartheid, and the Afrikaner Civil Religion* (Berkeley: University of California Press, 1975) 42.

trials in terms of God's Providence and sees in sorrow, hope for the future."[5] His epic poem *By die Monument* (1908, in conjunction with the National Women's Monument project, 1906–1913) memorializes those, especially women and children, who died in the British concentration camps, and his *Verse van Potgieter's Trek* (1909—Andries Hendrik Potgieter was a leader among the Voortrekkers or Trekboers) celebrates the Great Trek of 1838 as a religious pilgrimage, comparable to Abraham's trek from Ur of the Chaldees and the Exodus from Egyptian bondage.

> But see! the world becomes wilder;
> > the fierce vermin worsen,
> stark naked black hordes,
> > following tyrants.
> How the handful of trekkers suffer,
> > the freedom seekers, creators of a People.
> Just like another Israel,
> > by enemies surrounded, lost in the veld,
> but for another Canaan elected,
> > led forward by God's plan.[6]

There is a note of tragic realism in the following lines from the same poem. The Ndebele chief Mzilikazi is speaking:

> We were here from the beginning,
> > the white man will not win;
> one day he will be vanquished;
> > one day we will drive him away!
> Yes! the land we'll sweep clean,
> > and kaffir justice will reappear.

By die Monument includes Totius's most famous poem, "Vergewe and Vergeet," based on Deuteronomy 4:9, "That you not forget the things your eyes have seen," which gives poignant expression to the truth of Crapanzano's observation that Afrikaner self-understanding is founded on a wound, a sense of having been a victim. The poem tells of a little thorn tree growing by the side of a wagon track. One day a great wagon rides over it, the wheels cutting into its stem and almost severing it, because once the thorn tree had scratched the wagon. The wagon rolls on, and the little tree struggles upright again, healing its wound by its own gum:

---

[5]Hexham, *The Irony of Apartheid*, 35.
[6]As quoted in Hexham, *The Irony of Apartheid*, 37.

In course of time the hurt-marks
    fade where the wheels had lunged—
only one place endures
    that cannot be expunged.

The wounds grew healed and healthy,
    with years that come and go,
but that one scar grew greater
    and does not cease to grow.[7]

The scar that grew greater is the memory of British injustice and cruelty that fueled the energy of the Afrikaner nationalists after the second Boer (Freedom) war, secured their political triumph in 1948, and led to the policy of Apartheid as it has been applied during the last three decades. That memory of injustice was symbolized by the Slagtersnek myth, memorialized in the inimitable lyric poetry of Totius, and politicized in the rhetoric of the Nationalist Party.

Such transfigurations of history into myth, however, should not obscure the fact that the Boers were indeed the victims of British imperial arrogance, and that they responded with extraordinary dignity and resourcefulness. In the face of great opposition they created a new culture and forged a new nation. Let us not forget that Paul Kruger was a heroic figure in most of continental Europe at the turn of the century, a symbol of freedom and dignity in the face of arrogant power. The Boers were the Sandinistas of the turn of the century.

If Slagtersnek was a symbol of victimage in the Afrikaner mythology, Blood River is a symbol of victory. On December 16, 1838, a commando of 468 Boers led by Andries Pretorius defeated a Zulu army of approximately ten thousand strong on the banks of the Ncome river in Natal. The Zulus left three thousand on the field of battle around the laager, while the Boers suffered no casualties at all (three Boers suffered minor wounds). The Boers renamed the river Blood River, because it was tinged with the blood of the fallen after the battle. This is the stuff legends are made of, and of the subsequent treatment of this event Thompson writes:

> Here . . . are all the hallmarks of a classic political myth: its partial concordance with historical reality, its delayed codification followed by rapid development and fervent deployment for political purposes, and its adaptation to changing circumstances.[8]

The Battle of Blood River has been celebrated in the Orange Free State since 1894, in the Transvaal since 1903, and in the four provinces since the Union of

---

[7]As quoted in Moodie, *The Rise of Afrikanerdom*, 43-44.
[8]Thompson, *The Political Mythology of Apartheid*, 146.

1910, as a public holiday, known until 1952 as Dingaan's day and since then as "Geloftedag," the "Day of the Covenant" or "Vow."[9] In 1938 the Great Trek of 1838 was reenacted by several ox-wagon parties trekking by various routes from Cape Town to Pretoria. This celebration was a watershed in the history of Nationalist politics in this century; it aroused a spirit that eventually carried Daniel François Malan to the premiership in 1948 at the head of a Nationalist government. The Great Trek is the center of the Afrikaner mythology and it is summed up in the vow of Blood River. Hendrik or Henning Klopper, the chief organizer of the 1938 celebration, sent off the ox-wagons *Piet Retief* and *Andries Pretorius* on their memorial journey to Pretoria from the foot of the statue of Jan van Riebeeck in Cape Town with the following words:

> On this solemn occasion, at this spot where almost three centuries ago Jan van Riebeeck stepped ashore, it is fitting, in view of the great ethnic deed [*volksdaad*] which we now begin to celebrate, that we should remember the vow of Sarel Cilliers: "Brothers and fellow-countrymen, we stand here before the Holy God of Heaven and Earth to make a vow that, if He will be with us and protect us and give the foe into our hands, we shall ever celebrate the day and date as a Day of Thanksgiving like the Sabbath in His honor. We shall enjoin our children that they must take part with us in this, for a remembrance even for our posterity. For the honor of God shall herein be glorified, and to Him shall be given the fame and the honor of the victory." . . . We bring praise to those who won for us a land and a future and we give honor to the Almighty, in the firm belief that He will make us a powerful People before His countenance."[10]

The vow quoted by Klopper was taken in approximately that form on December 7, 1838, at a place called Danskraal (or another place called Wasbank). In the absence of a chaplain, Cilliers was the religious leader of the commando, and the version of the vow just quoted goes back to his death-bed recollection in 1871, as recorded by H. J. Hoftstede, in his *Geschiedenis van den Oranje-Vrijstaat*.[11] It has been displayed on the walls of patriotic houses for generations in that form, and recent scholarship, which has raised awkward

[9]Floris van Jaarsveld, *Die Evolusie van Apartheid. En ander geskiedkundige Opstelle* (Cape Town: Kaapstad, 1979). Dingaan (or Dingane) was the Zulu king whose "day of reckoning" came at the Blood River.

[10]Klopper's version of the vow, in Thompson, *The Political Mythology of Apartheid*, 184, as excerpted from Moodie's full translation in *The Rise of Afrikanerdom*, 179; cf. Thompson's variant translation in *The Political Mythology of Apartheid*, 167.

[11]H. J. Hoftstede, *Geschiedenis van den Orange-Vrijstaat* (The Hague: D. A. Thieme, 1876) 57-58.

questions about the text of the vow and its importance in the history of the battle, has been met with dramatic intolerance from the Afrikaner right.

In March 1979 at a conference on "Problems in the Interpretation of History with Possible Reference to Examples from South African History Such as the Battle of Blood River," the following occurred, as reported by the Johannesburg *Sunday Times* (April 1, 1979). When Floris van Jaarsveld, a leading Afrikaner historian went to the podium, a group of men rushed up before he could begin his presentation, grabbed him,

> emptied a tin of tar over him and plastered him with feathers. During the assault, a man who identified himself as Eugene Terreblanche, of the *Afrikaanse Weerstandbeweging* (Afrikaans Resistance Movement) seized the microphone and swung the tail of a sjambok [braided whip] through the air. Standing behind the Vierkleur flag of the South African Boer Republic, he said: "We as young Afrikaners are tired of seeing spiritual traditions and everything that is sacred to the Afrikaner desecrated and degraded by liberal politicians, dissipated academics, and false prophets who hide under the mantel of learning and a false faith—just as Professor Floors van Jaarsveld now, at this symposium, attacks the sanctity of the Afrikaner in his deepest essence. . . . this standpoint draws a line through the significance of the Afrikaner's history and is blasphemous.[12]

The first recorded memorial observance of the covenant vow was in 1865, but it was not until the covenant was renewed at Paardekraal in December 1880—which marked the beginning of armed resistance to the British rule of the Transvaal—that it began to play its mythic role. After the victorious Boer rebellion in 1880–1881 (the "First Boer War"), the covenant was celebrated at Paardekraal in that year and in every subsequent fifth year, and some of Paul Kruger's choicest religiopolitical sentiments were aired on those occasions. It is also in connection with these observances and Kruger's role in them that the idea of the Afrikaners as a chosen people was expressed with seriousness and consistency for the first time.[13]

At Paardekraal in 1881 Kruger stated that God gave them victory at Blood River and at Majuba and Doornkop, that it was he who had given them freedom and a land. Often he warned that his burghers should not think that their own prowess had earned them victory but rather to remember that God had supported them and that "General Jesus" has fought for them, and that their leaders had been mere tools in the divine hand.[14] The debate in the Transvaal turned on

---

[12]*Sunday Times* (Johannesburg), April 1, 1979, as quoted in Thompson, *The Political Mythology of Apartheid*, 213-14.

[13]Thompson, *The Political Mythology of Apartheid*, 169-71.

[14]van Jaarsveld, *The Afrikaner's Interpretation*, 12; and *Die Evolusie van*

whether it was God or good marksmanship that had defeated the British; it did not take into account the glaring deficiency in British generalship and tactics, which clearly contributed as much to the lopsided victory as did good Boer shooting.

The civil religion that sustained the Afrikaners until quite recently was given form, therefore, in the late nineteenth and early twentieth centuries under the impulse of British imperialism and Dopper Calvinism. Dopper Calvinism comes from the theology of Abraham Kuyper (called "Abraham the Mighty," 1837–1920), who presented a religious alternative to the liberal rationalism of the nineteenth-century Calvinism of Holland. In South Africa the Doppers broke away from the Reformed Church of the Transvaal, which had, in turn, broken away from the Cape Dutch Reformed Church to be the church of the trekkers. The Cape church had become English and evangelical through the advent of many Scottish ministers during the nineteenth century, who came as part of a deliberate British strategy to Anglicize the Dutch. Indeed, the most influential figure in the Cape Dutch church during the nineteenth century was Andrew Murray, a Scotsman, and a revivalist evangelical.

There is no need here to go into the theological nuances of differences among these three churches. It is sufficient to note only that the Doppers were and are explicitly Calvinist, with a theology of history including election or chosenness, and a strong emphasis on providence. Hence, to the extent that Calvinism is to be blamed or credited for the South African ideology, it is the Calvinism of Kuyper, not of Calvin or even the Dutch Reformed Church, that is in question. Furthermore, it is understandable that the ideology of separateness should be most strongly advocated by the church that was most sectarian in theology and social situation. Recently, as it became clear that racism was a more influential factor than Calvinism in the politics of the Afrikaners, the Calvinists of Potchefstroom have sought to distance themselves from the government. Today the Afrikaners practice a much more pragmatic than ideological politics, whose basic inspiration is what it in fact has always been, namely, racism.

There are other elements in the Afrikaner myth that are as important as the victimage, victory, and chosenness we have focused on, but since they seem to come from sources essentially other than the Bible we shall only mention them in closing this section. Thompson suggests that "the concept that human 'races' are unassimilable, is the heart of the Afrikaner nationalist mythology, and of the political economy that it endorses."[15] The chief working ingredients of the current mythology are: (1) legitimate authority is not to be questioned; (2) whites are

---

Apartheid, 65-67.

[15]Thompson, *The Political Mythology of Apartheid*, 105.

superior, blacks are inferior; (3) the Afrikaner has a special relationship with God (a biblical element); and (4) South Africa rightfully belongs to the Afrikaner.[16]

Having considered the elements of victimage, victory, and chosenness in the Afrikaner national mythology, all elements that, although they are universally human as attitudes, receive a special support from the biblical record, we turn now to the specific texts that are used to justify Apartheid. In fact, in October 1976 the General Synod of the Dutch Reformed Church approved and accepted a report on the biblical justification for apartheid entitled *Human Relations and the South African Scene in the Light of Scripture*, the English translation of a report entitled, revealingly, *Ras, Volk, en Nasie: Volkerverhoudinge in die Lig van die Skrif (Race, Volk, and Nation . . .).*[17]

Douglas Bax, after an analysis of the report, concludes that although it cites almost fifty texts, it actually bases its case on the five texts that the Dutch Reformed Church has traditionally called on to support the separation of the races: Gen. 1:28, Gen. 11:1-9, Deut. 32:8, Acts 2:5-13, and Acts 17:26.[18] Willem Vorster questions the hermeneutic the report employs, specifically the assumption that the Bible contains universally and eternally valid principles of conduct, and argues for a more modern and more flexible hermeneutic, while Bax argues that even within the guidelines of this questionable hermeneutic the report misunderstands the texts.[19]

To take only the two most glaring instances of misunderstanding, it argues that the Tower of Babel story intends to say that God purposed the diversity of language and culture and that the realization of that diversity was an unfolding of the intention of God in creation expressed in the command to be fruitful and multiply. Bax has no difficulty in establishing, along with the consensus of interpretation, that the confusion of language at Babel is a negative not a positive thing, God's reaction to human pride, not an unfolding of his original purpose in creation. Furthermore, he can point to the hermeneutical and ethical mistake of arguing from what is to what ought to be, from providence to principle. George Edward Moore called this the "naturalistic fallacy" in moral reasoning, and Bax is right to point it out.[20]

---

[16]J. M. du Preez, *Africana Afrikaner: Master Symbols in South African School Textbooks* (Alberton, 1983) 71, as cited in Thompson, *The Political Mythology of Apartheid*, 233.

[17](Cape Town-Pretoria: N. G. Kerk-Uitgewers [Dutch Reformed Church Publishers], 1975).

[18]Douglas Bax, in *Apartheid Is a Heresy*, ed. John W. DeGruchy and Charles Villa-Vicencio (Cape Town: Eerdmans, 1983) 114.

[19]Bax, in *Apartheid is a Heresy*, 94-111.

[20]Bax, in *Apartheid is a Heresy*, 123, 133.

The Tower of Babel is the cardinal text in the Dutch Reformed Church's attempt to provide a biblical justification of Apartheid, followed closely by the two texts from Acts, of which we shall remark on only one. The report argues that the miracle of Pentecost shows that God intends us to hear the gospel in our own languages and that this justifies cultural separation. The miracle of Pentecost, however, is presented as the reversal of the fate of Babel, as different people are brought into the one church by the ability of Peter to communicate with them all, over the barriers of their diversity. So, Acts 2 apparently teaches the opposite of what the report claims.

It is not profitable to discuss each of the passages marshalled in support of racial separation, because of the defective hermeneutical principles on which such a discussion would be based. It is no longer intellectually possible to take texts and passages out of context the way the report does, in order to justify cultural attitudes. Clearly one has to argue from a broader biblical base, as Vorster points out in his review of the report. Nevertheless, it is important to note that the Dutch Reformed Church as recently as 1974 was seeking to provide biblical justification for Apartheid. In 1986 a representative group of Dutch Reformed theologians published a collection of essays repudiating the attempt to find biblical or theological justification for the traditional racial attitude and practice.[21] In some circles it seems, thinking has changed in the last twelve years.

It is only fair to observe that the present leaders of South Africa disavow the term Apartheid, and describe the aims of their policy as "democratic pluralism."[22] One does not need to be a cynic to see that this is yet another description of a situation based on the conviction that the white group, now including the descendants of the British imperialists, should maintain power over its own destiny, and not be subject to a black government. You might call such conviction racist, but in my opinion that would be an oversimplification: there are other important factors such as economics involved, as those who favor a Marxist analysis would readily acknowledge. In any case it is clear that the use of the Bible to support and justify a political or cultural program is fraught with difficulty.

Indeed, the record is so bad, as our brief review of only one among many histories of the misuse of the Bible to justify the actions of national self-interest shows, that one is encouraged to abandon the whole notion of providence, of God acting in history, as the existentialist hermeneutic has done. If one is not willing to abandon the notion of God acting in history—and there do seem to me to be both logical and theological difficulties in the existentialist confinement of God-talk to the realm of the individual—then clearly one must be careful not to keep making the same mistake. This seems to me to be a challenge that faces the

---

[21]J. Kinghorn, ed., *Die N. G. Kerk en Apartheid* (Johannesburg, 1986).
[22]van Jaarsveld, *Did Evolusie van Apartheid*, 2.

theologies of liberation. Do the liberation theologies make the same mistake as the Boers did, of identifying their own group interest with the activity of God in the world? Is it possible to identify certain historical forces as the activity of God without idolizing certain groups (the poor, the oppressed, the blacks, the males, the heterosexuals, the Jews)?

For my own part, I should like to think that the myth of God acting in history need not be abandoned because so many people have misused it so often; "abuse does not prohibit use," is an ancient principle of moral reasoning. Rather we should exercise due care, and especially a clear-eyed self-criticism, whenever we invoke providence.

The Iranian Revolution: Five Frames for Understanding

Michael M. J. Fischer

I am interested in the Islamic form of the Iranian revolution first as part of the sociology and anthropology of the Islamic world, second as part of general questions of comparative sociology about the possibilities for revolution in the late twentieth century, and third as part of general questions about the role of ideologies in relation to changes in class structure. The late twentieth century provides quite different conditions for revolutionary initiatives than did the early modern world of Europe (the time of the English, American, and French revolutions). In part this is because of the hegemonic force of the modern inter-dependent world economy. The current Islamic resurgence is perhaps parallel in some ways to the upheaval in the Buddhist world during the 1950s and 1960s.

Let me suggest two preliminary thoughts about the role of religion in sociopolitical context. Religion is a kind of language or idiom and, like all languages, it is used as a medium of debate, dispute, and conflict. It is never just a list of dogmas that can be looked up in a canonic source such as the Qur'an; interpretation and point of view are always necessary components. Moreover, religious interpretations differ in sociologically patterned ways. Think, for instance, of the sociology of Protestantism—the best-developed area of the sociology of religion—and the correlation between class and denomination. In New England, Unitarians and Congregationalists tend to be in the upper strata of society, Methodists and Presbyterians at the next level, Baptists and Pentecos-tals below that. So too, there are rough class-linked differences in the interpre-tations of Islam. Differences in religious interpretation can provide an important tool for comprehending critical social cleavages within a society.

In the following pages, I want to suggest five frames for thinking about the current Islamic revolution in Iran, the most dramatic example of the recent Islamic currents of renewal. The first two frames are historical: first, we need to place this revolution within the context of five generations of Islamic movements over the past two centuries; and second, we need to place it within the history of Iran itself over the past century. The third frame reminds us that revolutions have a processual form—they are not events, but unfold over time—and to ask whether this revolution fits into the pattern of other revolutions. Fourth, we need to consider the Shi'ite form which served as the mobilizing idiom of this revolution. Finally, we need to consider the social agendas of the revolution.

The high drama of religious revolt has marked the turn of the fifteenth century of the Islamic era. The overthrow of the Pahlavi dynasty on behalf of an Islamic republic in Iran; the seizure of the grand mosque in Mecca by anti-Saudi dissidents in the name of a *mahdi* (or "messiah"); the assassination of President Anwar Sadat, a series of armed confrontations with the state, and militant withdrawals (*hijra*, patterned after the tactical withdrawal of Muhammad from Mecca to Medina) by fundamentalist groups in Egypt; the millenarian revolt, resulting in bloodbath in Kano, Nigeria; and even the attempted assassination of the pope by a member of the Turkish National Action Party, possibly hired by the Russians under the cover of defense of Islam against the imperialist, Westernizing, Christian "crusades"—all have focused attention on painful social discontents in the Islamic world.

What these revolts seem to have in common is their class basis and their traditionalizing, but nontraditional, ideology. These traditionalizing ideologies may claim to be a return to pure, original Islam, but are in fact responses to a modern situation and would have looked quite out of place thirteen or even three centuries ago.

Middle Eastern intellectuals describe the development of ideologies in the Islamic world over the past two centuries as progressive changes in response to challenges from the West, with various initiatives that did not work, ranging from liberalism in the 1930s to socialism in the 1950s. These failures, Moroccan social historian Abdullah Laroui suggests, produced a crisis: Middle Eastern intellectuals seemed to face a choice between two unpalatable alternatives. On the one hand, they could attempt to speak the language of the masses (Islam) in an effort at political mobilization. The problem here, according to Laroui, is that religious language is not tailored to modern politics and, at a certain point leads to obscurantism. It is fine for mobilizing, less appropriate for analysis of strategic moves.

On the other hand, intellectuals can turn to revolutionary Marxism. The problem here is that since this is not the language of the masses, it leads to isolation of the intellectuals from the masses and the need to develop a disciplined cadre of activists. Should this cadre be able to seize power (as happened in South Yemen and more messily in Afghanistan), then the more backward the country is at the time of the coup, the more totalitarian the succeeding regime will have to be. Laroui and other intellectuals have posed the dilemmas in intellectual terms. As an anthropologist, I see them as not merely intellectual or strategic dilemmas, but as fundamentally linked to shifts in the class structure of most Middle Eastern countries.

An important question is why intellectuals and politicians in the 1930s were able to take a public position that Islam was what kept the Muslim world backward, while no public figure dared to take such a secularist stand in the

1970s. The quick answer is that there has been a massive demographic shift in many Middle Eastern countries toward ruralization of the urban political arenas. The rural folk who come to the city bring with them their traditional styles of religion, and in the city they become politicized. While they cannot control or direct politics, they can constrain politics through strikes and demonstrations. A few statistics may indicate the dimensions of the problem. Between 1960 and 1979, Cairo doubled in size from four to eight million people, without commensurate increases in infrastructure and services; similar growth affected other major cities of the Middle East, including Tehran.

As important as simple growth are the bottlenecks in the structure of opportunity. In the 1970s, some 300,000 high school graduates took the university entrance examination, but only some 30,000 places were available at the universities. In Cairo, the ratio of males to females at the top three universities in 1952 was 13–1; by 1975 the ratio was 2–1, and the overall number of students had increased fivefold. The consequences are deeply upsetting for young people from provincial and relatively traditional families who are suddenly thrown into the anonymous, fast-paced big-city life: traditional patterns of behavioral propriety are put under tremendous strain at these big universities, and many students react by withdrawing into the safety of tradition. Women who went without veils in the provincial towns might now veil in the big city. Young members of the Muslim Brotherhood of both sexes interviewed in jail said that among their deep concerns was to find a pure member of the opposite sex.

Let us review the five generations of Islamic response to the challenges of Westernization and modernization (see chart 1). Each generation has left a positive legacy that could be incorporated by the following generations; each generation also experienced flaws and failures that limited its own effectiveness. During the eighteenth and early nineteenth centuries there was what may be called a movement of puritanical religious reform. This was the age of the Wahhābis who eventually created the state of Saudi Arabia, the Sanūsi who similarly provided the backbone of a state in Libya, the Fulani movements in West Africa, the Mahdi of the Sudan who was briefly able to expel the British, and in Iran, the Usulis who were to become the dominant school of clerics to the present day.

The four key characteristics of this "generation" of Islamic ideology were: (a) the effort to purify Islam of superstitious accretions such as shrine worship and mindless ritualism; (b) the free use of *ijtihād*, a disciplined form of reasoning by which new problems could be submitted to theological solutions; (c) the primacy of sociomoral issues over metaphysical-philosophical ones, and (d) political militancy. All of these slogans and efforts are still visible today. That early generation, however, was criticized by its children for lack of modern technological skills, and for too quickly jettisoning the critical intellectual skills of traditional scholarship.

The second generation followed at the turn of the twentieth century, initiating what is often called modernist reformism. This was the period of constitutional experiments in Egypt, Turkey, Iran, and Iraq. It is the era of Sayyid Jamāl ad-Din al-Afghāni, of Muhammad 'Abduh in Egypt, Sir Sayyid Ahmad Khan in India, and Sir Muhammad Iqbāl in Pakistan. The modernists operated under the conviction that Islam was fully compatible with science and democracy. There were efforts to reinterpret Islamic terminology to fit liberal ideas. Thus *shūrā*, which traditionally meant "consultation," now came to mean parliamentary democracy; *ijmā*, which traditionally meant "consensus of the learned," now was equated with public opinion. It was a period of experimentation with secularization, of separation of state and religion, the time of Kemal Atatürk's (1881–1938) modernization of Turkey and Reza Shah Pahlavi's (1878–1944) similar efforts in Iran. Perhaps the leading defects of this generation were the underestimation of the political economy of dependency: simple adoption of Western education and constitutional forms would not be sufficient to catch up with European economic, technological, and military superiority, and a sense of elitism pitted the upper class and educated middle-class modernizers against the lower class. (They knew best, they assumed, and would force the backward lower classes to change.)

The 1930s saw the peak of secularist, Westernizing, and constitutionalist faith. Both politicians (Atatürk, Reza Shah) and intellectuals (Taha Hussein in Egypt, Sādeq Hedāyat and Ahmad Kasravi in Iran) openly spoke of Islam as keeping their countries backward. Atatürk's reforms were the most drastic: outlawing traditional garb, having the state control prayer leaders, banning Sufi orders, imposing the Latin script (even for a time having the call to prayer in Turkish instead of Arabic). But the 1930s also saw the rise of anticolonialist movements incorporating fundamentalist reactions to the failures of the modernists and appealing to the frustrations of the increasing numbers of migrants from rural areas into the urban lower classes. The success of Japan in 1905 against Russia, and the rise of the Bolsheviks and the Nazis suggested that the ways of Western Europe were neither invincible nor necessarily the way of the future.

This was the period of the founding in Egypt of the Muslim Brotherhood, which grew into the second largest political party, with 1,200,000 members by 1952. Led by déclassé intellectuals and professionals (the educated who could find jobs commensurate with their capabilities), the Muslim Brotherhood's rank and file were largely the rural migrants who had become urban workers. On the Indo-Pakistani subcontinent, Abu al-Ala Mawdudi's (1903–1979) Jama'at-i Islami was a parallel movement. In Iran, there was the smaller Fida'iyyan-i Islam, led by Mujtaba Nawwab Safavi (1923–1955, now honored on a stamp of the Islamic Republic of Iran): in 1946, the Fida'iyyan assassinated Ahmad Kasravi as well as two prime ministers, but was suppressed in 1955 with the execution of its major leaders. The enduring legacy of this generation of neofundamentalists was the development of political organization and an Islamic-language populism that called for a single leader (an "amir" ["emir"] or "imam"), for consultation rather than democracy, and an activist Islam freed of the dominance by clerics interested only in ritual. Despite the involvement of key clerics, these movements were led by committed laymen. The failings of the neofundamentalists were their continued devaluation of historical skills and their totalitarian attitudes towards nonmembers.

The 1950s and 1960s saw the growth of what may loosely be called Islamic socialisms: Gamal Nasser (1918–1970) in Egypt, the Destour party in Tunisia, the Ba'th in Syria and Iraq, Zulfikar Ali Bhutto (1928–1979) a bit later in Pakistan, and the White Revolution of Muhammad Reza Shah Pahlavi (1919–1980) in Iran. This was the beginning of serious democratic mass politics, responding to the demands of the politicized masses, recognizing the responsibility of governments for economic reconstruction and social welfare, and taking full account of the unequal trade relations and dependency structures of the world economy which had vitiated the liberals' hopes. The strategy—like that of Germany and Japan before them—was to use the state to coordinate economic and social modernization. On the debit side, the need for control easily decayed into corrupt authoritarianisms.

The Islamic resurgence or renewal of the 1970s and 1980s thus came as a series of reactions against these corrupt authoritarianisms, constituting a search for moral identity in the language pioneered by the neofundamentalists of the 1930s. The problems, of course, are those of inability to live up to Islamic ideals of justice (corruption by power) and lack of clarity about fundamentalist-versus-modernist programs.

It should be clear from this brief and schematic review that Islam is not a single ideology but a language used in rich and diverse ways, to articulate varying ideologies. Muslims themselves are ambivalent about the relative weight to assign to Islamic rhetoric, as (1) a decayed cultural legacy about which the masses can be reeducated by *mujaddid* ("renewers"); (2) a vehicle for anti-imperialist nationalism (*ta'asob* is a key slogan word, meaning "fanaticism" perjoratively but "tenacity of moral purpose" positively); (3) a language of class conflict (against Western-educated, secularized elites—the *taqhuti*, or "idolators" of materialism, in the rhetoric of Iranian revolution—and against hidebound conservative clerics, the *ulama-yi gishri* who teach a *din-i khoshk* or dry, lifeless religion); (4) a cynical tool of elites' foreign policy and domestic efforts to mobilize symbols of legitimacy; or (5) an irrationalist force against which vigilance must be vigorous.

II

We shall now turn more directly to Iran. It is certainly possible to apply the five-generation schema to the history of Iran (see chart 2). But for our purposes it may suffice to remind ourselves of two basic things: that the 1977–1979 revolution did not come from nowhere—it has a history almost a century long; and that it is a revolutionary process that needs to be seen as an unfolding temporal structure, not as a unified event.

The 1977–1979 revolution is not the first, but the fifth time since 1872 that an alliance between secular reformers and religious leaders has forced either major policy change on the government or indeed change in the form of the government itself. For the secularist middle-class faction of the revolution, the most important predecessors were the second and fourth generations by the schema of section 1, the Constitutional Revolution of 1905–1911 and the effort in 1952–1953 under Mohammad Mosaddeq (1880–1967) to replace the monarchy with a republic and to seize control of Iranian resources. For these middle classes, the 1977–1979 revolution was supposed to be the completion of a bourgeois revolution that would transfer political power into their hands.

Although the 1977–1979 revolution was the fifth time a powerful alliance between similar forces was formed, it was the first time the religious leaders were able to seize control of such an alliance. This was due in large part to the Pahlavi monarchy's success in suppressing open political discourse during the 1960s and 1970s, so that Islam became the umbrella language of protest for all factions, however different their objectives. This gave special prominence to the voice of the clerics who were masters of Islamic moral discourse and could speak for the interests of more powerful sectors of society. It is indeed an old political tactic of merchants in the bazaar to fund clerical speakers, so as to deflect attention from their own direct political interests, while indirectly furthering such interests.

This time it was not only the merchants who allowed the clerics to speak for them. For the religious leaders, the 1977–1979 revolution was also a third revolution: in their eyes the 1905–1911 Constitutional Revolution had been betrayed by the secularists, and Ayatollah Abu al-Qasim Kashani (initially an ally of Mosaddeq) had been betrayed by Mosaddeq; hence the determination of the religious leaders not to be sold out again in this revolution. This is one reason offered for the insistence on placing a *faqih* or religious expert over the officials of the government, and a Council of Guardians as well as a Supreme Judicial Council in the new constitution. The 1905 Constitution had a clause empowering a panel of five *mujtahids* (experts in Islamic jurisprudence) to veto any proposed legislation not in accord with Islam. But this clause had been ignored, and the Ayatollah Ruhollah Khomeini faction of the 1977–1979 revolution wanted to make sure that such betrayal would not occur again.

Other factions of the 1977–1979 revolution had other visions of what the revolution was supposed to be. There were important clerics such as the more liberal Ayatollah Mohammad Kazim Shariatmadari and the more leftist Sayyid Mahmud Taleqani who opposed the new constitution proposed by the Khomeini faction. The secular Marxists, and the Tudeh party (Moscow-linked communists) in particular, thought there would be a two-stage revolution, in which first the liberals and the mullahs would seize control, and after their ability to govern had collapsed, conditions would be ripe for a marxist or communist coup. The Islamic leftists, the Mujāhidin-i Khalq (People's Mujāhidin Organization of Iran), after 1982 the most important remaining opposition faction to Khomeini's Islamic Republican Party, attracted a constituency of progressive Muslim political thinkers and actors, all of whom, however, were outmaneuvered by the Khomeini faction. Their lineage is grounded in the activities of laymen such as Engineer Mehdi Bazargan and clerics such as Sayyid Mahmud Taleqani in the 1960s and especially the 1970s lay leader, 'Ali Shariati (1933–1977), who contemplated the renewal of Islam in the context of the modern technological world and who launched a major critique against the monopoly of religion by the clerics.

In other words, it is of primary importance to remember that political alliances such as the revolutionary coalition of 1977–1979 have a long history in Iran. To understand the fate of changing balance within these alliances, one needs to look at both a class-linkage of different religious ideologies or formulations and at the dynamics of the revolutionary process itself.

The 1977–1979 revolution fits remarkably well the schematic pattern of revolution analyzed by Crane Brinton in his *Anatomy of Revolution* (1938). Brinton drew his schema from a comparison of the four great democratic, popular revolutions of England, America, France, and Russia. In all these cases, and in Iran as well, the initial conditions were those of a society with a rising prosperity and standard of living that suddenly encountered a severe recession or depression, placing a financial squeeze upon the government. The government reacted by taxing the leading sectors of society, thereby turning what had been its primary social base of support into part of the opposition. These leading sectors joined an oppositional ideology that saw the government as illegitimate. (In Iran, of course, this oppositional ideology was Shi'ism.) The attribution of illegitimacy to the government in turn paralyzed the operation of the government, blocking it from using the means of force normally available to it, and allowing the first phase of the revolution to proceed with an ease unanticipated by the revolutionary coalition. This first phase, the sweeping away of the old regime, is then followed by a stage of dual sovereignty (a public government, with a private power cabal behind the scenes), a reign of terror, and a series of crises which gradually narrow the social base of the revolution. Finally there is a third state, thermidor, consisting of the long painful period of reconstruction.

In the Iranian case, one should distinguish the long-term structural causes of the revolution and the short-term ones. The long-term causes are manifold, but for our purposes can conveniently be collapsed into two: unbalanced economic growth (with support being given to large-scale enterprises at the expense of smaller and traditional enterprises), and refusal to allow the gradual increasing participation of wider segments of society in the political arena (oil revenues, in effect, made the state financially independent of its own population, and this in turn translated into indifference or inability to gather feedback from or negotiate among the interests of the various segments of the society). Radicals of the 1960s and 1970s predicted that Iran would blow up in the 1990s, when it was estimated that Iran would run out of easily recoverable oil reserves. That the revolution came much sooner has to do with the short-term causes, and these fit Crane Brinton's model quite well.

In 1973 oil prices increased tremendously. This led to reckless spending so that within eighteen months Iran had become overcommitted, suffered serious cash flow problems, and had become a major borrower on the international capital markets. Inflation followed. An initial construction boom increased the flow of rural migrants into the cities where excellent wages could be earned for simple manual labor. Problems with bottlenecks in the transportation and supply systems in conjunction with inflation, caused the implementation of recessionary policies. The first to be hurt were construction workers, who were laid off and remained as an unemployed mass in Tehran and other big cities. But almost all sectors had serious complaints. The swollen bureaucracy chafed under a three-year wage freeze during the period of high inflation. Since 1975 the government had complained that consumer prices were due to the illegitimate markups by middle men, making the bazaar a scapegoat for the inflation. The business community complained of capricious changes in the laws allowing foreign capital investment and mandating the sale of public shares. As early as 1975 many businessmen were already stripping their assets and moving their money abroad. At the same time as these economic pressures mounted, there was political tightening. A new party, the Rastakhiz Party (National Resurrection Party), was formed, and all Iranians were intimidated into joining.

In other words, when the revolution arrived it was not simply an explosion of fanatics and powerful mullahs. On the contrary, it was a revolution by all parts of the society against a repressive government. The first stage began in the summer and fall of 1977. At that point President Carter's human rights initiatives encouraged Iran's writers and lawyers to demand to be allowed to form public organizations. Slum dwellers were bulldozed from their homes in south Tehran. In the fall Khomeini's elder son mysteriously died; many thought he had died at the hands of the secret police, a suspicion exacerbated by not being allowed to publicly mourn him. There was an ill-advised attack on Khomeini in a government-controlled newspaper and in January 1978, demonstrators in Qum were killed. This initiated a cycle of demonstrations spaced forty days apart. For Muslims, the fortieth day is an important memorial date after death and as deaths of each demonstration were memorialized, new clashes between government forces and demonstrators brought new deaths. These demonstrations spread to cities throughout Iran. On August 19, the Rex Cinema in Abadan was torched; 430

people were trapped inside and died: this radicalized the revolutionary movement. A second turning point came on September 8, when troops opened fire on a demonstration in Tehran, the day after a massive march that ended the month Ramadān. Demonstrations increased in size during the following months, with millions turning out on the ninth and tenth of Muharram (anniversary of the martyrdom of Husayn—see below—and a key Islamic holy day), December 19-20. Violence increased throughout December and in January the shah was finally eased out (he left the country on January 16). On February 1 Khomeini triumphantly returned from exile. Important events of 1978 included not only the street demonstrations, but strikes by such critical sectors of the economy as oil workers, bank employees, and public utilities employees.

The second stage—dual sovereignty—followed: a public government was formed under Engineer Mehdi Bazargan, with Houstonian Ibrahim Yazdi as Foreign Minister; behind the scenes a Revolutionary Council made its own decisions. This dual sovereignty lasted until the hostage crisis of November 1979. A reign of terror was part of this second stage. It began with executions of generals and members of SAVAK (secret police). Bazargan attempted to speak out against the escalation of executions as early as March, but the executions seemed to operate as a way of political muscle flexing by certain factions of the revolution. Cycles of executions can be correlated with political competition between factions. The great fury of executions began after the bombing of the Islamic Republican Party headquarters in June 1980, when "seventy-two" IRP leaders were killed. Some 2,000 were executed in the next four months.

Through the competition of political factions, the base of the revolution began to narrow. The liberals were forced out and dual sovereignty ended by November 1979. At this time the American embassy was taken and its staff held hostage. It was a spectacular device which worked to ward off the efforts of the liberals to reestablish relations with the United States (and thereby short-circuit the revolution, or so the activists thought) and to ensure the passage of the new constitution which had been facing widespread opposition. Bani-Sadr was forced out in June 1980, and the next year saw a concerted campaign against the Islamic leftists (Mujahidin). The conservative-liberal Ayatollah Shariatmadari was put under house arrest in April 1982. During December 1983–January 1984, the Tudeh Party was rounded up. As the Islamic Republican Party consolidated control, the most interesting political arena was the struggle of factions within the party. But before we turn to that, or rather to the associated agendas for the Revolution, we need to slow down and retrace the momentum of the revolution in terms of the Shi'ite ideology that was used to mobilize it.

III

Shi'ism, the branch of Islam to which the vast majority of Iranians belong, distinguishes itself from Sunni Islam, the branch of Islam to which most of the

Arab world belongs, originally through a dispute over the succession to the Prophet Muhammad through his cousin and son-in-law 'Ali ibn Abi Tālib, to 'Ali's sons Hasan and Husayn, and then through the line of the Twelve Imams (spiritual leaders succeeding Muhammad through 'Ali). (The twelfth Imam did not die, but withdrew from this world and will return at the end of time as the Mahdi or messiah.) Sunnis say that the succession should go, as it historically did, through a consultative-elective process. Muhammad was succeeded by four caliphs—Abu Bakr, 'Umar, 'Uthman, and 'Ali. After 'Ali, the political leadership of the new Islamic empire went to the Umayyad Dynasty, centered in Damascus, and led by Mu'awiyah and his son Yazid. Husayn, the grandson of the prophet, contested the leadership of Yazid in the Battle of Karbalā'.

Husayn was martyred on the tenth of Muharram in the Battle of Karbalā', and his story is central to Shi'ite notions of identity and sense of purpose. It is known in all its details by every Iranian. Each year it is reenacted in "passion plays" and parade floats: how after the hajj (annual pilgrimage to Mecca), during which Yazid tried to have Husayn killed, the people of al-Kufa in southern Iraq asked Husayn to come and lead them in a revolt against the tyrannical Yazid; how Husayn set out with seventy-two loyal followers; how by the time he reached southern Iran the Kufans had been co-opted by Yazid; how the seventy-two were encircled by the Syrian forces; how in the desert heat they were inhumanely denied water; and how each of them was martyred. The stories are told in rich, tear-jerking detail: 'Abbas, the half-brother of Husayn, slipped through the enemy lines to the Euphrates to get water for the thirsty women and children; he was caught as he returned; his hand carrying the goatskin was cut by a Syrian sword, so he grabbed the waterskin by his other hand; it was slashed, so he grabbed the skin with his teeth; the skin was punctured and he suffered martyrdom. Even more dolorous is the story of Husain's three-year-old daughter, who cried and cried for her father and would not sleep: "What have I done, " she cried, "that my father does not come to me?" Finally, when Husayn's head was brought to her on a platter, she looked at it, was quiet, and died. These stories are not only enacted and retold during the month of Muharram, but are reference frames for sermons throughout the year.

The story of Karbala' is the key Shi'ite paradigm of existential tragedy: In this world evil usually triumphs over good and justice, yet there is a need for Muslims to fight for justice. Husayn knew he would die, but he went to Karbala' to witness for the truth. He wanted his martyrdom to shock people into recognizing and returning to the just cause. Tears shed at the commemoration of Husayn's martyrdom are partly over the corruption of Islam imposed by the Umayyids and their Sunni followers, and partly because Husayn will act as an intercessor for his partisans at their judgment in the hereafter. Mainly, however, the lamentation is rooted in a remorseful identification with the people of al-Kufa who allowed evil to triumph, and in the spirit of rededication to the fight for the values of Husayn. Throughout the 1960s and 1970s, preachers identified the arch-tyrant Yazid with the shah, and the goals of Islamic justice with such figures as Ayatollah Khomeini.

This political inflection of the Karbala' story was a powerful device, not only for honing political consciousness in the prerevolutionary era, but for mobilizing demonstrators during the revolution. Remember the young men dressed in shrouds who positioned themselves in the vanguard between ordinary demonstrators and the shah's troops. During Muharram 1978 (December–January 1978–1979), as the first phase of the revolution came to its emotional climax, Khomeini still in Paris called on people to abandon the traditional processions of flagellation and mourning for Husayn, and to honor Husayn instead by marching in the largest political demonstrations Tehran could muster. A year later, during Muharram 1979, there should have been thanksgiving for the overthrow of the shah, but the United States, by announcing it would allow the entry of the shah for medical treatment handed Khomeini a powerful device for getting his new constitution. "How," Khomeini thundered, "is this year different from all other years? Last year we faced the offspring of the mother of corruption [the shah] but this year we face the mother of corruption herself" [American imperialism and the fear that the U.S. would bring back the shah].

We have seen that the first phase of the revolution was carried by a coalition, that mullahs could speak in behalf of factions with differing objectives, and that Shi'ite Islam served as an umbrella language. In this context the Karbala' story could serve as a powerful umbrella device for unifying demonstrations. But we also need to see how Shi'ism is used by different portions of the coalition and by different strata of the society.

Before the revolution and during the revolution's first phase, the dramatic enactments during Muharram of the Karbala' story were associated with village and working-class neighborhoods. It was a colorful, community-organized religious idiom. It was ambivalently viewed by the more learned members of the clergy, who thought it smacked a bit too much of idolatry—too much passion and too little reason.

The traditional middle classes (the clergy, the old-style landowners and bazaar merchants) practiced a different style of religion, focused on weekly discussion groups that were rationalistic, argumentative, and more concerned with a social code of morality. Islam, they insisted, requires each Muslim to think for himself or herself; only when a Muslim is no longer competent may he or she turn to someone more learned for guidance. These "more learned ones" are, of course, the clergy. They formed a hierarchy, at the top of which were a series of ayatollahs who were not merely legal experts but who also administered religious taxes which they redistributed in such a manner as to run and control the religious institution. This financial independence of the clergy is one of their greatest sources of strength (one that the new Islamic Republican Party wanted to centralize under its own control). For this traditional set of middle classes, religion was not merely a personal code of ethics, but a socially enforced code for creating a just world. It included a legal system with rules of evidence and witnesses.

One often hears from yellow journalists about the severe penalties of Islamic law: the stoning of an adulteress, the cutting off of the hand of a thief. Less often does one hear that, to impose such a severe penalty on a thief, twenty-two separate conditions of evidence must be met; or that, technically, for an adulteress to be stoned there must be four witnesses to the act (hence, in the hands of a liberal judge, it is a penalty that could almost never be imposed). Islamic law includes a set of economic rules as well: individual rights to property are protected, but ultimately all property belongs to God or the community. The individual has usufruct privileges as long as the property is productive and taxes are paid so as to redistribute some of the inequalities of wealth that inevitably build up. The ultimate ownership by God and the community provides a rationale for the regulation of trade relations as well: there are rules of fair price and rules against biting usury (even—in conservative interpretations—against all interest entirely).

A third interpretation of Shi'ism was that of the new middle and upper classes with secular education. For these people, religion was a more individualistic and privatized ethic. Often, such people were interested in mystical traditions of Islam. They rejected both excessive ritualism and the old tax, judicial, and economic rules elaborated by the clergy as outdated, as nonessential to the spirit of Islam.

Finally, a fourth, critical interpretation was that of modernizers such as Ali Shariati, S. Mahmud Taleqani, and Engineer Mehdi Bazargan who attempted to find a mediating path between the traditional middle class and the individualized secular middle-class interpretations. They wished to reform and to renew Islam—possibly even without the clergy—so as to provide a moral support for a modern technological society. Ali Shariati, in particular, appealed to the newly literate youth of Iran to help him recover such an Islam. Being literate, this new generation had no need, and no right to depend upon the clergy to tell them what Islam required. They could read the old books for themselves, and they could reason for themselves. Shariati's appeal was enormously infectious, and one the clergy has treated cautiously. The Islamic Republican Party is attempting to claim Shariati's legacy for itself and to reedit his works in a manner helpful to its own objective. The Mujahidin is attempting to preserve Shariati's legacy as a source of opposition to the Islamic Republican Party.

These four interpretations of Shi'ism, and their associated social strata, provide a simplified way of understanding the struggle over the definition of what an Islamic Republic of Iran should be. For more detailed understandings of the struggle in the current phase of the revolution, one must turn to the factional struggles within the Islamic Republican Party and especially to the social agendas being proposed for the revolution. The factions themselves are somewhat shifting and difficult to chart, though they have some interesting ideological forms resonant still with the ideological battles of the nineteenth century.

The Hojjatiyya faction took the conservative nineteenth-century position that the world will be renewed only after it has fallen into corruption. It will be renewed by the mahdi, and one cannot force the pace. Indeed, to do so is blasphemous. Members of this faction went so far as to question Khomeini's claim that he is a representative of the imam or mahdi. This faction only paid lip service to the export of the revolution, and was opposed to the notion of a unitary *faqih* (Islamic law expert) as authoritative leader of the community. The dominant Maktabi faction, by contrast, took up the cry of the Shaikhis and the Babis of the nineteenth century: one cannot wait for the Mahdi, but must prepare the way; revolution will help precipitate the return of the Mahdi, and it must be exported; there should be a unitary *faqih*. Of key importance for institution building are such Maktabi notions as the transformation of the consciousness of the masses, an enforceable authoritative set of interpretations of Islam which are *maktabi* (by the Book as interpreted by the *faqih* or party), and the absence of class conflict or interest-group politics since an Islamic society is *tawhidi* ("one," that is, classless).

IV

The social agendas of the revolution are of course still being fought over. But one can at least construct a series of questions about the political system, economic policy, and social policy. Let us first consider the political system.

Initially, the slogans of the revolution in 1977–1978 were to implement the 1905 Constitution. First, there was a demand to allow Parliament to be more than a rubber stamp for the shah's programs, and to implement the clause allowing five mujtahids to veto legislation that conflicted with Islam. Second, there was a call to reform the judicial system and allow open trials and due process. Third, there was a call for political pluralism, decentralization, and regional autonomy, particularly in allowing education in languages other than Persian and in allowing greater freedom for the local administration of revenues.

With the radicalization of the revolution during 1979–1981, a new Islamic constitution replaced the 1905 Constitution. Khomeini laid stress on swift justice, criticizing the graft in long trials, and the ability of criminals to be released on technicalities. Criminals need no defense lawyers, he repeatedly insisted, despite the stress in Shi'ism on its own due-process procedures. Although he criticized democratic elections as mindless popularity contests, Khomeini was forced to respect the form of electoral processes. The Islamic Republican Party in large part simply seized the existing state, and added to it parallel institutions under its own aegis. Thus, the Revolutionary Guards became a parallel military force, and revolutionary committees were set up in ministries and economic enterprises.

The Maktabi faction was very much opposed to any decentralization. It was as insistent as was the shah on Persian as the single language of government and education. The establishment of a new legal system has been slow. Much of the workings of the court system in the early postrevolutionary years must be considered revolutionary justice rather than Islamic justice, and the government admitted its need for trained lawyers.

Slowly the Islamic Republic consolidated itself. There have been regular elections. A parliamentary structure has been set up, overseen by a Council of Guardians (six mujtahids and six lawyers) as well as by the *faqih* (Khomeini, succeeded by Ali Khamenei). A party structure was established—despite the assassination of more than eighty of its leaders in June 1980—with a politburo, central committee, central committee secretariat, and military (Revolutionary Guards) and paramilitary (Basij) units. A far-reaching ideological campaign was instituted, including a purging of the universities, utilization of prisons for reeducation, calls on children to turn in their parents for antistate activities, and use of the Hajj and international conferences as forums for spreading the message of the new republic. Struggle for control of these institutions continues.

In the economic sphere, the original slogans of the revolution concerned the reduction of oil production, so as to more effectively utilize its revenue to stimulate other domestic economic production, and reorientation of trade so as to break out of dependency relations with the West, especially the United States. Iran lowered its oil production from the six million barrels a day it produced before the revolution to between two and three million barrels a day, and was able to maintain this production despite the war with Iraq. It shifted the pattern of trade, reducing its exports to developed countries from 88% in 1977 to 74% in 1983. It expanded its markets in Sri Lanka, Malaysia, Brazil, Turkey, and India. Trade with India doubled, trade with Turkey went up from $41 million in 1977 to $774 million in 1982. Trade relations with Japan returned to near-prerevolutionary levels by 1983 (some $2 billion). One-third of its imports came from Germany, Japan, and Italy. There were efforts to settle claims with the United States; in 1982 the U.S. exported some $200 million worth of wheat, rice, and manufactured goods to Iran, buying in return 1.8 million barrels of Iranian oil for its strategic reserves. There have been various negotiations to get economic projects going again. The Russian-built steel mill outside Isfahan opened a second furnace in 1984. Yugoslavs helped put the Sar Chesmeh copper mines back into production. Japan continued construction on a petrochemical complex. There is talk about completing two nuclear power plants that were 85% and 70% complete at the time of the revolution. Banks have been nationalized, and foreign trade has been centralized. New land reform legislation has been debated repeatedly, if somewhat inconclusively, by parliament.

As in the political sphere, so in economic policy much remains to be worked out. The war with Iraq created shortages, need for rationing, and fluctuations in trade policy depending on a tightrope negotiation between sound management of foreign reserves and placating of consumer demand. There are antiprofiteering squads, as there were under the shah, now called *ansar ul-allah* ("helpers of God"), who harass and regulate shopkeepers and merchants. There have been a series of industrial strikes (as little reported as under the shah) over broken promises for higher pay, rehiring fired workers, and casting aspersions on the workers as troublemakers.

In social policy, women's rights and the position of minorities have been two contested arenas over the course of the revolution. During the first phase of the revolution, women's rights became an important component of the campaign for general civil rights. As the liberals were beginning to be pushed aside after the return of Khomeini, there were several marches and counterdemonstrations in which women's rights remained a last open battle for the liberal program. Since then the age of permitted marriage for women has been lowered from sixteen to thirteen, coeducation has been abolished, dress codes established, the middle-class feminist movement driven underground (or abroad), and the rules for polygamy eased. Yet there is also new legislation making it easier (under contract law, rather than family law, so as to circumvent conservative opinions on the latter) for women to obtain divorces and support. In the area of minority rights, the first phase of the revolution was remarkably protective of non-Muslims and non-Shi'ite Muslims. Since then, non-Muslims have been driven from public sector jobs; even non-Muslim schools now have Muslim principals and teachers. Armenian schools have been closed because their teachers refused to teach religion classes in Persian rather than Armenian. Bahā'is are subject to a campaign of constant harassment, their leaders imprisoned, tortured and executed, often on bogus charges of being spies.

A government has been consolidated, but political, social, and economic agendas have not yet been fully worked out. There is still considerable political competition occurring within the forces of the revolution. It is impossible to tell how much active and passive resistance there is to the government. One hears jokes about people asking for American rice but fearing to name the imperialist satan, and so asking for the *bereng-i marq bar amrika* ("death-to-American rice"), an indication that a long tradition of coping with repressive politics is not likely to be dead. The credible showing Iran kept up in the war against Iraq is an indication that Iranian nationalism remains strong.

Iran remains a fascinating exemplar of change in the modern world. In the 1970s Iran served as a principal model for modernization theory. Here was a case of a third-world country that had the best chance, so one thought, to break into the industrial first world, because it was a case where the constraint of capital had been removed. In the 1980s Iran served as a major case for thinking about what happens under conditions of demographic explosion, economic strain, and social change for a population with strong cultural traditions that feels oppressed by an alien culture and world economy, and that attempts to use its traditional religious resources as a vehicle of moral protest. An important part of what is at issue is the reconstruction of a meaningful world in which people do not feel themselves devalued by more powerful outside forces, and in which they can feel proud of their identity and in control of their own destiny.

Many ugly things take place in revolutions, yet one cannot but hope and wish the Iranian people well in their painful struggle. They are in the midst of a dynamic process the results of which are as yet very unclear. To monitor and make sense of this process we need to continue to ask the kinds of questions I hope I have suggested in the five frameworks posed above, frameworks that take account of generations of Islamic response to Westernization, of the history of Iranian revolutions, of the structural pattern of revolutions, of the dynamics of Shi'ism and of the social agendas being contested and proposed.

Chart 1. Contributions and Failings of the Five Generations

	Enduring Contributions	Failings
Puritanical religious reformism (premodern fundamentalism—18th–19th centuries)	Ijtihad Sociopolitical engagements	Loss of old scholarly historical and evaluative skills. Lack of new technocratic skills.
Modernist reformism (Afghani, Abduh, Sir Sayyid Ahmad Khan, Ataturk, Iqbal—early 20th century)	Science and technology Democracy	Underestimation of the political economy of dependency. Elitism vis-à-vis the lower classes.
Neofundamentalists (Muslim Brotherhood, Maududi's *Jamiat-i Islam*—1930s, 1940s	Political organization Populism (ademocratic)	Continued devaluation of historical skills. Totalitarian (antiplurist attitude toward nonmembers).
Islamic socialism (Nasser, Destour, Ba'th, Bhutto—post-World War II	Economic reconstruction Social Welfare	Need for dictatorial means: decay into corrupt authoritarianism.
Islamic Resurgence of the 1970s, 1980s	Leverage against corruption Search for moral identity	Inability to live up to Islamic ideals of justice (corruption). Lack of clarity about fundamentalist versus modernist program.

Chart 2. Clerical Struggles in Iran

Generation (1-5)	Internal Factions (a vs b vs c)	State-Clergy Relations	No. of Seminary Students
Safavid Dynasty (1501–1722) a. activist, dominance-seeking immigrant clergy (Majlesi) vs b. native gentry, tolerant, philosophically catholic Afghan invasion		[patronage by the state of:] seminary students, shaykh-ul-Islam, judges, and endowments administrators [withdrawl of clergy to Iraq and into quietism (Akhbari)]	
Qajar Dynasty (1785–1925) [1. puritanical reformism] a. activist, dominance-seeking Usulis vs b. scholarly, quietist (Ansari) [2. modernist reformism: al-Afghani, Dowlatabadi, Roshdiyeh] a. conservatives: anticonstitution and antimodernist (Nuri, Imam, Jom'eh) b. moderates: proconsition, antimodern schools (Khorasani, Behbehani, Modarris) c. modernists: Dowlatabadi, Roshdiyeh		[competition] [struggles for constitution and against foreign debt-enslavement:] 1873 de Reuter protest 1891–1892 tobacco protest 1905–1911 constitutional revolution secularization of schools 1851 Dar al-Fanun 1911 123 elementary schools (Tehran)	

Pahlavi Dynasty (1925–1979)
1925–1941
[3. neofundamentalists: Fada'iyan-e Islam;
    Kashani]

[4. "socialist" issues: Mosaddeq]

1941–1960
a. conservative, clerical elite: prostability
   (Borujerdi, Behbehani, Shahrestani)
b. neofundamentalist, nonelite clergy:
   Kashani

c. leftist clergy (Borqe'i, Lajevardi)

1960–1977
[5. Islamic revival]
a. conservative, clerical elite (Shari'at-
   madari, Golpayegani, Khonsari, Kho'i)

b. oppositional clerics (Islamic renewal:
   Khomeini, Shirazi, Sadeq Rohani,
   Taleqani, Mahallati, Montazeri)

c. mediating reformers (Motahhari, Be-
   heshti)

d. royalists (Mahdavi, Imam Jum'eh of
   Tehran)

[suppression of clergy]   1924: 5,000–6,000
secularization of schools,   1935: 3,000
law, endowments, dress code 1940: 740

[reemergence of clergy]
cooperation with the crown: 1947: 5,000–6,000
1949 Borujerdi convocation
1953 Behbehani and Sharestani praise shah;
     state puts more religion in schools;
1955 anti-Bahai campaign

[opposition to the state in parliament and extrale-
gally; struggle against becoming a déclassé
stratum]
1960 Borujerdi breaks state-clergy truce
1960–1963 Goftar-e Mah; an inquiry into the
1962 principle of Marja'iyyat and the clergy
1963 15th of Khordad—demonstrations against
     the White Revolution
1965–1973 Hosayniyeh Ershad
1970 arrest of Taleqani;
     exile of 48 Qum teachers
1971 Khomeini: stay away from 25,000-year
     celebrations; guerillas
1972 five Mojahedin guerillas executed
     (students of Taleqani)
1975 15th of Khordad demonstrations
     against the Rastakhiz Party
1977–1979 revolution against Pahlavi monarchy

For Further Reading

Abrahamian, Ervand. *Iran Between Two Revolutions*. Princeton: Princeton University Press, 1982.

Akhavi, Shahrough. *Religion and Politics in Contemporary Iran*. Albany: SUNY Press, 1980.

Algar, Hamid. *Religion and State in Qajar Iran 1785–1906*. Berkeley: University of California Press, 1969.

Bashiriyeh, Hassein. *The State and Revolution in Iran 1962–1982*. New York: St. Martins, 1984.

Benard, Cheryl, and Zalmay Khalilzad. *The Government of God: Iran's Islamic Republic*. New York: Columbia University Press, 1984.

Bill, James. *The Politics of Iran: Groups, Classes and Modernization*. New York: Merrill, 1972.

Binder, Leonard. *Iran: Political Development in a Changing Society*. Berkeley: University of California Press, 1962.

Bonine, Michael E., and Nikki R. Keddie, eds. *Modern Iran: The Dialectics of Continuity and Change*. Albany: SUNY Press, 1981.

Brinton, Crane. *Anatomy of Revolution*. New York: Random House, 1938.

Cottam, Richard. *Nationalism in Iran*. Pittsburgh: University of Pittsburgh Press, 1964.

Esposito, John, ed. *Voices of Resurgent Islam*. New York: Oxford University Press. (1983.

Fischer, Michael M. J. *Iran: From Religious Dispute to Revolution*. Cambridge MA: Harvard University Press, 1980.

_____. "Iran and Islamic Justice." *Middle East Executive Reports* (January 1980).

_____. "Becoming Mullah: Reflections on Iranian Clerics in a Revolutionary Age." *Iranian Studies* 12/1-4 (1980): 83-118.

_____. "Legal Postulates in Flux: Justice, Wit, and Hierarchy in Iran." In *Law and Islam in the Middle East*, ed. D. Dwyer. Westport CT: Bergin and Garvey Publishers, 1989.

_____. "Islam and the Revolt of the Petit Bourgeoisie." *Daedalus* 3/1 (1982): 101-25.

_____. "Imam Khomeini: Four Ways of Understanding." In *Voices of Resurgent Islam*, ed. J. Esposito. New York: Oxford University Press, 1983.

Fischer, Michael M. J., and Mehdi Abedi. Foreword to *A Clarification of Questions: An Unabridged Translation of Resaleh Towzih al-Masael* by Ayatollah Sayyed Ruhollah Mousavi Khomeini. Boulder CO: Westview Press, 1984.

Graham, Robert. *Iran: The Illusion of Power*. New York: St. Martins, 1979.

Halliday, Fred. *Iran: Dictatorship and Development*. London and New York: Penguin, 1979.

Hooglund, Eric. *Reform and Revolution in Rural Iran*. Austin: University of Texas Press, 1982.

Irfani, Suroosh. *Revolutionary Islam in Iran*. London: Zed Press, 1983.

Katouzian, H. *The Political Economy of Modern Iran*. New York: New York University Press, 1981.

Kazemi, Farhad. *Poverty and Revolution in Iran*. New York: New York University Press, 1980.

Keddie, Nikki, *Religion and Rebellion in Iran: The Tobacco Protest of 1881–1892*. London : Frank Cass and Co., 1966.

———. *Roots of Revolution: An Interpretive History of Modern Iran*. New Haven: Yale University Press, 1981.

———, ed. *Religion and Politics in Iran*. New Haven: Yale University Press, 1983.

Khomeini, Ruhullah Musavi. *Islam and Revolution: Writings and Declarations of Imam Khomeini*. Trans. Hamid Algar. Berkeley: Mizan Press, 1981.

———. *A Clarification of Questions: An Unabridged Translation of Resaleh Towzih al-Masael*. Trans. J. Borujerdi. Boulder CO: Westview Press, 1984.

Laroui, Abdullah. *The Crisis of the Arab Intellectual*. Berkeley: University of California Press, 1976.

Zonis, Marvin. *The Political Elite of Iran*. Princeton: Princeton University Press, 1971.

Nuclear Ethics—
"The Challenge of Peace"

Kenneth Keulman

The intensity of critical national debates often rises and falls according to some obscure rhythm. Ultimately they either become archaic, when the times have so changed that they are trivial, or else they are resolved and left behind as a settled matter. The arousal of anxiety over nuclear weapons issues in the early 1980s, particularly in Western Europe and the United States, was unprecedented in scope. Previous public concern centered on specific issues: the early protests of the Committee on Nuclear Disarmament in England focused on the placement of antiballistic missiles in suburban areas. The renewal of activity in the 1980s possibly had its origins in the prolonged negotiations of SALT II and the anticlimax of its not being ratified. Then the beginning of the Reagan administration marked further deterioration of U.S.-Soviet relations. An accelerated U.S. military buildup was accompanied by rhetoric that emphasized the war-fighting capabilities of United States' nuclear weaponry.

The commitment to democratic politics is one the policy of nuclear deterrence claims to sustain. Yet a case can be made that in fact, the two are in opposition—that the inherent structural logic of deterrence strategy is not conducive to public debate and democratic choice, both among the populace at large and their elected representatives. How menacing is the world we live in? To what degree is that precariousness generated, and to what degree limited, by deterrence strategies? If people are unable to provide reasonably informed answers to questions such as these, the possibility of democratic choice is weakened. But many believe they cannot answer—because of the complexities of the issues, the all-pervasive secrecy, and because of the abstruse character of whatever technical data is made public.[1]

The collective effect of all these dynamics has been to focus the attention of many Americans on the possibility of nuclear war, perhaps for the first time. Organizations such as Physicians for Social Responsibility expanded this aware-

---

[1]For a development of this argument, see Michael Walzer, "Deterrence and Democracy," *The New Republic* (2 July 1984): 16-21.

ness by emphasizing the complete inadequacy of medical care after a nuclear attack. A grass-roots nuclear freeze movement gathered momentum, and in the 1982 elections various forms of a nuclear freeze were endorsed by referenda in eight states and numerous cities. Large sections of the population thus have voiced their desire to play a role in determining the direction of nuclear weapons policy.

While the nuclear predicament is political, military, and diplomatic, it is also an unprecedented ethical dilemma. The moral gravity of the issues posed by the situation in which the United States and the former Soviet Union possessed about 50,000 nuclear devices, was beyond question. It is possible, though it may be arduous, to reconcile the "realistic" approach to international relations with the requirements of ethics. Neither these requirements nor competition among nation-states—their striving for power, their search for superiority, their insecurity—will disappear. The type of realism that finds ethical behavior in international relations implausible, or allots to nations a privileged sphere of operation fundamentally different from that of persons or groups within the nation, may be the inheritor of a long tradition. Yet the desire for a type of behavior that does not result in duplicity and violence, cannot simply be repressed. Nations are governed by human beings whose decisions have an impact on other people. Considerations of ethical or unethical conduct are consequently both necessary and justifiable.[2]

In Western religious tradition, reflection on the nature of conflict and its resolution has varied, both in intensity and depth. Christian attitudes toward war have traditionally taken the form of the pacifist stance, the just-war tradition, and the crusading spirit—which emerged historically in that order.[3] The nuclear age has created a fourth response, nuclear pacifism, which understands the just-war tradition as prohibiting any use of nuclear weapons. During the last several years, the moral questions posed by nuclear weapons have moved to the central place in political and religious concerns. The intensified public awareness of the danger of nuclear war has stimulated a new controversy within religious communities on the ethics of deterrence policy.

In the late 1950s and early 1960s, there began a widening debate over the just war, pacifism, and nuclear armaments among Protestant and Catholic theologians and political thinkers, with the former taking on a leading role in developing new analytic approaches and the latter reacting by refining the traditional just-war theory. In the area of international law, a similar reevaluation has taken place. International law has become more demanding and less accommodating

---

[2]See Stanley Hoffmann, *Duties Beyond Borders* (Syracuse: Syracuse University Press, 1981).

[3]For a historical overview of these positions, see Roland Bainton, *Christian Attitudes toward War and Peace* (Nashville: Abingdon, 1960).

of national sovereignty than it had been in the nineteenth century. This is especially the case in an area that is one of the mainstays of sovereignty—the right to wage war. This right was intact in nineteenth-century law, restricted after the First World War, and severely curbed in the United Nations Charter, which recognizes its legitimacy only in self-defense or in collective resistance to aggression.

Roman Catholic thinking over the last century has developed in a direction parallel to that taken in international law. For Pope Pius XII, aggression was identical with offensive use of force and was not a moral alternative. Later, John XXIII went further than either Pius XII or international law in proscribing any use of force to redress a "violation of justice" that had already taken place. Paul VI echoed the sentiments of the Kellogg-Briand Pact of 1928, when he declared before the United Nations, "Never again war!" Yet he still maintained the justice of defense—though not offensive use of force.[4]

In the 1950s, Pius XII saw in nuclear weapons a destructive capacity far exceeding that of previous military technologies, yet he nonetheless acknowledged the right of national self-defense against aggression. The 1950s came to a close with the just-war theory maintained by the church. Catholics were free to question policy options as they related to U.S. nuclear strategy, but such objections could not call into question the moral foundations on which military policy, and nuclear strategy in particular, claimed to be founded.

Yet changes were beginning to take place. The changes had begun modestly as early as the 1950s, during the pontificate of Pius XII. Like almost all popes, he was theologically conservative. Yet he took an interest in all aspects of the modern world and delivered addresses on an amazing variety of subjects. He initiated few innovations himself, except in the Easter liturgy, which had remained substantially the same for a thousand years. Yet it frequently happens that when ritual is altered, it heralds the beginning of a social revolution. What Pius XII began, John XXIII and Paul VI carried forward. The most significant event of their pontificates was the Second Vatican Council (1962–1965), the most ecumenical, democratic, and theologically progressive council in the history of the church.

The 1960s witnessed a reorientation of the church in its teaching on war and peace. Pope John XXIII's encyclical *Pacem in terris*[5] and the Second Vatican

---

[4]Pope Paul VI, *Never Again War!* (New York: United Nations Office of Public Information, 1965).

[5]"Peace on Earth," deliberately dated on Maundy Thursday (11 April 1963), was vital to himself and so near his death (on 3 June 1963) that it is often called "John's last will and testament." (The title—as with other encyclicals and concili-

Council provided the theological and ethical framework for this reevaluation. Both provided the ecclesiological authority for reconsideration of the just-war doctrine.

The first step in a new direction was taken by John XXIII in April 1963. The encyclical *Pacem in terris* spoke directly to the issue of nuclear weapons:

> Justice, right reason, and humanity . . . urgently demand that the arms race should cease; that the stockpiles which exist in various countries should be reduced equally and simultaneously by the parties concerned; that nuclear weapons should be banned; and that a general agreement should eventually be reached about progressive disarmament and an effective method of control.[6]

In a later passage the pope writes that "it is hardly possible to imagine that in the atomic era war could be used as an instrument of justice."[7] The encyclical stands out as a clear-cut indictment of nuclear weapons. *Pacem in terris* acknowledged that nuclear weapons challenge traditional teaching on war and peace. Traditional notions of self-defense, resistance to aggression, criteria for involvement in war, and conduct in war had to be reevaluated. The encyclical signified a new sensitivity to the realities of the nuclear age.

The Second Vatican Council stands as the second major event in the postwar reexamination of war and peace within the church. *Gaudium et spes* ("Joy and hope")—subtitled the "Pastoral Constitution on the Church in the Modern World"—condemns the use of a wide range of modern "scientific weapons."[8] It

---

ar documents—follows the ancient custom of naming documents by the first word[s] in the document. *Pacem in terris*, "Peace on Earth," are the first three words of the encyclical text.)

[6]John XXIII, encyclical letter *Pacem in terris*, Peace on Earth (Washington DC: National Catholic Welfare Conference, 11 April 1963) n. 112. ("N.," here as also below, refers to the numbered section [or "paragraph"] of the document.) For general distribution, the text was published by America Press (New York, 1963), from which it is conveniently reprinted in *The Gospel of Peace and Justice: Catholic Social Teaching since Pope John*, ed. Joseph Gremillion (Maryknoll NY: Orbis Books, 1976) 201-39.

[7]Ibid., n. 127.

[8]See Vatican II, 64. *Gaudium et spes* (7 December 1965) n. 80, as it appears in *The Documents of Vatican II, with Notes and Comments by Catholic, Protestant, and Orthodox Authorities*, gen. ed. Walter M. Abbott, trans. ed. Joseph Gallagher (New York: Herder & Herder/Crossroad, 1966; New York: America Press; London: Geoffrey Chapman, 1966). For a later translation of the documents (and in the order of their promulgation—internal section/paragraph numbers remain the same), see *Vatican Council II. The Conciliar and Post-*

strongly implies that these weapons call into question traditional assumptions about the conduct of warfare. The Council also affirms the morality of the pacifist option,[9] and calls on the state to make provision for those who for reasons of conscience cannot participate in war.[10]

The Council recognizes that the savagery of war is magnified by the new weapons of massive destruction: "All these considerations compel us to undertake an evaluation of war with an entirely new attitude."[11] This echoes *Pacem in terris*, which maintains that war is no longer a means of vindication of violated rights. In the text itself of the Constitution, the just-war principle of discrimination is implicitly applied to the use of nuclear weapons. The strongest condemnation of the entire Council is an explicit application of the just-war principle of discrimination: "Any act of war aimed indiscriminately at the destruction of entire cities or of extensive areas along with their population is a crime against God and man himself. It merits unequivocal and unhesitating condemnation."[12] Subsequent papal teaching has been in continuity with that of the Council.

Vatican II did accept the policy of deterrence, and left unresolved the dilemma of whether a nation can continue to possess nuclear weapons, designed precisely to wreak the type of destruction condemned by the Constitution, that it may not use. Still, the Second Vatican Council was a decisive moment in the history of Catholic teaching on war and peace because, like *Pacem in terris*, it moved the church further away from an unquestioning endorsement of warfare in a nuclear age. The mood of the church thus changed dramatically with the *aggiornamento* of John XXIII, Vatican II, and the *Ostpolitik* of Paul VI on behalf of the church in Eastern Europe.

By the late 1960s the Catholic Church in the United States was prepared to take up the mandate of the Second Vatican Council to evaluate war with an entirely new attitude. The Council provided the authoritative context for the debate. Yet the impact of Vatican II in itself does not explain the specific direction in which the American Catholic Church was to move in the next fifteen years. The European Church had the same mandate but moved in a quite different direction. The answer lies in the effect of the Vietnam War on the American psyche.

Conciliar Documents, gen. ed. Austin Flannery (Northport NY: Costello Publishing; Collegeville MN: The Liturgical Press; Wilmington DE: Scholarly Resources, 1975). *Gaudium et spes* is also cited—especially in Catholic literature—as the "Pastoral Consitution" or as just the "Constitution."

[9]Ibid., n. 78.
[10]Ibid., n. 79.
[11]Ibid., n. 80.
[12]Ibid.

Although the entire moral-political controversy about Vietnam had nothing directly to do with nuclear weapons, it paved the way for the development of nuclear pacifism in the Catholic Church in the United States. From 1968 onward, the American bishops—who had traditionally supported the war policies of the government—became increasingly critical of the nation's military policy, especially nuclear-weapons policy once the Vietnam war had ended.

Another factor in the changing attitude of the American Catholic Church was the composition of the United States bishops during the post-Vatican II era. The overwhelming majority of them was consecrated after January 1, 1968, the year in which domestic opposition to the war in Southeast Asia became strong enough to force President Johnson to decide he could not run for reelection. The Vietnam War created in the church a generation gap no less wide and enduring than in any other segment of American society. But the impact of that war most likely could not have changed the thinking of the bishops as decisively as it did except in tandem with the type of change in the church's outlook on the world that found articulate expression in the Second Vatican Council. There were many bishops who were prepared to accept a connection between opposition to the Vietnam War and opposition not only to the government's nuclear weapons policy but also to American military efforts in general. The late 1960s saw the gradual movement of the American Catholic Church toward a more critical evaluation of the just-war doctrine and an increasing skepticism toward the morality of the use, threat, and more recently, the possession of nuclear weapons.

Catholics in the United States have in fact been examining the issues of nuclear conflict, deterrence, and disarmament since the end of the Second World War. Theologians wrote about nuclear weapons within the context of traditional just-war principles of discrimination and proportionality.[13] Thus the ferment over the affront posed by nuclear weapons to human conscience is not entirely new. Thoughtful Catholics, like thoughtful people everywhere, have been involved in these issues for decades. What is new on the Catholic side is the democratization of a crucial debate in a church known for authoritative pronouncements.

In the light of the Second Vatican Council and of subsequent papal teachings, the United States Catholic bishops have made corporate statements on war and peace. The most significant are the pastoral letter "Human Life in Our Day" (1968), the pastoral letter "To Live in Christ Jesus" (1976), Cardinal John Krol's congressional testimony representing the policy of the United States Catholic

---

[13]See, e.g., Francis J. Connell, "Is the H-Bomb Right or Wrong?," *Sign* 29 (1950): 11-13; Connell, "Problems of War," *American Ecclesiastical Review* 125 (1951): 64-65; John C. Ford, "The Hydrogen Bombing of Cities," *Theology Digest* 5 (1957): 6-9; and John Courtney Murray, "Remarks on the Moral Problem of War," *Theological Studies* 20 (1960): 40-61.

Conference on the SALT II treaty (1979), and the administrative board's statement on registration and the draft (1980).

In "Human Life in Our Day," in accord with the Vatican Council, the bishops accept the legitimacy of pacifism and call for the recognition of both conscientious objection and selective conscientious objection by the legal system.[14] The letter also makes reference to the problematic nature of possession of weapons that cannot be used. The bishops urged that the United States stop trying to maintain "nuclear superiority" since "any effort to achieve superiority leads to ever higher levels of armaments."[15]

By the mid-1970s the bishops had moved beyond a simple reaffirmation of Vatican II and had begun to chart a new and in many ways distinctive contribution to the issues. The 1976 pastoral letter deals with many aspects of the ethical life and devotes some reflection to the nuclear question.[16] This document contains a sentence that has not been in previous statements of the universal magisterium or of the American bishops:

> As possessors of a vast nuclear arsenal, we must also be aware that not only is it wrong to attack civilian populations but it is also wrong to threaten to attack them as part of a strategy of deterrence.

This statement maintains that it is morally wrong to *threaten to do* what one cannot morally do since the threat involves the immoral intention to do evil. It follows that counterpopulation deterrence is morally wrong and must be condemned. The document does not explicitly raise the question of how deterrence can continue to exist in the light of this or how deterrence can be effective without the intention to use weapons. The bishops' statement, in some of its specific recommendations, represents a major divergence on the part of the American Catholic episcopacy from the national and international security policies to which the United States has been committed since the advent of the nuclear age.

For the past several years, a primary consideration in discussing the morality of deterrence has been *intentionality*. The government of a pluralistic society cannot enter into any significant public debate over such ideas as the morality of threat and intention. These are reserved to ethicists and bishops, who have great

---

[14]National Conference of Catholic Bishops, pastoral letter "Human Life in Our Day," 15 Nov. 1976 (Washington DC: United States Catholic Conference, 1968).

[15]Ibid.

[16]National Conference of Catholic Bishops, pastoral letter "To Live in Christ Jesus: A Pastoral Reflection on the Moral Life," 11 November 1976 (Washington DC: United States Catholic Conference, 1976).

difficulty agreeing among themselves. Nevertheless, the dilemma raised by the issue of intention became clear in the 1976 statement. The role is pivotal in any consideration, not only of war but of deterrence of war. Deterrence contains an implied threat, or a conditioned threat to use. The dilemma arises from the traditional understanding that it is unethical to threaten seriously or intend to do what it is morally wrong to do.[17]

The question was addressed in 1979 when Cardinal John Krol, testifying for the United States Catholic Conference on behalf of SALT II before the Senate Foreign Relations Committee, stated that "not only the use of strategic weapons but also the declared intent to use them involved in American deterrence policy is wrong."[18] Krol distinguished between the use of arms, the threat to use arms, and their possession. He maintained that no use or declared intent to use nuclear weapons was acceptable, but the possession of nuclear arms lacking the declared intent to use them was tolerable for the sake of a deterrent while arms talks proceed. The reasoning of this position is that possession requires no declared intent and so is morally permissible. Obviously the credibility of the argument rises or falls on the persuasiveness of the distinction between intent and possession. Since 1979 that distinction has been under challenge. There is a human chain of command that is primed and ready to act so that weapons can be launched. There is a structural intent to the nuclear weapons a nation possesses because it is not only weapons that are possessed, but an entire human and technological system of nuclear weaponry.

The bishops became even more troubled by the prospect of nuclear war for the same reasons as did the Western world at large. In July 1980, President Carter had issued Presidential Directive 59, expanding the range of targets of nuclear weapons beyond the urban-industrial area that had been the focus of strategic planning for two decades. This directive aimed to improve deterrence by increasing the capacity for a prolonged but limited nuclear war. Concurrently, the Pentagon seemed to be equipping itself to fortify offensive capabilities of nuclear strategy.

Ronald Reagan entered office with a desire to confront the Soviet Union with a demonstration of United States power. He viewed the Soviet Union as an expansionist nation committed to achieving global hegemony principally by military domination. He discerned "unrelenting" momentum in the Soviet acquisition of arms and warned that a hazardous "margin of superiority" over the United States had been consolidated. He estimated the measures of agreed restraint on strategic weapons included in the two principal arms control treaties

---

[17]Some representative thinkers who have maintained this are Abelard, Aquinas, Butler, Bentham, and Kant.

[18]Cardinal John Krol, "Testimony on Salt II," *Origins* (1979): 197.

(SALT I and SALT II) to be "fatally flawed," a codification of disadvantage for the United States. Employing weapons inventories and defense expenditures as major gauges of military position, he dedicated himself to prodigious sustained increases in the defense budget.

The strident rhetoric of the Reagan campaign alarmed many bishops. Cardinal Krol's testimony had previously set the stage for a thorough study of war and peace issues by the National Conference of Catholic Bishops. A vocal "Mennonite Caucus" had also emerged among the bishops. With these immediate factors juxtaposed against the significant changes that had occurred within the church from *Pacem in terris* to Cardinal Krol's testimony, the Conference established an ad hoc committee in November 1980 to draft a pastoral letter on war and peace.

The committee, chaired by then-Archbishop Joseph Bernardin, began working on the document in the spring of 1981. The committee held many meetings, heard testimony from more than thirty-five expert witnesses, and issued a first draft in June 1982. A second draft was discussed at the annual bishops' meeting in November 1982. The third draft was issued in early spring 1983 and served as the basis for the final document—"The Challenge of Peace: God's Promise and Our Response"—approved at the May meeting of the conference.[19]

The document runs to more than 30,000 words. A synopsis is therefore in order. The letter begins with a recognition of a most important sign of the times: we live in a moment of crisis because of the real possibility of the destruction of our world through nuclear war. The present-day situation is balanced by the call for peace as an ethical demand arising from an interdependent world.

The pastoral letter states that the church's teaching recognizes the international common good and calls for structures commensurate to that good. The absence of adequate structures at the present time places an even greater responsibility on the part of individual nations which are called to interpret their national interests in the light of the broader global interest. A realistic assessment of the contemporary global situation dominated by the major powers in a divided world is called for. In spite of the fundamental differences between United States

---

[19]National Conference of Catholic Bishops, pastoral letter "The Challenge of Peace: God's Promise and Our Response," A Pastoral Letter on War and Peace, 3 May 1983 (Washington DC: United States Catholic Conference, 1983); dist. *Origins. National Catholic Documentary Service* 13/1 (19 May 1983). The pastoral letter went through three drafts, written by the NCCB Ad Hoc Committee on War and Peace. The three drafts were presented in turn to the bishops for comment. The fourth and final draft was formally approved by the bishops on 3 May 1983.

and other political systems, mutual interests do exist. These mutual interests provide the starting point for structural change, beginning with negotiations. The bishops want to emphasize the significance of political dialogue and negotiation based on a common interest in preventing a nuclear holocaust. They do not issue a call for Western political initiatives aimed at bringing about more freedom for people in the Soviet Union and the Eastern bloc. In this regard, they seem to advocate realpolitik—practical, commonsense polity and policies.

The document spells out the just-war criteria under the traditional headings of *jus ad bellum* and *jus in bello*. Pacifism and just war are seen as distinct but interdependent methods of judging warfare. The bishops' letter applies the principles of a just war to the contemporary situation. In the light of the destructive capacity of nuclear weapons it becomes imperative to condemn their use. The document takes three positions on the use of nuclear weapons: it condemns any use of nuclear weapons against civilian population targets and any first use of nuclear weapons; yet, while highly skeptical of the possibility of limiting any nuclear war, it does not absolutely reject the use of counterforce weapons in response to a nuclear attack. The statement gives a strictly conditioned moral acceptance of a limited nuclear deterrence that can never be the foundation for an authentic peace.

The drafts show relatively little change on the issue of the use of nuclear weaponry. The first draft consistently condemns the use of nuclear weapons or any weapons used against population centers or civilian targets. The second draft condemns the first use of nuclear weapons. The third draft abhors the notion of initiating nuclear war on however restricted a scale. The entire thrust of the letter's reasoning goes against any use of counterforce nuclear weapons as first use or in retaliation.

Now let us begin a more detailed analysis of "The Challenge of Peace." The preliminary draft of the pastoral letter condemned the use of nuclear weapons to counter an assault waged by conventional warfare since "nonnuclear attacks by another state must be deterred by other than nuclear means." The statement reiterates the 1976 assertion of the bishops that not only is it immoral to launch an attack on civilian populations, but it is also immoral to threaten to attack them as part of a strategy of deterrence. The report concludes that "we cannot lightly demand abandonment of possession of all nuclear weapons at this moment." A "temporary toleration" is permitted. Toleration of the possession of nuclear weapons, the report insists, is not "a comforting moral judgment," but "an urgent call to efforts to change the present relationship among nuclear powers."

The initial draft of the pastoral letter wavered between nuclear pacifism and a reformulation of the just-war theory for a nuclear age. It was a mixture of utopian hopes and pragmatic compromises. It manifested a troubled ambivalence and a desire for compromise on fundamentally irreconcilable issues. There is an ambiguity in the nature of what the report "tolerates." Is that which is tolerated the intention to threaten population centers? Or is that which is tolerated the possession of weapons? Policymakers regard the distinction between possession and use as quaint. Government and military officials who possess weapons intend to use them. Consequently, there exists no such situation as possessing nuclear weapons with no intention to use them.[20] The statement appears to be calling for an ethically acceptable deterrent without a militarily credible plan to back it up.

One of the commentators on the first draft of the pastoral believed that the document distorted reality. "The letter misrepresents the mainline of American nuclear strategy," stated Philip Odeen, a former assistant secretary of defense and a professional defense planner. Mr. Odeen asserted that "the focus of our strategy and targeting is Soviet military power not Soviet population." As a result, he believed the pastoral accepts a "caricature of mutual assured destruction," followed in the United States, he suggests, by "a small minority on the right pushing 'war-winning' approaches."[21]

But was it Mr. Odeen's perception of reality, rather than that of the bishops, that was distorted? United States nuclear weapons policy has always claimed to be predicated on deterrence, but it has not always been content to stop with that. It has also been concerned with the possibility of fighting a nuclear war as well as deterring one. The argument runs that it is essential to prepare to engage in a nuclear war on all levels, from the most limited to the most widespread. Such a nuclear war is thought of as though it were an endurance contest, with triumph going to the side that lasts the longest. Conquest rather than deterrence would enjoin plans for a prolonged, escalatory nuclear battle. A nuclear-fighting program demands flexible preparations for a war that has no compass and whose nature cannot be predicted.

The nuclear-fighting doctrine was lodged in Presidential Directive 59, and later confirmed by President Reagan. This directive was justified by former Secretary of Defense Harold Brown on the ground that it was compatible with deterrence and allowed the United States more "options" than one of simple retaliation. The presupposition is that the failure of deterrence would not be fatal; it would instead signal the beginning of a protracted nuclear conflict.

Speeches and statements by Secretaries Weinberger and Haig, together with a speech by Assistant for National Security Affairs William P. Clark on May 21, 1982, prepared the nation for the Pentagon's new strategy for nuclear conflict,

---

[20]As the Joint Chiefs of Staff put it: "Deterrence depends upon the assured capability and *manifest will* to inflict damage on the Soviet Union disproportionate to any goals that rational Soviet leaders might hope to achieve." "U.S. Military Posture for FY 1983" (Washington DC: Government Printing Office, 1982) 19; emphasis added.

[21]"The Bishops and the Bomb," *Commonweal* (13 August 1982): 430.

disclosed by Richard Halloran in the *New York Times* of May 30, 1982. This strategy, advocated by Secretary Weinberger the previous March without any public announcement or debate, made explicit what had formerly been implicit—planning for an extended nuclear conflict. The policy calls for a nuclear weapons escalation geared for a "protracted" nuclear war. United States nuclear forces "must prevail and be able to force the Soviet Union to seek earliest termination of hostilities on terms favorable to the United States."

This new program assumed the need to prepare for waging a nuclear conflict for an indefinite period, as though it could be controlled by both adversaries. It also presupposes that America could impose favorable terms—a circumlocution for conquest—on the Soviets, after both sides had inflicted incredible suffering on each other.

The policy was ominous. It assumed that a nuclear conflict could take place "over a protracted period" without devastation of the nations involved. It presumed that "favorable terms" would have some human significance after such a nuclear war. Preparations for it would be so incredibly expensive that it would indenture the economy to the Pentagon's desire for development and production of more, and more advanced, conventional and nuclear armaments. Implementation of this proposal would result in the eventual militarization of the economy. The Atlantic Alliance also could not survive this scheme; no European ally could even think about engaging in a "protracted" nuclear conflict. The only conflict of this type would directly involve the United States and the Soviet Union, consequently the most destructive long-range ICBMs would be used, most likely from the outset.[22]

In November 1982, the bishops issued a second draft of their letter. The language about "toleration" of the possession of nuclear weapons was changed, but the general approach was not altered in any meaningful way. The refusal to discuss possible uses of nuclear weapons can be seen as a responsible way to shift the argument away from ways to use nuclear weapons to ways to avoid using them. The second draft also addresses, in a way that the first draft did not, concrete policy positions of the government and, in doing so, places the statement in opposition to United States policy. Besides the broader concern relative to deterrence strategy, the second draft specifically rejects the MX missile and calls for an "immediate . . . halt [to the] testing, production and deployment of new strategic systems."[23]

---

[22]See the discussion in the first chapter of Theodore Draper, *Present History* (New York: Random House, 1983).

[23]"The Challenge of Peace: God's Promise and Our Response" (second draft), *Origins* 12 (28 October 1982): 312.

In May 1983, the bishops voted on the final text of "The Challenge of Peace: God's Promise and Our Response." Whereas the first and second drafts seemed to equate pacifism and just war as credible responses to the political problem of war, the third draft and final text distinguish between the renunciation of violence as an alternative for an individual and the mandate of the state to deploy force as a last resort to defend the common good and the lives of its citizens. This theme was strengthened following a Vatican consultation, which made the American bishops more "conscious of the consequences our teaching will have not only for our nation but for the lives of others."[24] The bishops write: "War is permissible only to confront 'a real and certain danger,' that is, to protect innocent life, to preserve conditions necessary for decent human existence and to secure fundamental human rights."[25]

The problem with this statement is that it constitutes a broad warrant. Might it have justified, for example, an intervention by NATO forces in Poland if in some future crisis involving the activity of Solidarity, Soviet troops would have invaded Poland? Apart from the question of whether the bishops' statement implies that America and its allies should respond with force to secure the fundamental human rights of the Poles, if the Polish people, under overt Soviet military invasion and suppression, should appeal to the West for aid, the more relevant issue is whether the bishops considered this dilemma before approving the statement quoted earlier. Their words can be interpreted to include a military intervention by Western forces in Eastern Europe under specific circumstances—an action that NATO, aware of the security apprehensions of the U.S.S.R., did not consider during the Hungarian uprising in 1956, the Warsaw Pact invasion of Czechoslovakia in 1968, or the Polish crisis from mid-1980 onward.

The vast majority of bishops wanted their statement to offer a clear and specific critique of prevailing nuclear weapons strategy. At the same time, they were reluctant to place themselves outside the political realities of public policy. The final draft, like its predecessors, rejects countercity warfare, opposes first use of nuclear weapons, and is skeptical about the possibility of "limited" nuclear war. Furthermore, the letter, while sidestepping a direct analysis of threat and intention and their relationship to deterrence, accepts deterrence on a strictly conditional basis providing it is used as a step toward disarmament. The final draft also builds a case for the validity of a nonviolent or pacifist witness for individuals. In brief, the final draft of the letter represents the culmination of Catholic thinking on issues of war and peace that finds its roots in *Pacem in terris* and the Second Vatican Council.

---

[24]Precis on the third draft, ii-iii.

[25]"The Challenge of Peace: God's Promise and Our Response," n. 86.

Part 2 is the core of the document. Here, the letter accepts the challenge posed by nuclear weapons as demanding "fresh applications of traditional moral principles." The bishops admit that "the political paradox of deterrence has also strained our moral conception." Then they pose a series of questions: "May a nation threaten what it may never do? May it possess what it may never use? Who is involved in the threat each great power makes: Government officials? Or military personnel? Or the citizenry in whose defense the threat is made?"

In responding to these questions posed by the bishops, an even more fundamental question needs to be asked: Why do the great powers continue to possess strategic nuclear armaments, and not only to possess them but to add to them? The answer provided by policymakers is primarily their perceived deterrent capability: there have been no wars among the major powers since the advent of the nuclear age. Though deterrence is hazardous, it has held up. The problem with this type of reasoning is that it does not demonstrate the cause-effect connection. The fact that the United States has followed a policy of deterrence and has not had war with the former Soviet Union does not itself prove that deterrence has prevented war.

Another reason for perennially escalating arms production is that, from the perspective of nation-states, no clear path exists to the removal of dependence on nuclear arsenals for the end they serve. One-sided escalation or disarmament tends to bring about strategic instability. Likewise, practices for targeting strategic weaponry other than the threat of full-scale counterpopulation warfare tends, in the minds of many policymakers, to weaken the effectiveness of the deterrent, consequently, the likelihood of nuclear conflict is lessened by increasing the possibility of mutually assured destruction were nuclear weapons to be used.

There are, though, two reasons why it is imperative to transcend this stage in thinking about the nuclear dilemma. The first is that deterrence hinges mainly on perception. If the threat is of such a type as to make carrying it out irrational, then it loses its efficacy. In the context of current strategic debates, this concern is expressed in the argument that an irrationally destructive deterrent force deters only an equivalently irrational destructive force, leaving untouched the possibility of use of force at lower levels. While neither the United States nor the former Soviet Union would want to risk almost certain annihilation of its own major cities and its industrial base by a countercity strike against the other, some form of limited nuclear weapons use could occur, especially if the targets were the nuclear forces of the other side.

The most controverted section of the pastoral letter revolves around this issue of deterrence. Even a minimalist notion of deterrence maintains that at the time the Soviet Union and the United States would in every imaginable situation hold fast to the possibility of assailing one another with nuclear warheads; and that while neither adversary could be sure that the other would initiate a first strike, each could also not be sure that the other would not initiate a first strike.

But this naive conception of deterrence has never been adequate for those who make policy. The doctrine of deterrence involves issues that hinge on both political-psychological and technical decisions. As such, these issues are inherently volatile, since both political psychology and technology change. They are also contingent, since the individuals on whose judgments the exposition of the deterrent threat depends are themselves executors of political and technological change.

The permutation of threat into doctrine is consequently marked by irresolution. Thus, successive generations of nuclear-weapons policymakers, desiring an impossible "certainty" in deterrence, have met with problems in selecting among different weapons, and have ended by selecting the instruments of fighting a nuclear war. In the search for the unattainable goal of certain deterrence, successive governments have attempted to make deterrence more extensive, both psychologically and technologically. There must exist no "window" through which the adversary might discern a lack of will or technical competence on the part of the other.[26]

A section of the letter, "The Moral Assessment of Deterrence," provides a detailed criticism of the doctrine. Two specific issues are at the center of the letter's unease with deterrence: the targeting practice envisioned by United States policy, and the fear that deterrence will increase the possibility of nuclear war.

With regard to the targeting issue, the letter maintains that assured destruction is immoral because it makes nuclear weapons appear more usable and demands increasingly more war-fighting capabilities: there is no limit on the number of targets and weapons, consequently the infinite needs of the nuclear arsenal will compete with other moral claims on the resources of society. Moreover, destruction of large parts of civilian society is an unavoidable part of any large-scale strategic nuclear war.

Prior to the August 1980 announcement of the countervailing strategy in Presidential Directive 59, it had been assumed on both sides of the Atlantic that the McNamara Doctrine implied a threat of retaliation against Russian urban centers. One result of the debate over the bishops' pastoral, especially with its proscription of any strategy that aimed at destruction of cities, was that it elicited from Secretary of Defense Caspar Weinberger and National Security Adviser William P. Clark the first clear statement ever given by high-ranking government officials that the United States is not committed to a strategy of annihilation of cities. Clark wrote to Bernardin on January 15, 1983, as follows:

---

[26]See Emma Rothschild, "The Delusions of Deterrence," in *The New York Review of Books* (14 April 1983): 40-50.

For moral, political and military reasons, the United States does not target the Soviet civilian population as such. There is no deliberately opaque meaning conveyed in the last two words. We do not threaten the existence of Soviet civilization by threatening Soviet cities. Rather, we hold at risk the warmaking capability of the Soviet Union—its armed forces, and the industrial capacity to sustain war. It would be irresponsible for us to issue policy statements which might suggest to the Soviets that it would be to their advantage to establish privileged sanctuaries within heavily populated areas, thus inducing them to locate much of their warfighting capability within those urban sanctuaries.[27]

It is true that Soviet strategic airfields, missile silos, naval bases, submarines at sea, weapons manufacturing and storage locales, and civilian early warning facilities, are probable targets. Many of the above targets, however, are very near or colocated with cities, especially in Europe. In addition, there is an industrial targeting category. Modern nuclear doctrines require that "war-supporting" facilities be attacked. Many of these facilities are necessarily industrial in nature and engage a workforce of considerable size. They are almost always situated near major transportation centers, so that raw materials and finished products can be efficiently transported to other industrial sectors, or to forces in the field. A major countervalue attack therefore might involve nearly all large cities in the United States and the Soviet Union, and possibly most of the large cities in the Northern Hemisphere.[28] There are fewer than 2,500 cities in the world with populations of more than 100,000 inhabitants, so the devastation of all such cities is well within the means of the world nuclear arsenals.

In regard to the second issue—the increased likelihood of war resulting from deterrence—the fear is expressed in the letter that a counterforce strategy aimed at military targets and nuclear weapons will make deterrence unstable, presumably by stimulating the arms race and by prompting one or the other side to initiate a nuclear strike in order to prevent it from being attacked first.

The bishops conclude that the policy of deterrence creates and keeps in place a balance of terror that all too easily could lead to nuclear war. They also criticize the cost of maintaining deterrence, which takes money away from

---

[27]This quotation from Clark and a similar statement from Weinberger were included in the text of the third draft, nn. 83-84. A reaffirmation of the administration's policy can also be found in Secretary Weinberger's "Annual Report to the Congress," 1 February 1983, 55: "The Reagan Administration's policy is that under no circumstances may such weapons be used deliberately for the purpose of destroying populations."

[28]J. Peterson, ed., "Nuclear War: The Aftermath," ed. J. Peterson, *Ambio* (special issue) 2/2-3 (Royal Swedish Academy of Sciences, 1982).

programs for the poor. Their overall conclusion is to render a "strictly conditioned moral acceptance,"[29] as long as the deterrent strategy is viewed as a step on the way toward progressive disarmament and not as an end in itself. No use of nuclear weapons that violates the principles of discrimination or proportionality may be intended as a strategy of deterrence, since Catholic teaching maintains that one ought not to intend or do moral evil. This reasoning on deterrence is much sharper than positions found in previous episcopal statements on this issue. It shifts from an argument maintained in an earlier pastoral (1976) which, as we have seen, condemned not only attacks against civilian populations but also threats to attack them as a strategy of deterrence.

The bishops write: "Although reasons exist which move some to condemn reliance on nuclear weapons for deterrence, we have not reached this conclusion."[30] They would thus disagree with those who see the threat of massive retaliation implicit in the policy of deterrence, as immoral in itself.[31] The letter views the situation in a different light. It sees the duty not to threaten innocent persons as a prima facie principle, one which is counterbalanced in the present situation by the obligation to preserve the lives and liberties of the innocent (assuming the dubious proposition that deterrence has achieved this). The difference is that the pastoral letter implies that deterrence is justified, rather than that immoral behavior is tolerated out of necessity. Given that overridden obligations continue to exert some moral force, there would still exist a duty to extricate oneself from circumstances in which the obligation not to threaten had to be overridden in order to fulfill a more stringent obligation. The bishops intimate that seeing deterrence as intrinsically immoral would place us in a perpetual state of moral tension in which ethical criteria, rather than being overridden by other ethical principles, are disregarded because of consequences that may result.[32]

Yet this conclusion seems to be inconsistent, for the bishops have judged morally objectionable nearly every aspect of deterrence policy, principally massive civilian casualties whether directly intended or not; first use under any circumstances; and any so-called limited use of nuclear weaponry. The bishops demonstrate that they are ill at ease with their conclusion. They make reference to "the moral and political paradox posed by deterrence" and to their own strictly conditional acceptance of it. By conditional acceptance they mean that deterrence is permissible only if negotiations move toward reducing the arsenal of nuclear

---

[29]"The Challenge of Peace: God's Promise and Our Response," n. 186.

[30]Ibid., n. 192.

[31]Michael Walzer, *Just and Unjust Wars* (New York: Basic Books, 1977) 272.

[32]Cf. William H. Shaw, "Nuclear Deterrence and Deontology," *Ethics* 94/2 (January 1984): 248-60.

weapons, that the goal is nuclear parity and not superiority. But in spite of all mention of paradoxes and conditions, the conclusion does not seem to follow from the principles that were set out. To ethically repudiate deterrence, only to tolerate it as a practical necessity, is to consider too rapidly the suspension of moral principle.

It can be argued that the intention of nuclear weapons policy during the time of this debate was not the commendable one of deterring war but the reprehensible one of using nuclear weapons for the purpose of inflicting massive destruction if deterrence fails, and is consequently immoral. Ethicist Germain Grisez maintains that what he calls "the precise intent to kill" renders it impossible to consider deterrence tolerable or justifiable as a lesser evil awaiting progress in arms control or disarmament, as it means either that a moral evil may be done to avoid some other evil, or the killing of millions of innocent persons may be morally acceptable on the basis of proportionality.[33]

Any criticism of deterrence has to be informed by an awareness of the way in which current technological developments have destabilized deterrence: what is the effect on crisis stability when both sides attempt to deter, not with threats of mutual destruction, but with war-fighting, counterforce arsenals? Such a criticism must also reflect on what would occur if deterrence failed.

It is the elite of experts, not democratic decision making, that has brought about this situation. That speaks well for the experts, some would say: deterrence has prevented nuclear conflict. On the other hand, risks of disaster have increased over the decades along with the increase in the number and destructiveness of the weapons. Deterrence has not been a steady state but a race, and every forward movement in the race endangers the balance upon which our lives depend. This forward movement endangered the lives of the Russians, and theirs endangered ours; and we were both driven to keep moving forward. Possibly the experts have not done well enough. We need to question their competence.

One of the difficulties a close reading of the pastoral letter reveals is that, despite admirable intentions, the bishops' inability to reach a consensus is sometimes masked as objectivity. They advocate a "conditional" acceptance of deterrence "on the way toward progressive disarmament." The problem is that, in practice, these are not congruent realities. Military strategists, for example, argue that it is not sufficient for the United States to possess strategic forces merely capable of deterring a nuclear attack or retaliating in the event of such an attack. To make deterrence "credible," it is necessary to have, among other elements, some "damage limitation" capability. In other words, there must exist

---

[33]Germain Grisez, "The Moral Implications of a Nuclear Deterrent," *Center Journal* 2 (Winter 1982): 9-24.

some weapons capable of destroying an adversary's missiles before they are launched. These counterforce weapons are highly destabilizing. If the erstwhile Soviets were aware that their missiles were threatened by those of the United States, they may have been tempted to launch theirs first, which is the last thing America wanted them to do. One man's damage limitation, at a certain point, becomes another man's feared first strike.

Another double-bind situation arises. The document supports "immediate, bilateral verifiable agreements to halt the testing, production and deployment of new nuclear weapons systems." Yet even a "conditional" support of deterrence implies that some weapons—those that enhance a credible deterrence—are necessary. Why put a stop to development of such weapons? It is not clear, however, why an outright ban on arms development and deployment would be more difficult to negotiate than a complex agreement involving qualified bans and various ceilings and numerical limits. It can be argued that the speed at which technological development pushes the world toward war—by making missiles more accurate, for instance, and increasing the chances of a successful first strike—outweighs the "benefits" that a new weapons system might bring.

There is further territory in which the bishops' conditional acceptance of deterrence and their desire for disarmament puts them in a difficult position. Deterrence, in practice, implies the use of "bargaining chips"—weapons developed in order to exact concessions from the former Soviets. It was the United States' failure to part with multiple-warhead (MIRV) missiles—the bargaining chip of the late 1960s—that became one of the most destabilizing steps in the history of the arms race. The U.S. deployment of MIRVs led to the Soviet deployment of MIRVs, contributing, in turn to the so-called "window of vulnerability" panic of the late 1970s. And American infatuation with cruise missiles (the SALT II talks bargaining chips that the Pentagon refused to part with) and the MX missile (advertised as the "chip" needed to force the Soviet hand in the disarmament talks at Geneva) added further to the balance of terror existing in the 1980s.

The recognition that a nuclear war, probably even a conventional war in Central Europe, would be fatal and senseless for the people who live there; the realization that the supposedly stable deterrence system (MAD) is a psychological construct based on dubious assumptions; the knowledge that the manufacture of armaments in West and East serves the interests of a minority—all these factors demand an understanding of the causes of conflict and the unmasking of the motives behind the arms race. The international system has drastically changed. Analyzing world affairs in military, bipolar terms has become a hindrance to understanding the contemporary world. The very unusability of nuclear arsenals, the emergence of new nations, the intractability of various conflicts independent of the cold war and the development of transnational links have strained or broken the blocs and multiplied the actors.

Throughout their analysis of nuclear deterrence the bishops oscillate between contradictory positions which they never reconcile. This is in part because deterrence involves a paradox which strained their moral conception. The paradoxes of deterrence are not the bishops' responsibility. But the ambiguities in their argument arise partly from the nature of the problem and partly from the fact that they appointed for the drafting of their letter a committee sufficiently representative of a broad spectrum of opinion. They then voted for or against scores of amendments to the text, much like a legislative body formulating a multiple-issue bill to satisfy diverse constituencies. Consequently, the statement does not provide a single logically consistent analysis of the issues, but at times moves simultaneously in various directions. Yet seen from a broader perspective, the statement is not simply a middle-of-the-road one which tries to arrive at a lowest common denominator consensus among the representative opinions. It is rather an important development in ethical discourse.

In one particularly trenchant analysis, the statement notes that "strategies have been developed which previous generations would have found unintelligible," for the declared purpose of never having to use the weapons produced. But "threats are made which would be suicidal to implement,"[34] and these strategies depend on perceptions of what is rational and how convincing one adversary's threat is to the other. In this way they formulate the ethical dilemmas, while emphasizing that the fundamental issue is how to prevent nuclear conflict, acknowledging the distinction between "declaratory policy" and "action policy," and adding that "there has been substantial continuity in United States' action policy in spite of significant changes in declaratory policy."[35] In a thinly veiled criticism of written assurances from administration officials that it is not policy to target civilian populations, the bishops deny that the assertion of an intention not to attack a civilian population directly constitutes a moral policy.

The ownership and control of nuclear weapons defines relationships of power. The moment in 1981 when Giscard d'Estaing handed to François Mitterand the codes for launching France's nuclear weapons was considered by the media to be the moment when Mitterrand officially entered office. Over the last four decades, an elaborate ritual, couched in the jargon of deterrence, has been fashioned to justify, explain, and solidify the nexus of power established by nuclear weapons. And yet this pattern does not necessarily correspond to patterns of economic and political power. In fact, the ritual has become more and more distant from wider political and economic realities—specifically, the economic growth of Western Europe and Japan, the increasing political significance of

---

[34]"The Challenge of Peace: God's Promise and Our Response," n. 136.
[35]Ibid., nn. 164-65.

West Germany, the independence of the Third World, and the widespread popular demand in Western industrialized nations for more extensive political participation. The risk is that this disjunction could precipitate a major conflict. As the model of power etched by nuclear weapons begins to disintegrate, the ritual could be called to account. That is, any attempt to reverse the perceived decline in American power since the Vietnam War is likely to involve an increased emphasis on the use of nuclear armaments because other instruments of economic and political power are losing their potency.[36]

One of the most urgent issues in international politics thus hinges on developing ways to eliminate dependence on nuclear weapons as instruments of foreign policy. The pastoral letter offers at least one suggestion to mitigate the hazards involved in such dependence. It should first be noted that there will continue to be discussion over the conclusions reached by the bishops' statement. But situations marked by debates about appropriate ethical responses are not ordinarily the most perilous. To the extent ethical discernment looks for a response that is equivalent to the threat and the questions involved, such discernment ordinarily signifies that the problems spawning conflict are still in the foreground. The flash point is that at which the violent confrontation begins to break free of the issues that provoke it and becomes impelled by a need for supremacy.

The statement advocates the establishment of an international mediating agency. Judging from the urgency with which the prospect of this agency is discussed, the authors may view it as the most significant of their recommendations. Confidence in the utility of an international mediating agency is well founded in reference to the former, manageable stage of conflict because an intractable dispute ordinarily has its origin in a confrontation capable of arbitration. Its application to the latter, less manageable stage of conflict is more problematic. In general, the pastoral letter addresses the danger of rampant violence by advocating arbitration in the initial stages of conflict as the means of impeding escalation. While this is a pragmatic measure, and justifies attempts to create such a body, it does not come to terms fully with the issues. The reason is that early arbitration, which may avert serious confrontation in some instances, is not capable of doing so in all. Successful mediation presumes some degree of willingness among the disputing parties to cooperate. But it is exactly the lack of this willingness that is the source of the danger intractable conflicts generate and arbitration cannot contain, and which lies behind the possibility of full-scale nuclear war.

This type of recommendation on the part of the bishops raises, at least obliquely, the larger question correlative with the issuing of the statement itself:

---

[36]See Mary Kaldor, *The Baroque Arsenal* (New York: Hill and Wang, 1981).

that of the perennial issue of church-state relations. One may draw the conclusion from their pastoral letter that, while the bishops believe in the political wisdom of the separation of church and state, they resist any effort to transform the separation of church and state into the division of religion and politics. The pastoral letter subjects nuclear policy to ethical and intellectual scrutiny. It insists that political and military practices be judged according to ethical standards. The letter sanctions the existence of a breach between ethical standards for private conduct and ethical standards for governmental conduct. But it draws limits, as when it rejects the idea of "limited" nuclear conflict, maintaining that to cross the nuclear threshold is "to enter a world where we have no experience of control, much testimony against [limited war's] possibility, and therefore no moral justification for submitting the human community to this risk."

The bishops thus recognize a distinction between ethics and public policy. They note that there can exist legitimate disagreement on the application of ethical principles. The implication is that ethics and politics are both related and distinct. The two are related because laws and policies are inevitably formed by the ethical beliefs of the policymakers. But they are distinct in that only those moral principles that have an effect on the common good are the proper objects for legislation. The bishops' statement situates itself on the middle ground between the position that there is no relation at all between the political order and ethics, and the position that the two are identical.

The bishops nevertheless find themselves in a dilemma. If they withdraw from the attempt to influence public consensus and public policy, they may in fact mobilize support for a critical stand within the church, even if it opens the community to charges of public irresponsibility. On the other side, they may begin to view issues from the perspective of decision makers, become overly understanding of their problems and accept only the limited alternatives that appear to be currently at hand. If they move in one direction they appear utopian, unrealistic, and irresponsible. If they move in the other they seem to have given over their integrity by acquiescing in situations they themselves have branded unjust and unethical.

The response to "The Challenge of Peace" clearly reflects this dilemma. While individual bishops have adopted one or another of these conflicting positions, the conference of bishops as a body has continued to maintain that they can be both responsible participants in the public debate and faithful interpreters of their tradition. The bishops continue to insist that integration is possible, that Christian participation in a pluralistic society need not become a contradiction in terms. The task before them is to renew their community's traditional attitude toward public life in ways appropriate to the new, endangered world it confronts.

In summary, "The Challenge of Peace" is the most significant American Catholic episcopal statement to date on the ethical issues of nuclear warfare, deterrence, and disarmament. Earlier documents, which marked stages of development in the bishops' teaching on modern warfare, did not analyze nuclear strategies within the framework of the traditional just-war theory. This one reiterates Vatican II's condemnation of nuclear or conventional counterpopulation warfare, but it explicitly cites this as a violation of the *jus in bello* principle of discrimination. The statement, moreover, advances episcopal teaching when, on the basis of the principle of proportionality, it condemns first-use of nuclear weapons and counterforce nuclear warfare that entails massive civilian casualties. The rationale for this position is the letter's "extreme skepticism" about the prospects of controlling nuclear war.

The bishops' statement calls into question some of the basic assumptions and defense strategies of modern nation-states. Initiation of nuclear war cannot be morally justified in any conceivable situation. Nations should adhere to a "no first-use" policy. The document opposes the first use of nuclear weapons by the United States. It also criticizes the deployment of new MX missiles on the ground that they would intensify the arms race. It condemns any strategy of assured destruction that involves indiscriminate targeting of civilian populations. The condemnation of assured destruction and first-use strikes was at the heart of United States policies.

The bishops thus go on record against first-strike weapons, against any nuclear war-fighting capability that exceeds the limited function of deterrence sketched in their statement, and any proposal to lower the nuclear threshold or to blur the distinction between nuclear and conventional weapons.

They support a number of proposals to curb the arms race. They back immediate, bilateral, verifiable agreements to end the testing, production, and deployment of new nuclear weapons systems. They support negotiated bilateral deep cuts in the arsenals of both major powers, particularly among destabilizing weapon systems. They also support negotiations on a comprehensive test-ban treaty. They advocate bilateral removal of short-range nuclear weapons and bilateral removal of nuclear weapons from regions where they are likely to be overrun in the early stages of war, consequently forcing rapid and uncontrollable decisions for their use.

The bishops go on record in support of several unilateral, bilateral, and multilateral arms-control measures they believe would ease international tensions. Some of these did not provoke debate among arms controllers in the United States; for example, negotiated deep cuts in the arsenals of both major powers, such as the proposals for consideration in the Geneva START and INF talks, particularly if they would lead to reductions in destabilizing weapons.[37] Their proposals for removal by all sides of short-range nuclear weapons and nuclear

---

[37]"The Challenge of Peace: God's Promise and Our Response," n. 191.

weapons likely to be overrun in the early stages of war were favored by U.S. arms controllers, dependent on consultation with and approval by allies, correlative with adequate verification procedures. Their opposition to proposals "which have the effect of lowering the nuclear threshold and blurring the difference between nuclear and conventional weapons" is sensible.[38]

The statement's call for a comprehensive test-ban treaty is a more complicated situation, in a world in which some nuclear powers (for example, China and France) would not subscribe to a test ban, and where verification would constitute a problem. The major powers have been involved intermittently in negotiations for a comprehensive test ban since 1958. Although it could be argued that a comprehensive test ban would be a barrier to nuclear weapons proliferation, it does not appear likely that the nuclear-weapons nations will permanently forego underground testing except as part of a comprehensive arms limitation and reduction program to which all nuclear powers adhere.[39]

The U.N. Declaration on Human Rights and the two United Nations covenants embody a sense of moral obligation after the crimes and horrors of World War II. In this regard, the fashioning of a legal framework was especially significant. The relationships between legal and ethical rights and duties are complicated. In international relations, moral obligations can exist regardless of the indifference of law. The various strictures of "The Challenge of Peace" relating to nuclear weapons go far beyond the sanctions of either the United Nations charter or the conventions that control the *jus in bello*. The latter do not expressly concern themselves with nuclear weaponry; the former does not exclude use of these weapons in retaliation against conventional or nuclear warfare. Human conscience is often in advance of treaties and laws, and insinuates itself, not through legislation, but through unilateral policy decisions or diplomatic understandings.

Yet, it must also be said that, in writing their pastoral letter, the bishops deferred implicitly to the testimony of men whose expertise they had presumed to call into question. They concluded that international stability may well depend not only on the maintenance of present levels of nuclear forces, but also on spiraling escalations involved in the maintenance of a system of deterrence. They consequently admitted that there can be a difference of opinion on the issue of nuclear weapons, but in doing so they blunted their own attempt to have a significant impact on the arms race. They were lauded by those who agreed with them and dismissed by those who did not. They found it impossible to confront

---

[38]Ibid., n. 190.

[39]The placing of "The Challenge of Peace" in a wider foreign policy context is a theme of James Dougherty, *The Bishops and Nuclear Weapons* (Cambridge MA: Archon Books, 1984).

the issue with anything resembling the authority they ordinarily exercise on other complicated, though much less menacing, questions of personal morality.

The pastoral letter is specific in judgment but flexible in interpretation. While it has frequently been called prophetic, its policy recommendations are actually mainstream; they would appear far more moderate in a different political climate. Their support for nuclear sufficiency to maintain a deterrent is hardly pacifist. Their opposition to destabilizing new nuclear-weapons systems and to weapons and policies that blur the distinction between conventional and nuclear war is not novel. Their call for a nuclear freeze was supported by a majority in the House of Representatives, many former government officials, and seventy percent of the American people. Their support for a no-first-use pledge is also mainstream, and they acknowledge that such a pledge cannot be implemented without time. Their call for deep reductions in U.S.-Soviet nuclear stockpiles reflected the stated aim of U.S. proposals at the time.

While the episcopal letter marks a significant step in the history of the Roman Catholic Church in the United States, it is not the end of debate on these issues, both because new questions about nuclear weapons policy have arisen as a result of changes in technology and international politics, and because the statement itself has left several crucial issues (notably with regard to the ethics of deterrence) unresolved. It also remains to be seen whether the complex balancing of considerations that produced the bishops' consensus around certain key positions and its unifying line of argument can withstand further critical scrutiny. The ultimate success of the pastoral letter will depend on whether it accomplishes its stated goal of forming the consciences of individuals and of involving the religious community in public policy debate on nuclear weapons. Once all the publicity died down, however, there did not seem to exist any sense of urgency on the part of the majority of the bishops about systematically following through on the initiatives provided by the highly publicized peace pastoral.

Even more decisive in time will be the nature of the response to the letter by the wider public to which it has been addressed. One of the most significant functions of the debate around the statement was the opportunity to make explicit the questions of many Americans who were concerned about the deterioration of U.S.-Soviet relations, who were anxious to avoid a new arms race in space, and who were at the same time distrustful of the Soviet Union.

In the recent history of the Roman Catholic Church, 1983 will be remembered as the year of bishops' conferences on war and peace. At no time since the end of the Second World War have so many conferences reflected on issues of war and peace in such a penetrating way. The year began with a pastoral letter of the Berlin Bishops Conference, the governing body of the Catholic Church in the German Democratic Republic, issued on January 1, 1983. This was followed by a statement of the Hungarian Bishops and by a peace appeal made by the Austrian Bishops. More substantive statements followed with the letter of the

Bishops' Conference of the Federal Republic of Germany, the final draft of the pastoral of the National Conference of Catholic Bishops of the United States, and a statement on nuclear arms by the Dutch Bishops' Conference, in April and May 1983. A letter on peace was issued by the Catholic Bishops' Conference of Japan in July, followed by the declaration of the Belgian bishops and a joint statement by the Bishops of Ireland. The last document came in November from the French Bishops' Conference.

The pastoral letters vary in range and depth. The Bishops' Conferences of the Federal Republic of Germany and the United States produced a thorough survey, whereas other statements limited their message to a few generalizations. Most of the pastoral letters refer to the statement of the United States Bishops as a challenge to take up their own position.

International issues—particularly those of war and peace—affect our lives intimately and directly. Yet there exists a justified public cynicism—a belief that few elected officials are making much sense, that most of these leaders are simply playing politics, and that there is not much that can be done about any of it. All the more serious, then, is the statement of the bishops, in their entry into the public debate over nuclear weapons. They have spoken with the authority of their office, and their statement has been widely publicized and debated. The bishops' presence in American political life indicates a shift in the internal nature and also an extension of the range of democratic argument.

The evolution of American Catholic thinking on war and peace over the last two decades reflects the fact that American Catholics, who less than fifty years ago believed they possessed a coherent view of their world with which to approach social issues, now discovered that they were sharply divided over the most crucial predicament of our age. The events of the last twenty years have fragmented the historical synthesis of civil religion and Catholicism and made clear that problems of war and peace cannot be encountered apart from the political-cultural matrix in which they are embedded. Catholics in the United States are confronted with the imperative to transcend arguments between the just-war tradition and pacifism and to consider the cultural issues that have most divided them on questions of war and peace. The most recent period of development in Catholic thought on these questions indicates the extent of disagreement over the nature of political community and the limits of obligation. The reality of war has, during the past twenty years, forced American Catholics again to confront the issue of their relationship with their society, which they first encountered in the early days of the Maryland colony. Only by accepting this summons can they hope meaningfully to consider the questions that the existence of the global nuclear arsenal poses for human survival.

What of the immediate political impact of "The Challenge of Peace"? Although the statement was skeptical of all new nuclear weapons programs, including the MX and new missiles for NATO, within several weeks after the letter was issued, the Reagan administration won a congressional test vote on the MX and, at the Williamsburg Summit, gained allied approval for the on-schedule deployment of cruise and Pershing II missiles. These programs were not likely to be affected as a result of the episcopacy's censure.

The bishops raised difficult questions about the administration's policy, and introduced a moral tone into the national debate over nuclear-weapons policy. They reminded the nation that democratic politics cannot allow the public consideration of the most crucial matters to be cut off from the ethical convictions of the people.

Contributors

Kenneth Keulman is a professor of Ethics at Loyola University and currently a visiting fellow at the Center of International Studies of the Woodrow Wilson School, Princeton University. He is the author of *The Balance of Consciousness* (Pennsylvania State University Press, 1990). He has been a visiting scholar at Harvard Law School and research associate at the Center for European Studies at Harvard University, and has taught at Harvard University and Rice University.

Baruch A. Brody is the Leon Jaworski Professor of Biomedical Ethics and director of the Center for Ethics, Medicine, and Public Issues at Baylor College of Medicine, and professor of Philosophy at Rice University. His major scholarly works are *Abortion and the Sanctity of Human Life* (M.I.T. Press, 1975), *Identity and Essence* (Princeton University Press, 1981), and *Life and Death Decision Making* (Oxford, 1988).

Werner Kelber, Turner Professor of Biblical Studies at Rice University, is the author of *The Kingdom in Mark* (1974), *Mark's Story of Jesus* (1979), and *The Oral and the Written Gospel* (1983).

Richard Smith is professor of History and chair of Asian Studies, Rice University. His most recent book is *Fortune-Tellers and Philosophers: Divination in Traditional Chinese Society* (Westview Press, 1991).

Clement J. McNaspy, S.J., university professor emeritus at Loyola University, New Orleans, is the author of *Crescent of Christianity*, *Lost Cities of Paraguay*, and *Conquistador without Sword*, among other works. He is also one of the translators of Antonio Ruiz de Montoya's *Conquista Espiritual*.

Jesse Nash teaches in the Test Review Institute at Loyola University, New Orleans.

John Boles, Cline Professor of History at Rice University and managing editor of the *Journal of Southern History*, is author or editor of nine volumes on Southern history.

William Martin teaches sociology at Rice University. He writes frequently about fundamentalism and evangelicalism, with particular attention to television evangelism. His latest book is *A Prophet With Honor: The Billy Graham Story*.

Robert Hamerton-Kelly is senior research scholar in Ethics and member-in-residence, Center for International Security and Arms Control, Stanford University. He is the author of *Sacred Violence: Paul's Hermeneutic of the Cross* (1991), and editor of *Violent Origins* (1987).

Michael M. J. Fischer teaches anthropology and is director of the Center for Cultural Studies at Rice University. He is the author of *Iran: From Religious Dispute to Revolution* (Harvard University Press, 1980), *Anthropology as Cultural Critique: An Experimental Moment in the Human Sciences* (with George Marcus, University of Chicago Press, 1986), and *Debating Muslims: Cultural Dialogues in Postmodernity and Tradition* (with Mehdi Abedi, University of Wisconsin Press, 1990).

Index